AMERICA'S
TEST KITCHEN

Also by America's Test Kitchen

Desserts Illustrated

Modern Bistro

Vegan Cooking for Two

Boards

More Mediterranean

The Everyday Athlete Cookbook

The New Cooking School
Cookbook: Fundamentals

Cooking with Plant-Based Meat

The Savory Baker

The Complete Autumn and Winter
Cookbook

Five-Ingredient Dinners

One-Hour Comfort

The Complete Plant-Based
Cookbook

Cook for Your Gut Health

Foolproof Fish

The Complete Salad Cookbook

Meat Illustrated

Vegetables Illustrated

Bowls

The Ultimate Meal-Prep Cookbook

The Chicken Bible

The Side Dish Bible

The Complete One Pot

Cooking for One

How Can It Be Gluten-Free
Cookbook Collection

The Complete Summer Cookbook

100 Techniques

Easy Everyday Keto

Everything Chocolate

The Perfect Pie

The Perfect Cake

The Perfect Cookie

How to Cocktail

Spiced

The Ultimate Burger

The New Essentials Cookbook

Dinner Illustrated

America's Test Kitchen Menu
Cookbook

Cook's Illustrated Revolutionary
Recipes

Tasting Italy: A Culinary Journey

Cooking at Home with Bridget
and Julia

The Complete Mediterranean
Cookbook

The Complete Vegetarian
Cookbook

The Complete Cooking for Two
Cookbook

The Complete Diabetes Cookbook

The Complete Slow Cooker

The Complete Make-Ahead
Cookbook

Just Add Sauce

How to Braise Everything

How to Roast Everything

Nutritious Delicious

What Good Cooks Know

Cook's Science

The Science of Good Cooking

Bread Illustrated

Master of the Grill

Kitchen Smarts

Kitchen Hacks

100 Recipes: The Absolute Best
Ways to Make the True Essentials

The New Family Cookbook

The Cook's Illustrated Baking Book

The Cook's Illustrated Cookbook

The America's Test Kitchen Family
Baking Book

The Best of America's Test Kitchen
(2007–2023 Editions)

America's Test Kitchen Twentieth
Anniversary TV Show Cookbook

The Complete America's Test
Kitchen TV Show
Cookbook 2001–2023

Healthy Air Fryer

Healthy and Delicious Instant Pot

Mediterranean Instant Pot

Cook It in Your Dutch Oven

Vegan for Everybody

Sous Vide for Everybody

Toaster Oven Perfection

Air Fryer Perfection

Multicooker Perfection

Food Processor Perfection

Pressure Cooker Perfection

Instant Pot Ace Blender Cookbook

Naturally Sweet

Foolproof Preserving

Paleo Perfected

The Best Mexican Recipes

Slow Cooker Revolution Volume 2:
The Easy-Prep Edition

Slow Cooker Revolution

The America's Test Kitchen D.I.Y.
Cookbook

THE COOK'S ILLUSTRATED ALL-TIME BEST SERIES:

All-Time Best Brunch

All-Time Best Dinners for Two

All-Time Best Sunday Suppers

All-Time Best Holiday Entertaining

All-Time Best Soups

COOK'S COUNTRY TITLES:

Big Flavors from Italian America

One-Pan Wonders

Cook It in Cast Iron

Cook's Country Eats Local

The Complete Cook's Country TV
Show Cookbook

FOR A FULL LISTING OF ALL OUR BOOKS:

CooksIllustrated.com

AmericasTestKitchen.com

Praise for America's Test Kitchen

"A mood board for one's food board is served up in this excellent guide . . . This has instant classic written all over it."

PUBLISHERS WEEKLY (STARRED REVIEW) ON BOARDS: STYLISH SPREADS FOR CASUAL GATHERINGS

"In this latest offering from the fertile minds at America's Test Kitchen the recipes focus on savory baked goods. Pizzas, flatbreads, crackers, and stuffed breads all shine here . . . Introductory essays for each recipe give background information and tips for making things come out perfectly."

BOOKLIST (STARRED REVIEW) ON THE SAVORY BAKER

"Reassuringly hefty and comprehensive, *The Complete Autumn and Winter Cookbook* by America's Test Kitchen has you covered with a seemingly endless array of seasonal fare . . . This overstuffed compendium is guaranteed to warm you from the inside out."

NPR ON THE COMPLETE AUTUMN AND WINTER COOKBOOK

Selected as the Cookbook Award Winner of 2021 in the General Cookbook Category

INTERNATIONAL ASSOCIATION OF CULINARY PROFESSIONALS (IACP) ON MEAT ILLUSTRATED

Selected as the Cookbook Award Winner of 2021 in the Health and Nutrition Category

INTERNATIONAL ASSOCIATION OF CULINARY PROFESSIONALS (IACP) ON THE COMPLETE PLANT-BASED COOKBOOK

"The book's depth, breadth, and practicality make it a must-have for seafood lovers."

PUBLISHERS WEEKLY (STARRED REVIEW) ON FOOLPROOF FISH

"Another flawless entry in the America's Test Kitchen canon, *Bowls* guides readers of all culinary skill levels in composing one-bowl meals from a variety of cuisines."

BUZZFEED BOOKS ON BOWLS

"Diabetics and all health-conscious home cooks will find great information on almost every page."

BOOKLIST (STARRED REVIEW) ON THE COMPLETE DIABETES COOKBOOK

"*The Perfect Cookie* . . . is, in a word, perfect. This is an important and substantial cookbook . . . If you love cookies, but have been a tad shy to bake on your own, all your fears will be dissipated. This is one book you can use for years with magnificently happy results."

THE HUFFINGTON POST ON THE PERFECT COOKIE

"True to its name, this smart and endlessly enlightening cookbook is about as definitive as it's possible to get in the modern vegetarian realm."

MEN'S JOURNAL ON THE COMPLETE VEGETARIAN COOKBOOK

"Filled with complete meals you can cook in your Instant Pot. Next time you're thinking of turning to takeout or convenience foods, prepare one of these one-pot meals instead."

NBC NEWS ON MEDITERRANEAN INSTANT POT

"If you're a home cook who loves long introductions that tell you why a dish works followed by lots of step-by-step hand holding, then you'll love *Vegetables Illustrated*."

THE WALL STREET JOURNAL ON VEGETABLES ILLUSTRATED

"Here are the words just about any vegan would be happy to read: 'Why This Recipe Works.' Fans of America's Test Kitchen are used to seeing the phrase, and now it applies to the growing collection of plant-based creations in *Vegan for Everybody*."

THE WASHINGTON POST ON VEGAN FOR EVERYBODY

"A one-volume kitchen seminar, addressing in one smart chapter after another the sometimes surprising whys behind a cook's best practices . . . You get the myth, the theory, the science, and the proof, all rigorously interrogated as only America's Test Kitchen can do."

NPR ON THE SCIENCE OF GOOD COOKING

"The 21st-century *Fannie Farmer Cookbook* or *The Joy of Cooking*. If you had to have one cookbook and that's all you could have, this one would do it."

CBS SAN FRANCISCO ON THE NEW FAMILY COOKBOOK

"The go-to gift book for newlyweds, small families, or empty nesters."

ORLANDO SENTINEL ON THE COMPLETE COOKING FOR TWO COOKBOOK

"The America's Test Kitchen team elevates the humble side dish to center stage in this excellent collection of 1,001 recipes . . . Benefiting from the clarity that comes from experience and experiments, ATK shows off its many sides in this comprehensive volume."

PUBLISHERS WEEKLY ON THE SIDE DISH BIBLE

FRESH PASTA AT HOME

10 Doughs, 20 Shapes, 100+ Recipes,
with or without a Machine

AMERICA'S TEST KITCHEN

Library of Congress Cataloging-in-Publication Data

Names: America's Test Kitchen (Firm), author.

Title: Fresh pasta at home : 10 doughs, 20 shapes, 100+ recipes, with or without a machine / America's Test Kitchen.

Description: Boston, MA : America's Test Kitchen, [2022] | Includes index.

Identifiers: LCCN 2022038758 (print) | LCCN 2022038759 (ebook) | ISBN 9781954210332 (paperback) | ISBN 9781954210349 (ebook)

Subjects: LCSH: Cooking (Pasta) | Dough. | Noodles. | LCGFT: Cookbooks.

Classification: LCC TX809.M17 F735 2022 (print) | LCC TX809.M17 (ebook) |DDC 641.82/2--dc23/eng/20220817

LC record available at https://lccn.loc.gov/2022038758

LC ebook record available at https://lccn.loc.gov/2022038759

America's Test Kitchen

21 Drydock Avenue, Boston, MA 02210

Printed in Canada

10 9 8 7 6 5 4 3 2 1

Distributed by Penguin Random House Publisher Services

Tel: 800.733.3000

Pictured on Front Cover **Three-Cheese Ravioli with Pumpkin Cream Sauce (page 144)**

Pictured on Back Cover **Semolina Dough (page 22), Orecchiette (page 52), Rabbit Ragù (page 236)**

Editorial Director, Books **Adam Kowit**

Executive Food Editor **Dan Zuccarello**

Deputy Food Editors **Leah Colins and Stephanie Pixley**

Executive Managing Editor **Debra Hudak**

Project Editor **Valerie Cimino**

Senior Editors **Camila Chaparro, Joseph Gitter, and Sara Mayer**

Editorial Support **Katrina Ávila Munichiello, April Poole, and Rachel Schowalter**

Test Cooks **Olivia Counter, Carmen Dongo, Hannah Fenton, Jacqueline Gochenouer, Eric Haessler, Hisham Hassan, José Maldonado, and Patricia Suarez**

Kitchen Intern **Olivia Goldstein**

Design Director **Lindsey Timko Chandler**

Deputy Art Director **Janet Taylor**

Associate Art Director **Molly Gillespie**

Photography Director **Julie Bozzo Cote**

Senior Photography Producer **Meredith Mulcahy**

Senior Staff Photographers **Steve Klise and Daniel J. van Ackere**

Staff Photographer **Kevin White**

Additional Photography **Joseph Keller and Carl Tremblay**

Food Styling **Joy Howard, Sheila Jarnes, Catrine Kelty, Chantal Lambeth, Gina McCreadie, Kendra McKnight, Ashley Moore, Christie Morrison, Marie Piraino, Elle Simone Scott, Kendra Smith, and Sally Staub**

Project Manager, Publishing Operations **Katie Kimmerer**

Senior Print Production Specialist **Lauren Robbins**

Production and Imaging Coordinator **Amanda Yong**

Production and Imaging Specialists **Tricia Neumyer and Dennis Noble**

Copy Editor **Rebecca Springer**

Proofreader **Vicki Rowland**

Indexer **Elizabeth Parson**

Chief Creative Officer **Jack Bishop**

Executive Editorial Directors **Julia Collin Davison and Bridget Lancaster**

Contents

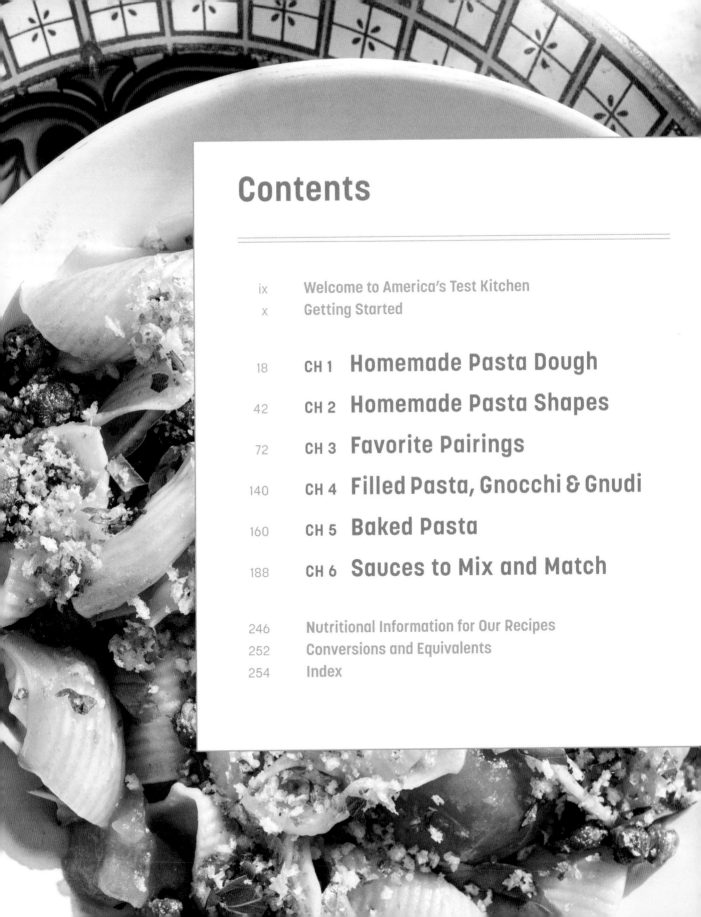

Welcome to America's Test Kitchen

This book has been tested, written, and edited by the folks at America's Test Kitchen, where curious cooks become confident cooks. Located in Boston's Seaport District in the historic Innovation and Design Building, it features 15,000 square feet of kitchen space including multiple photography and video studios. It is the home of *Cook's Illustrated* magazine and *Cook's Country* magazine and is the workday destination for more than 60 test cooks, editors, and cookware specialists. Our mission is to empower and inspire confidence, community, and creativity in the kitchen.

We start the process of testing a recipe with a complete lack of preconceptions, which means that we accept no claim, no technique, and no recipe at face value. We simply assemble as many variations as possible, test a half-dozen of the most promising, and taste the results blind. We then construct our own recipe and continue to test it, varying ingredients, techniques, and cooking times until we reach a consensus. As we like to say in the test kitchen, "We make the mistakes so you don't have to." The result, we hope, is the best version of a particular recipe, but we realize that only you can be the final judge of our success (or failure). We use the same rigorous approach when we test equipment and taste ingredients.

All of this would not be possible without a belief that good cooking, much like good music, is based on a foundation of objective technique. Some people like spicy foods and others don't, but there is a right way to sauté, there is a best way to cook a pot roast, and there are measurable scientific principles involved in producing perfectly beaten, stable egg whites. Our ultimate goal is to investigate the fundamental principles of cooking to give you the techniques, tools, and ingredients you need to become a better cook. It is as simple as that.

To see what goes on behind the scenes at America's Test Kitchen, check out our social media channels for kitchen snapshots, exclusive content, video tips, and much more. You can watch us work (in our actual test kitchen) by tuning in to *America's Test Kitchen* or *Cook's Country* on public television or on our websites. Listen to *Proof*, *Mystery Recipe*, and *The Walk-In* (AmericasTestKitchen.com/podcasts), to hear engaging, complex stories about people and food. Want to hone your cooking skills or finally learn how to bake—with an America's Test Kitchen test cook? Enroll in one of our online cooking classes. And you can engage the next generation of home cooks with kid-tested recipes from America's Test Kitchen Kids.

Our community of home recipe testers provides valuable feedback on recipes under development by ensuring that they are foolproof. You can help us investigate the how and why behind successful recipes from your home kitchen. (Sign up at AmericasTestKitchen.com/recipe_testing.)

However you choose to visit us, we welcome you into our kitchen, where you can stand by our side as we test our way to the best recipes in America.

Getting Started

Introduction

Making pasta from scratch is one of life's elemental culinary pleasures. This tactile (and fun!) kitchen exercise forces you to slow down and literally feel what you're doing. Practiced pasta makers already know this, of course; if you aren't one, we'd humbly like to suggest that you become one—and let this book show you the way.

We teach you how to make four master pasta doughs: egg dough, semolina dough, whole-wheat dough, and gluten-free dough, along with several flavor variations. With plenty of step-by-step photos, we also guide you through everything you need to know to roll out dough into sheets and cut it into strands, form dough into shapes, and make filled pastas and extruded pastas. Then, nearly 100 recipes for finished dishes help you really showcase your handmade creations.

Fresh pasta takes a bit of time, but it's not difficult. Unlike with bread baking, for example, there's no yeast, there's no starter, there's no proofing or rising time, and there's no extended baking time. There's primarily just flour, water, and egg (and sometimes there isn't even any egg). And you can choose how you want to make pasta; whether you prefer to do it entirely by hand, use a manual pasta machine, or use an electric extruder, we've got you covered with equipment recommendations and clear instruction.

Homemade fresh pasta is far superior to any commercially made fresh pasta you can purchase. What about dried pasta, which is available these days in a seemingly endless multitude of shapes? It's probably found in some form in nearly every pantry in America, and of course it has its place on the dining table—including ours. Think of the comparison this way: Fresh pasta is neither better nor worse than dried pasta; it's simply a different thing altogether.

The rewards of pasta making go beyond serving and enjoying a great dinner. Not only will you get to bask in the admiration of those around your table as they marvel at your pasta-making prowess, but you'll also have added a fantastic new skill to your kitchen repertoire. Perhaps most important, you'll have provided yourself a worthwhile break from the stresses of your day, and you will have cared for those you love in the best possible way, by providing them a delicious, truly from-scratch meal.

Ingredients for Fresh Pasta

There are four main pasta doughs in this book. Each is made with a different flour: all-purpose, semolina, whole-wheat, and rice (for gluten-free fresh pasta). All but the semolina recipe use eggs as well. There are also variations on these doughs that use other whole-grain flours and flavoring ingredients including spinach, herbs, and more. Here's what you'll need to make all of them.

Flours

WHITE FLOUR

Italians make fresh pasta using a particular type of lower-protein white flour called doppio zero, with a talcum powder–like grind. However, we created our fresh egg pasta dough recipe using readily available all-purpose flour. Our go-to in the test kitchen is Gold Medal Unbleached All-Purpose Flour, which has a moderate protein content. You can also successfully use a high-protein all-purpose flour, such as King Arthur Unbleached All-Purpose Flour. Don't use bleached all-purpose flour in our pasta dough recipes, as the bleach will weaken the proteins in the dough and will make the starches prone to bursting when they are boiled, resulting in pasta with pitted, pebbly surfaces.

SEMOLINA FLOUR

Semolina flour is made from whole-grain durum wheat and has a higher protein content than all-purpose flour. This is the type of flour typically used in commercial dried Italian pasta, but you can also use it to make fresh pasta. This golden-colored flour makes for an egg-free fresh pasta with a sturdier texture and a bit more "chew" than fresh pasta made with eggs and all-purpose flour. It also takes more elbow grease to roll it out. We developed our semolina pasta dough recipe using fine semolina (sometimes labeled semola rimacinata, extra-fancy, or #1), which is available in Italian markets, large supermarkets, and online. Don't use conventional semolina, which is too coarse.

- **Whole-wheat flour** contains the entire wheat kernel, including the germ, which means that it's higher in fiber, fat, and protein than all-purpose flour. Because the protein in the germ doesn't form gluten, we bolster our whole-wheat pasta dough recipe with some all-purpose flour.

- **Rye flour** contains less protein than whole-wheat flour, which can be an issue when baking but doesn't pose a problem for fresh pasta. Rye pasta has a slightly sweeter flavor than whole-wheat pasta. The darker the flour you use, the stronger the rye flavor will be.

- **Spelt flour** is ground from an ancient type of wheat that's rich in protein and minerals and has a rich, nutty flavor. Like rye flour, it has less protein than whole-wheat flour, but it works great in our whole-grain pasta recipe.

- **Farro flour** is ground from high-fiber, high-protein farro, also known as emmer. It has been used in Italian cuisine since Roman times, mostly in its whole-kernel form, in soups and risotto-type dishes. Its flour works well for fresh pasta.

BUCKWHEAT FLOUR

Buckwheat is a pseudograin that is naturally gluten-free and not related to wheat at all. It's an herb, more closely related to rhubarb and sorrel. The flour is made by grinding its triangular seeds, which contribute a dark color and earthy flavor. With its high protein content, it adds sturdy structure to pizzoccheri (see page 126), the traditional pasta shape made using this flour.

BROWN RICE FLOUR

Brown rice flour is essential for our gluten-free pasta dough. Because it still contains the bran, brown rice flour has more protein, fiber, and fat than white rice flour, which in turn provides more structure to gluten-free fresh pasta than white rice flour would. We developed our recipe for gluten-free pasta dough using Bob's Red Mill brown rice flour, which is finely ground.

Eggs

Egg whites contain water and protein, both essential for pasta dough. Many pasta doughs supplement whole eggs with extra yolks, and for good reason. While yolks contain about 50 percent water, they are also loaded with fat and emulsifiers, both of which limit gluten development and help create suppleness in the dough. But because their proteins coagulate when heated, adding structure, egg yolks also help ensure that the shaped pasta is strong enough to stay intact when boiled. In addition to using whole eggs, we add six or seven extra yolks from large eggs to our fresh egg pasta dough (depending on whether you use moderate-protein or high-protein all-purpose flour).

FREEZING LEFTOVER EGG WHITES

As you've probably guessed, you will have leftover egg whites from making our fresh egg pasta dough. Here's our favorite way to freeze them for later use: Pour each leftover egg white into one well of an ice cube tray; cover and freeze. Use a paring knife or small spatula to remove the frozen egg white cubes; defrost in a small bowl in the refrigerator as needed.

WHAT TO DO WITH LEFTOVER EGG WHITES

- Use them to seal a big batch of homemade ravioli or other stuffed pasta.

- Add some extra egg whites to your next omelet, frittata, or batch of scrambled eggs.

- When breading chicken cutlets or fish fillets, you can use just egg whites instead of whole eggs with minimal difference in flavor.

- Defrost a cube any time you need to brush a pie crust, bread loaf, or other item with egg white before baking.

- Make dessert! Meringues, mousses, custards, marshmallows, pavlovas, and chiffon cakes are all fantastic ways to use up extra egg whites.

Extra-Virgin Olive Oil

Olive oil is not always added to fresh pasta recipes, but we use it in our fresh egg pasta dough and in our gluten-free pasta dough because it makes these doughs more supple and easier to roll, especially when rolling out pasta sheets by hand. It coats the proteins in the flour and controls their ability to develop gluten, which would otherwise cause snapback and make the dough harder to roll out.

Gluten-Free Necessities

TAPIOCA STARCH

Made from the starchy, tuberous root of the cassava plant, this white powder provides chew, elasticity, and structure to fresh pasta made with gluten-free dough. Tapioca starch is sometimes labeled tapioca flour even though it contains no protein and is a pure starch. Either product can be used in our recipe for gluten-free pasta dough.

XANTHAN GUM

Made by using the microorganism *Xanthomonas campestris* to ferment simple sugars, xanthan gum is used widely in commercial food products as a thickener. Because gluten-free flours have less protein than wheat flours and aren't capable of forming the same network required to stretch and surround starch granules, they need reinforcement. Xanthan gum strengthens these networks and also makes them more elastic. Essentially, adding xanthan gum is like adding glue to the proteins in gluten-free flour.

Flavorings for Dough

You can add subtle flavor and dramatic color to your homemade pasta dough by adding additional ingredients (see pages 28–29 for instructions). The process of flavoring dough is all about managing moisture so that you don't upset the dough's hydration balance.

SPINACH

We use convenient frozen spinach to flavor and color our spinach pasta dough. Squeezing it dry as much as possible after thawing and very finely chopping it before mixing produces the best results.

TOMATO

It's easy to get subtle tomato flavor and a lovely hue without excess moisture by blending tomato paste with the liquid ingredients before mixing them with the flour.

HERBS

You can experiment with any kind of soft fresh herb, including basil, parsley, dill, and tarragon. Just be sure to mince the herb thoroughly so that it incorporates smoothly into the pasta dough.

SPICES

Saffron is a classic choice for flavoring fresh pasta in Sardinia, where malloreddus made with saffron (see pages 18 and 57) is a local specialty. To make the most of its flavor, we steep the saffron first in a small amount of hot water to bloom it. For spices like black pepper, make sure that they are very finely ground.

LEMON

Finely grated lemon zest adds subtle citrusy flavor to fresh pasta dough without any excess moisture.

SQUID INK

An Italian classic, squid or cuttlefish ink brings a rich, ocean-y flavor to fresh pasta along with a startling blue-black color. Although you can purchase squid with the ink sac still attached in fish markets all over coastal Italy, in the U.S., squid ink is most often sold in a jar.

Equipment For Fresh Pasta

You can go minimalist and use just a rolling pin and elbow grease to make fresh pasta, but a few pieces of special equipment will help you do the job more quickly and easily. Here's a rundown of some options for preparing fresh pasta by hand, using a manual pasta machine, or using an extruder.

FOOD PROCESSOR

Mixing fresh egg pasta dough by hand is an art and a skill worth learning (see pages 20–21 for instructions), but a food processor undeniably speeds up the process. For its ease of use and its quick cleanup, we recommend the Cuisinart Custom 14 Cup Food Processor.

ROLLING PIN

For rolling pasta dough by hand, you'll need a sturdy rolling pin. We like the J.K. Adams Plain Maple Rolling Dowel (which is long and straight with no handles) and the J.K. Adams Gourmet Rolling Pin (which has handles). Their slightly textured surfaces hold a light dusting of flour for less sticking.

MANUAL PASTA MACHINE

Pasta machines make the process of rolling out sheets of dough and cutting them into noodles faster and easier and the results more uniform. Hand-cranked pasta machines are the most prevalent and affordable options. Our longtime favorite is the Marcato Atlas 150 Wellness Pasta Machine. It sports thickness settings from very wide to very narrow and produces gossamer-thin pasta sheets, and its noodle-cutting attachments work perfectly every time.

ELECTRIC PASTA EXTRUDER

These easy-to-use machines are more expensive than manual pasta machines, but if you want to make tubular shapes such as penne or ziti and round strands including spaghetti, you'll need one. They also mix the dough for you in a process similar to a bread machine; you just put the ingredients into the hopper and press a button. Our favorite is the Philips Pasta Maker, which comes with four pasta shaping disks (more can be purchased). We formulated our extruder doughs to work with any machine.

STAND MIXER ATTACHMENTS

A stand mixer with a dough hook will help you make our semolina pasta dough (see page 22). If you have a KitchenAid mixer, you can purchase their 3-Piece Pasta Roller & Cutter set to roll pasta sheets and cut them into linguine and fettuccine. They also have a Pasta Press attachment that allows you to extrude pasta strands and shapes. If you already own a Kitchen-Aid and you are trying to limit the number of appliances in your kitchen, this is a solid option for extruding pasta.

BAKING SHEETS

Nordic Ware Baker's Half Sheet Pan makes an ideal landing place for your fresh pasta after you've cut or extruded it. You can even buy a plastic lid for it that lets you slide the whole baking sheet into the freezer to freeze a batch of fresh pasta before transferring it to smaller containers or zipper-lock bags for storage.

ROLLING CUTTERS

To get those hallmark zigzag edges on farfalle, square ravioli, agnolotti, and other pasta shapes, you'll want to have a fluted pastry wheel on hand. A pizza cutter (or even a sharp knife) will work just as well for straight-edged pasta shapes.

RAVIOLI STAMP OR COOKIE CUTTER

Ravioli stamps range from simple to ornate and are a fun and traditional way to cut out rounds for filled pastas such as round ravioli and mezzelune. A cookie cutter also works great. You'll need a 2½-inch round stamp or cutter for round ravioli and tortellini and a 3-inch stamp or cutter for mezzelune.

RICER OR FOOD MILL

For lump-free potato gnocchi, we suggest a ricer or food mill to get the smoothest mash on the cooked potatoes. Lumps in the dough can result in the gnocchi breaking apart when you boil it. We like the RSVP International Potato Ricer.

GNOCCHI BOARD
MALLOREDDUS BOARD
GARGANELLI BOARD

While you can use a wire rack or even the tines of an inverted fork to achieve the ridged shapes characteristic of gnocchi, cavatelli, malloreddus, and garganelli, you can also use dedicated small wooden rolling boards for these shapes. They are inexpensive, fun to collect, and, especially in the case of intricately carved garganelli boards, allow you to imprint beautiful patterns on your handmade pasta shapes.

CHITARRA

The Marcato Atlas pasta machine is available with a chitarra attachment, but if you'd like to make this traditional squared-off strand pasta by hand, you'll want a chitarra. Similar to the musical instrument (guitar) for which it's named, this traditional tool is made of a rectangular wooden frame with thin metal strings running lengthwise between the ends of the frame. You lay the dough sheet over the strings and then roll over it with a rolling pin so that the sheet is cut into strands, which fall below.

Storing, Cooking, and Saucing Fresh Pasta

Fresh pasta freezes beautifully, so you can make a big batch ahead and stash it in your freezer like treasure to make any of the recipes in this book at any time. When it comes to cooking, the process is unsurprisingly similar to dried pasta, but there are a few things to watch out for to make sure that your fresh creations don't overcook.

STORING AND FREEZING FRESH PASTA

Unless you're planning to freeze your fresh pasta, it is best served on the day it is made. You can hold freshly made pasta at room temperature for up to 30 minutes or refrigerate it for up to 4 hours. Don't push it to overnight or longer, though; the noodles will start to clump together. This is caused by water in the pasta migrating outward and moistening the flour coating. The pasta will also take on a gray-green cast, a discoloration caused by oxidation of the iron in the dough's egg yolks (store-bought fresh pasta is packaged with nitrogen and carbon dioxide and less than 1 percent oxygen to prevent this discoloration).

Freezing fresh pasta works great, since it slows the chemical reactions that cause oxidation and keeps the water from migrating outward. To freeze your freshly made pasta, toss it with a bit of flour to help keep the pieces separate. Coil strand pasta into 2- to 4-ounce nests on a baking sheet, or spread shapes in a single layer and freeze on the sheet. Once frozen, transfer the pasta to zipper-lock bags and store in the freezer for up to 1 month.

To freeze stuffed pasta or gnocchi, place it on a single layer on a floured baking sheet and freeze for 1 hour. Transfer the partially frozen pasta or gnocchi to zipper-lock bags or containers and freeze for up to 1 month.

COOKING FROZEN PASTA

You can cook frozen pasta directly from the freezer, without thawing. Strands and shaped pasta will have the same cooking time as if they were not frozen. For filled pasta such as ravioli, increase the cooking time by a minute or two to ensure that the filling cooks through.

HOW MUCH WATER?

Our recommendation for cooking fresh pasta is generally the same as cooking dried pasta: Bring 4 quarts water to a boil in a large pot or Dutch oven, then add 1 tablespoon table salt and the pasta. When draining or removing the cooked pasta from the pot, reserve 1 cup cooking water to adjust the finished consistency of the sauce. You will likely need less of this cooking water with fresh pasta than with dried pasta.

Fresh pasta leaches starch into the cooking water just like dried pasta does. There are instances when we want extra-starchy cooking water to help emulsify a sauce, such as for Cacio e Pepe (page 88) or Pasta alla Gricia (page 98). In these cases, follow the instructions in the recipe for how much water and salt to bring to a boil.

DETERMINING DONENESS

Fresh pasta cooks more quickly than dried pasta, so there's a smaller margin for error. The last thing you want is to have all your efforts turn to mush. We recommend tasting fresh pasta early and often as it cooks, since it can be ready for draining in as little as 2 minutes. To test filled pasta such as ravioli, remove one from the pot, cut off a small corner, and taste that.

UNDERSTANDING AL DENTE

This term is the hallmark of any well-cooked pasta. Your teeth should feel some resistance when you take a bite, but the pasta will be tender. Whether fresh or dried, pasta is a complex network of starch granules held together by protein. As the pasta is boiled, the starch granules on the surface absorb water and swell, and some eventually burst, releasing starch into the cooking water. The granules beneath the pasta's surface don't become as hydrated and swell without bursting. There are differences between al dente fresh pasta and al dente dried pasta. By its very nature, fresh pasta is always going to be softer and more hydrated than dried pasta, so al dente fresh pasta will be softer and silkier in texture than al dente dried pasta.

SAUCING FRESH PASTA

Cooked fresh pasta readily absorbs sauce, so a light hand is better so that you can fully enjoy its delicate taste and texture without overwhelming it with sauce. Combining cooked pasta with hot sauce causes the pasta to keep cooking, which for fresh pasta in particular can easily lead to overcooking. In recipes where you need to finish your pasta and sauce together, such as Cacio e Uova (page 101), you will undercook the pasta slightly and then toss it with the sauce to finish. Likewise for baked pasta recipes, you will undercook the pasta when boiling it. For most recipes, though, a quick but gentle toss to combine pasta and sauce is sufficient. Since fresh pasta is more delicate and breaks more easily than dried pasta, we don't generally recommend that you stir the pasta and sauce together, since this action is more vigorous than tossing.

We treat filled pasta even more gently, saucing it more lightly than strand pasta or shaped pasta, since you want the flavors of the filling to shine as well. We also take extra care when tossing filled pasta with its sauce to prevent the pieces from bursting open.

Pairing Pasta Strands and Shapes with Sauces

Pairing particular shapes with complementary sauces makes for a more pleasurable eating experience, helping you to get a little bit of everything in each bite. Consider these suggestions as guidelines to get you started, rather than rules.

THIN PASTA STRANDS AND HOLLOW PASTA STRANDS

Pasta including linguine and spaghetti works well with light sauces like Browned Butter–Sage Sauce (page 192) and smooth sauces like Cacio e Pepe (page 88). Thin, hollow pasta strands like bucatini easily become coated inside and out with these sauces. Seafood is also a favorite traditional pairing with thin pasta strands.

THICK PASTA STRANDS

Fettuccine, tagliatelle, and pappardelle can stand up better to thicker, more substantial sauces like Pesto Calabrese (page 204) and creamy sauces like Gorgonzola-Walnut Cream Sauce (page 218) or Alfredo Sauce (page 220). They are often served with ragùs such as Ragù alla Bolognese (page 230), since the bits or shreds of meat are captured within their folds.

CURLY PASTA SHAPES

Twisted pasta shapes like busiate, trofie, and fileja nicely cradle sauces with little pieces of ingredients, including pestos, ground meat sauces, and thickened tomato sauces such as the one in Fileja with 'Nduja Tomato Sauce (page 82).

SHORT PASTA TUBES AND SHELLS

Tubular and shell-shaped pastas are great for holding onto chunky sauces, as in Pasta alla Norma (page 110). Pair larger shapes like rigatoni with sauces containing chunkier bits, and match smaller shapes like penne with more finely textured sauces. Tubular shapes are also classic for baking, as in our Baked Ziti on page 174.

SHORT ROLLED AND CUT PASTA SHAPES

Shapes including cavatelli, malloreddus, orecchiette, and farfalle are fun to pair with sauces where the ingredients are roughly the size of the pasta, including in dishes like Malloreddus with Fava Beans and Mint (page 118) and Farfalle with Sautéed Mushrooms (page 84). Orecchiette's little bowl shapes are particularly adept at catching saucy chunks, as in Pasta alla Norcina (page 104).

Pairing Filled Pasta with Sauces

When it comes to choosing a sauce for filled fresh pasta, consider the filling. Since they are already stuffed with something very flavorful, ravioli, agnolotti, and other filled pastas are often served with light-bodied sauces. Heavy or very chunky sauces will overwhelm delicate filled pasta. Regardless of which filled shape you make, here are some of our tips for pairing the fillings in Chapter 2 with the sauces that complement them best.

RICOTTA FILLING

For most of our cheese-based fillings, it's hard to go wrong with a simple tomato sauce like Fresh Tomato Sauce (page 210) or any of the pestos in Chapter 6. The Artichoke and Lemon Ricotta Filling (page 68) would pair especially well with the Garlic Oil Sauce with Lemon and Pine Nuts (page 191).

BRAISED SHORT RIB FILLING

Light but rich, Browned Butter–Hazelnut Sauce (page 192) or Browned Butter–Tomato Sauce (page 192) will enhance this smooth, meaty filling without overshadowing it.

GROUND PORK FILLING

The hearty flavor and more homestyle texture of this filling lets you get away with a bolder sauce. Try 'Nduja Tomato Sauce (page 82) or Creamy Tomato Sauce (page 214).

SQUASH, PROSCIUTTO, AND PARMESAN FILLING

The rich, sweet-salty qualities of this filling make it a swooningly great pairing with any of the browned butter sauces on page 192.

WILD MUSHROOM FILLING

The browned butter sauces on page 192 or the garlicky olive oil sauces on page 191 would work very well. Or go all out on the mushrooms and pair mushroom-filled pasta with Porcini Cream Sauce (page 219) or Mushroom Bolognese (page 240).

BITTER GREENS FILLING

One of the olive oil–based sauces on page 191 would really showcase the bold flavor of this filling. The traditional sauce in Liguria for pansotti stuffed with this filling is a walnut pesto called salsa di noci; find it on page 150.

LEEK FILLING

Since the leeks are cooked in butter, pair this filling with one of the browned butter sauces (page 192) or olive oil sauces (page 191). Creamy sauces like Alfredo Sauce (page 220) or Gorgonzola-Walnut Cream Sauce (page 218) also complement the leeks' mild flavor.

Pairing Flavored Fresh Pasta with Sauces

In addition to considering shapes when pairing fresh pasta with sauce, you should consider the flavor of the pasta itself, especially if you make a whole-grain pasta or one of our doughs flavored with spinach, tomato, herbs, lemon-pepper, or squid ink (see Chapter 2).

WHOLE-WHEAT AND WHOLE-GRAIN PASTA

The stronger, earthier flavors of these fresh pastas pair perfectly with sauces containing browned butter, mushrooms, nuts, strongly flavored herbs like sage, and assertive cheeses. Try these pastas with Toasted Nut and Parsley Pesto (page 196), Porcini Cream Sauce (page 219), or Mushroom Bolognese (page 240).

SPINACH PASTA

Pair spinach pasta with vegetable-based sauces, as in our Busiate with Spring Vegetables (page 128) or simple tomato sauces like Browned Butter–Tomato Sauce (page 192). It's also great for making filled pasta with one of our ricotta-based fillings on page 68 or for using in Three-Cheese Manicotti with Tomato Sauce (page 162).

TOMATO PASTA

Sauces with garlic or basil will enhance the delicate tomato flavor of this pasta. Pair tomato pasta with Garlic Oil Sauce with Parsley and Pecorino (page 190) or Classic Basil Pesto (page 194). It works well with ragùs that also use tomato paste for a touch of tomato flavor, including Beef and Onion Ragù (page 234). Or pair it with Sun-Dried Tomato Pesto (page 198) or No-Cook Fresh Tomato Sauce (page 208) for a multilayered tomato experience.

HERB PASTA

Butter- and olive oil–based sauces allow the delicate flavor of the herbs to come through (and let you see the pretty green flecks in the pasta). Try pastas made with herb dough with Garlic Oil Sauce with Parsley and Pecorino (and its variations, page 191, Browned Butter–Sage Sauce (and its variations, page 192), or White Clam Sauce (page 222).

LEMON-PEPPER PASTA

Since lemon and seafood have such a kinship, serve this pasta in tomato-free seafood dishes such as Linguine with Shrimp (page 96). Try it with a complementary vegetable, as in Tagliatelle with Artichokes, Bread Crumbs, and Parmesan (page 86). Or really highlight the lemon by serving it in Summer Squash Fettuccine with Ricotta and Lemon-Parmesan Bread Crumbs (page 130).

SQUID INK PASTA

Squid ink has a distinctive oceanic savoriness, so this pasta is a natural with any kind of seafood-based sauce, including in dishes like Linguine allo Scoglio (page 120) and Spaghetti al Tonno (page 112).

FRESH PASTA DO'S AND DON'TS

DO make big batches of fresh pasta ahead and freeze it for up to 1 month. Then you can serve your homemade fresh pasta any night of the week!

DO use a large pot and 4 quarts of salted water to cook most fresh pasta—the same recommendation that we give for cooking dried pasta.

DO pay close attention to the cooking time for fresh pasta—it cooks much faster than dried pasta, so start checking for doneness after just a minute or two.

DO reserve some of the pasta cooking water to adjust the consistency of your finished sauce, just as you would for dried pasta.

DO warm the serving bowls to help your finished creation stay hot longer.

DO finish fresh pasta dishes with a drizzle of extra-virgin olive oil.

DO feel free to add other garnishes such as the appropriate grated cheese, chopped fresh herb, or toasted bread crumbs.

DO feel free to substitute fresh pasta for dried when serving it with any sauces that have a fine, uniform texture, such as pestos or ground meat ragùs.

DO use 24 ounces of fresh pasta for every 16 ounces of dried when converting dried pasta recipes to fresh.

DON'T rush the process. The dough needs to rest after you make it so that the gluten can relax before you roll it out, and the shaped pasta needs to air-dry, or "cure" after you form it so that it doesn't stick together.

DON'T expect fresh pasta to be like dried pasta. No matter which of our doughs you use, your fresh pasta will have a smoother texture and be more tender than the same shape of dried pasta.

DON'T drain stuffed fresh pasta such as ravioli or tortellini in a colander, as this might cause the pieces to burst open. Instead, remove them from the cooking water using a slotted spoon or wire skimmer.

DON'T let your cooked fresh pasta sit unsauced for any length of time, or it will stick together hopelessly.

DON'T stir fresh pasta too vigorously when combining it with its sauce; this can break the delicate fresh strands or pieces.

DON'T add too much pasta cooking water when adjusting the finished consistency of the pasta and sauce. Since it's already so well hydrated, cooked fresh pasta won't absorb water to the same degree that cooked dried pasta does.

DON'T use fresh pasta in dishes that call for large pieces of ingredients such as broccoli or sausage. Because of its softer texture, fresh pasta has a greater tendency to clump, and the components won't combine evenly.

BUON APPETITO!

Feed a Crowd

Special-Occasion Showstoppers

Iconic Classics Made with Fresh Pasta

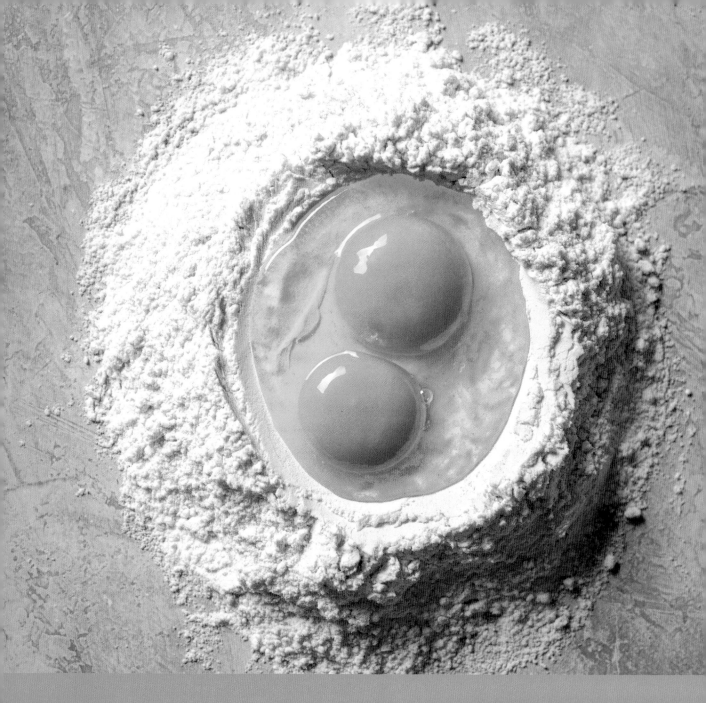

HOMEMADE PASTA DOUGH

Chapter 1

Doughs for Rolling, Cutting, and Shaping

Doughs for Extruding

Egg Pasta Dough

Makes about 1 pound
Total Time: 15 minutes

2 cups (10 ounces)
all-purpose flour,
plus extra as needed

2 large eggs plus
6 large yolks

2 tablespoons
extra-virgin olive oil

WHY THIS RECIPE WORKS: Use this tender, easy-to-roll dough for strand pasta, lasagna sheets, filled pasta, and any shape that you hand-cut from pasta sheets, such as farfalle, garganelli, and maltagliati. Six egg yolks, in addition to two whole eggs and a couple tablespoons of olive oil, make the dough incredibly supple while also adding great flavor. The addition of olive oil is a debated topic in Italy, but we find that it makes the dough easier to roll while still keeping it springy and delicate. In fact, you can roll this dough either in a manual pasta maker or by hand. Resting the dough for at least 30 minutes allows the gluten—the protein network that forms when flour and liquid interact and that makes doughs chewy—time to relax so that the dough won't contract after rolling out in a pasta machine or by hand. If using a high-protein all-purpose flour, such as King Arthur, increase the number of egg yolks to seven. See Chapter 2 for instructions on rolling, cutting, and shaping pasta dough as well as making filled pastas. See suggestions for flavoring your pasta dough on page 282.

1A For mixing and kneading with a machine Process flour, eggs and yolks, and oil together in food processor until mixture forms cohesive dough that feels soft and is barely tacky to touch, about 45 seconds. (If dough sticks to fingers, add up to ¼ cup flour, 1 tablespoon at a time, until barely tacky. If dough doesn't become cohesive, add up to 1 tablespoon water, 1 teaspoon at a time, until it just comes together; process 30 seconds longer.)

1B For mixing and kneading by hand Place flour in large bowl. Using fork, mix eggs, egg yolks, and oil together in separate bowl, then stir into flour. Using your hands, knead dough in bowl until mixture forms cohesive dough that feels soft and is barely tacky to touch, about 3 minutes. (If dough sticks to fingers after 3 minutes, add up to ¼ cup flour, 1 tablespoon at a time, until barely tacky. If dough doesn't become cohesive, add up to 1 tablespoon water, 1 teaspoon at a time, until it just comes together; knead 1 minute longer.)

2 Transfer dough to clean surface and knead by hand to form smooth, uniform ball, 1 to 2 minutes. Shape dough into 6-inch-long cylinder. Wrap with plastic wrap and set aside at room temperature to rest for at least 30 minutes or up to 4 hours.

Mixing and Kneading Egg Dough with a Food Processor

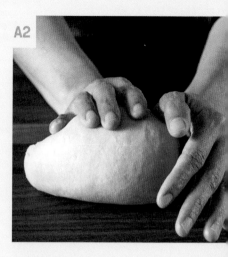

A1 Process the ingredients in a food processor until the mixture forms a cohesive dough that feels soft and is barely tacky to the touch.

A2 Transfer the dough to a clean surface and knead by hand to form a smooth, uniform ball, 1 to 2 minutes.

Mixing and Kneading Egg Dough by Hand

B1 Place the flour in a large bowl. Using a fork, mix the eggs, egg yolks, and oil together in a separate bowl, then stir them into the flour.

B2 Using your hands, knead the dough in the bowl until the mixture forms a cohesive dough that feels soft and is barely tacky to the touch, about 3 minutes.

B3 Transfer the dough to a clean surface and knead by hand to form a smooth, uniform ball, 1 to 2 minutes.

Semolina Pasta Dough

Makes about 1 pound
Total Time: 20 minutes

2¼ cups (11¼ ounces) fine semolina flour, plus extra as needed

⅔ cup (5⅓ ounces) warm water, plus extra as needed

WHY THIS RECIPE WORKS: Dried Italian pasta typically uses egg-free semolina dough, and it's also wonderful in its fresh form. This is a sturdy dough for making hand-formed shapes, including orecchiette, trofie, and malloreddus. You can also use it to make strand pasta, lasagna sheets, filled pasta, and hand-cut shapes (we do recommend using a machine to roll this dough). Doughs made with rougher semolina flour absorb sauces readily, so the pasta becomes permeated with the sauce's flavor. For the perfect chew, we use warm water, which jump-starts gluten development, and we give the dough a generous knead before resting it. Be sure to use fine semolina (often labeled rimacinata, extra-fancy, or #1); conventional semolina is too coarse. This recipe was developed using a 4.5-quart stand mixer. If using a 7-quart stand mixer, you will need to regularly push the dough into the center of the bowl so that the dough is properly kneaded. See Chapter 2 for instructions on rolling, cutting, and shaping pasta dough as well as making filled pastas. See suggestions for flavoring your pasta dough on pages 28–29.

1A For mixing and kneading with a machine
Add flour to bowl of stand mixer, then stir in warm water. Using your hands, knead dough in bowl until shaggy ball forms and no dry flour remains, about 3 minutes. (If dough sticks to fingers after 3 minutes, add up to ¼ cup flour, 1 tablespoon at a time, until barely tacky. If dough doesn't become cohesive, add up to 1 tablespoon water, 1 teaspoon at a time, until it just comes together; knead 1 minute longer.) Using dough hook, knead dough on medium speed until smooth and elastic, 10 to 12 minutes. (Dough may break into smaller pieces while kneading.) Transfer dough to clean surface and knead by hand to form smooth, uniform ball, 1 to 2 minutes.

1B For mixing and kneading by hand
Combine flour and water in large bowl. Using your hands, knead dough in bowl until shaggy ball forms and no dry flour remains, about 3 minutes. (If dough sticks to fingers after 3 minutes, add up to ¼ cup flour, 1 tablespoon at a time, until barely tacky. If dough doesn't become cohesive, add up to 1 tablespoon water, 1 teaspoon at a time, until it just comes together; knead 1 minute longer.) Transfer dough to clean surface and continue to knead by hand until dough is elastic and forms smooth, uniform ball, 10 to 12 minutes.

2 Shape dough into 6-inch-long cylinder. Wrap with plastic wrap and let rest at room temperature for 30 minutes or up to 4 hours.

Mixing and Kneading Semolina Dough with a Mixer

A1 Add the flour to the bowl of a stand mixer, then stir in the warm water. Using your hands, knead the dough in the bowl until a shaggy ball forms and no dry flour remains, about 3 minutes.

A2 Using the dough hook, knead the dough on medium speed until smooth and elastic, 10 to 12 minutes.

A3 Transfer the dough to a clean surface and knead by hand to form a uniform ball, 1 to 2 minutes.

A1

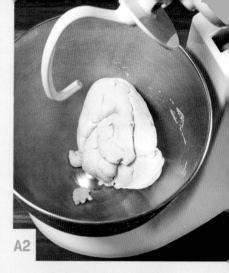
A2

A3

Mixing and Kneading Semolina Dough by Hand

B1 Combine the flour and water in a large bowl. Using your hands, knead the dough in the bowl until a shaggy ball forms and no dry flour remains, about 3 minutes.

B2 Transfer the dough to a clean surface and continue to knead by hand until the dough is smooth and elastic, 10 to 12 minutes. Form the dough into a uniform ball.

B1

B2

Whole-Wheat Pasta Dough

WHY THIS RECIPE WORKS: Use this hearty dough for strand pasta, lasagna sheets, filled pasta, and any hand-cut or hand-shaped pasta (we do recommend using a machine to roll it). A common complaint about commercial whole-wheat pasta is that it cooks up mushy. That's because whole wheat, with its bran and germ intact, tends to literally cut through the strands of gluten protein in the dough. To solve this problem and produce a malleable dough that rolls out easily and cooks up al dente, we use a blend of whole-wheat and all-purpose flours. The small amount of all-purpose flour helps keep the strands of gluten protein intact while still allowing for the nuttiness of the whole-wheat flavor to be front and center. You can substitute rye, spelt, or farro flour for the whole-wheat flour. See Chapter 2 for instructions on rolling, cutting, and shaping pasta dough as well as making filled pastas. You can flavor your whole-wheat pasta dough according to the instructions on pages 28–29, although the nuttiness of the whole-wheat flour will remain prominent.

Makes about
1 pound
Total Time:
15 minutes

1½ cups (8¼ ounces) whole-wheat flour

½ cup (2½ ounces) all-purpose flour, plus extra as needed

3 large eggs, lightly beaten

1½ tablespoons warm water

1A For mixing and kneading with a machine Process whole-wheat flour and all-purpose flour in food processor until combined, about 5 pulses. Add eggs and water and process until mixture forms cohesive dough that feels soft and is barely tacky to touch, about 45 seconds. (If dough sticks to fingers, add up to ¼ cup all-purpose flour, 1 tablespoon at a time, until barely tacky. If dough doesn't become cohesive, add up to 1 tablespoon water, 1 teaspoon at a time, until it just comes together; process 30 seconds longer.)

1B For mixing and kneading by hand Whisk whole-wheat flour and all-purpose flour together in large bowl. Stir eggs and water into flour mixture. Using your hands, knead dough in bowl until mixture forms cohesive dough that feels soft and is barely tacky to touch, about 3 minutes. (If dough sticks to fingers after 3 minutes, add up to ¼ cup flour, 1 tablespoon at a time, until barely tacky. If dough doesn't become cohesive, add up to 1 tablespoon water, 1 teaspoon at a time, until it just comes together; knead 1 minute longer.)

2 Transfer dough to clean surface and knead by hand to form smooth, uniform ball, 1 to 2 minutes. Shape dough into 6-inch-long cylinder. Wrap with plastic wrap and set aside at room temperature to rest for at least 1 hour or up to 4 hours.

VARIATION

Buckwheat Pasta Dough
Substitute ½ cup buckwheat flour for whole wheat flour; increase all-purpose flour to 1½ cups.

Gluten-Free Pasta Dough

Makes about 1 pound
Total Time: 15 minutes

1⅔ cups (7½ ounces) brown rice flour, plus extra as needed

½ cup plus 2 tablespoons (2½ ounces) tapioca starch

1 tablespoon xanthan gum

4 large eggs

1 tablespoon extra-virgin olive oil

WHY THIS RECIPE WORKS: Use this dough for strand pasta, lasagna sheets, filled pasta, and any shape that you hand-cut from pasta sheets, such as farfalle, garganelli, and maltagliati. While there are many dried gluten-free pastas available these days, fresh gluten-free pasta is still tricky. Because of the lack of gluten, the dough tears easily and can cook up mushy. For the best texture and flavor, we use a combination of brown rice flour for sturdy structure and tapioca starch for elasticity. Four whole eggs adds enough moisture and protein to ensure that the noodles hold together nicely once cooked. Xanthan gum is a must to help bolster the structure (see page 4 for more information on this ingredient), while a little extra-virgin olive oil helps with rolling. You need a machine to roll this dough; it will be too difficult to get the pasta thin enough using a rolling pin, and the dough will be much more likely to tear. See Chapter 2 for instructions on rolling, cutting, shaping pasta dough as well as making filled pastas. See suggestions for flavoring your pasta dough on pages 28–29.

1A For mixing and kneading with a machine Pulse rice flour, tapioca starch, and xanthan gum in food processor until combined, about 5 pulses. Add eggs and oil and process until cohesive dough forms and clears sides of bowl, about 10 seconds. (If dough sticks to sides of bowl, add up to ¼ cup rice flour, 1 tablespoon at a time, until barely tacky. If dough doesn't become cohesive, add up to 1 tablespoon water, 1 teaspoon at a time, until it just comes together; process 30 seconds longer.)

1B For mixing and kneading by hand Whisk rice flour, tapioca starch, and xanthan gum together in large bowl. Using fork, mix eggs and oil together in separate bowl, then stir into flour mixture. Using your hands, knead dough in bowl until mixture clears sides of bowl, about 3 minutes. (If dough sticks to sides of bowl after 3 minutes, add up to ¼ cup rice flour, 1 tablespoon at a time, until barely tacky. If dough doesn't become cohesive, add up to 1 tablespoon water, 1 teaspoon at a time, until it just comes together; knead 1 minute longer.)

2 Transfer dough to clean surface and knead by hand until dough comes together, about 30 seconds. (Dough should hold together but won't be smooth.) Shape dough into 6-inch-long cylinder. Wrap with plastic wrap if not using immediately (use within 4 hours).

Mixing Gluten-Free Dough with a Food Processor

A1 Process the dry ingredients together, then add the liquid ingredients and process until a cohesive dough forms and clears the sides of the work bowl.

Mixing and Kneading Gluten-Free Dough by Hand

B1 After stirring the liquid ingredients into the dry ingredients, knead the dough in the bowl until it is cohesive and clears the sides of the bowl.

B2 Transfer the dough to a clean surface and knead by hand until the dough completely comes together (it will not be smooth).

Creating Flavored Pasta

Adding additional ingredients to your homemade pasta dough brings eye-catching color and subtle flavor to your finished fresh pasta. You can add these ingredients to any of the pasta dough recipes in this chapter. Be prepared to adjust the consistency of each specific dough with extra water as needed. See page 14 for some suggestions to get started pairing flavored pastas with complementary sauces.

Herb Pasta

For dough mixed by hand or with a machine

Whisk 2 tablespoons minced fresh parsley, basil, dill, chives, and/or tarragon into the liquid ingredients before adding them to the flour.

For extruded dough

Whisk 2 tablespoons minced fresh parsley, basil, dill, chives, and/or tarragon into the liquid ingredients before adding them to the mixing chamber.

Lemon-Pepper Pasta

For dough mixed by hand or with a machine

Whisk 1 tablespoon grated lemon zest and 1 teaspoon finely ground pepper into the liquid ingredients before adding them to the flour.

For extruded dough

Whisk 1 tablespoon grated lemon zest and 1 teaspoon finely ground pepper into the liquid ingredients before adding them to the mixing chamber.

Spinach Pasta

For dough mixed by hand or with a machine

For egg and whole-wheat doughs, reduce the added egg yolks by half or omit the added water. For semolina dough, reduce the water by 2 tablespoons. For gluten-free dough, reduce the eggs to 3.

Process 4 ounces frozen spinach, thawed and thoroughly squeezed dry, with the liquid ingredients in a food processor until finely chopped. If mixing the dough with a food processor, add the flour to the processor and proceed with the recipe.

For extruded dough

For egg, whole-wheat, and gluten-free doughs, omit the added water. For semolina dough, reduce the water by 2 tablespoons.

Process 4 ounces frozen spinach, thawed and thoroughly squeezed dry, with the liquid ingredients in a food processor before adding them to the mixing chamber.

Tomato Pasta

For dough mixed by hand or with a machine

For egg and whole-wheat doughs, reduce the added egg yolks by half or omit the added water. For semolina dough, reduce the water by 2 tablespoons. For gluten-free dough, reduce the eggs to 3.

Whisk 2 tablespoons tomato paste into the liquid ingredients before adding them to the flour.

For extruded dough

For egg, whole-wheat, and gluten-free doughs, omit the added water. For semolina dough, reduce the water by 2 tablespoons.

Whisk 2 tablespoons tomato paste into the liquid ingredients before adding them to the mixing chamber.

Squid Ink Pasta

For dough mixed by hand or with a machine

For egg and whole-wheat doughs, reduce the added egg yolks by half or omit the added water. For semolina dough, reduce the water by 2 tablespoons. For gluten-free dough, reduce the eggs to 3.

Whisk 2 tablespoons squid or cuttlefish ink into the liquid ingredients before adding them to the flour.

For extruded dough

For egg, whole-wheat, and gluten-free doughs, omit the added water. For semolina dough, reduce the water by 2 tablespoons.

Whisk 2 tablespoons squid or cuttlefish ink into the liquid ingredients before adding them to the mixing chamber.

Saffron Pasta

For dough mixed by hand or with a machine

For semolina and whole-wheat doughs, bloom ½ teaspoon crumbled saffron threads in the specified amount of warm water for 15 minutes before adding the saffron mixture to the flour.

For egg dough, reduce the added egg yolks by half. For gluten-free dough, reduce the eggs to 3. Bloom the saffron in 1 tablespoon warm water, then whisk the saffron mixture into the eggs before adding it to the flour.

For extruded dough

Bloom ½ teaspoon crumbled saffron threads in the specified amount of warm water for 15 minutes before whisking the eggs and water together.

Egg Pasta Dough for an Extruder

Makes about 1 pound
Total Time: 25 minutes

WHY THIS RECIPE WORKS: You need a different dough if you're using a counter-top pasta extruder, no matter what kind of dough you are making. This is because too much hydration will cause the dough to gum up the works of the machine. Also, to end up with a pound of pasta, you need a slightly higher quantity of dough to begin with, since there will always be a bit left in the hopper at the end of the extruding process. Here, we adapt our fresh egg dough for an extruder, using three eggs and two extra egg yolks while omitting the olive oil altogether. Be aware that your extruder may have automatic mixing and extruding settings that will need to be adjusted to match the instructions given in this recipe. If using an extruding attachment for your stand mixer, combine the dough in the mixer bowl on low speed using the paddle attach-ment, then extrude the dough on low speed using an extruder attachment. For more information on using a pasta extruder, see pages 38–39. See suggestions for flavoring your pasta dough on pages 28–29.

2½ cups (12½ ounces) all-purpose flour, plus extra as needed

2 large eggs plus 4 large yolks

1 tablespoon warm water, plus extra as needed

1 Attach desired pasta die to pasta extruder and add flour to mixing chamber. Using fork, beat eggs and yolks, and water together in bowl. Select mixing setting, slowly add egg mixture to flour, and mix until no dry flour remains and mixture begins to form crumbles, about 3 minutes. (Mixture should not form cohesive dough.) Pause extruder and let dough rest for 10 minutes.

2 Lightly dust rimmed baking sheet with flour. Select extruding setting and allow about 3 inches of pasta to extrude through die; pause extruder. Cut off pasta, crumble into small pieces, and return to mixing chamber. Resume extruding, cutting pasta into desired lengths and transferring to prepared sheet. (If extruded pasta does not hold its shape, add up to 2 tablespoons water to mixing chamber, 1 teaspoon at a time, and mix for 30 seconds before extruding further.)

Achieving Properly Hydrated Egg Pasta Dough

Unlike traditional rolled pasta dough, extruded pasta dough needs to be much less hydrated and mixed in order to form shapes properly. Here are visual examples of over-hydrated, under-hydrated, and properly hydrated egg pasta dough to guide you to success.

Too wet   The mixture clumps and begins to form a cohesive dough in the mixing chamber, resulting in dough that cannot be extruded properly through the channel in the extruder.

Too dry   The mixture remains floury and barely clumps in the mixing chamber, resulting in pasta that is not able to hold its shape after being extruded.

Just right   The mixture begins to form crumbles with no dry flour remaining, resulting in pasta that extrudes properly and holds its shape.

too wet

too dry

just right

Semolina Pasta Dough for an Extruder

Makes about 1 pound
Total Time: 25 minutes

2¾ cups (13¾ ounces) fine
      semolina flour

⅔   cup (5⅓ ounces) warm
      water, plus extra as
      needed

WHY THIS RECIPE WORKS: To adapt our fresh semolina dough for use with an extruder, we add more flour while keeping the amount of water the same. Be sure to use fine semolina (often labeled rimacinata, extra-fancy, or #1); conventional semolina is too coarse. Be aware that your extruder may have automatic mixing and extruding settings that will need to be adjusted to match the instructions given in this recipe. If using an extruding attachment for your stand mixer, combine the dough in the mixer bowl on low speed using the paddle attachment, then extrude the dough on low speed using an extruder attachment. For more information on using a pasta extruder, see pages 38–39. See suggestions for flavoring your pasta dough on pages 28–29.

1 Attach desired pasta die to pasta extruder and add flour to mixing chamber. Select mixing setting, slowly add water to flour, and mix until no dry flour remains and mixture begins to form crumbles, about 3 minutes. (Mixture should not form cohesive dough.) Pause extruder and let dough rest for 10 minutes.

2 Lightly dust rimmed baking sheet with flour. Select extruding setting and allow about 3 inches of pasta to extrude through die; pause extruder. Cut off pasta, crumble into small pieces, and return to mixing chamber. Resume extruding, cutting pasta into desired lengths and transferring to prepared sheet. (If extruded pasta does not hold its shape, add up to 1 tablespoon extra water to mixing chamber, 1 teaspoon at a time, and mix for 30 seconds before extruding further.)

Achieving Properly Hydrated Semolina Pasta Dough

Unlike traditional rolled pasta dough, extruded pasta dough needs to be much less hydrated and mixed in order to form shapes properly. Here are visual examples of over-hydrated, under-hydrated, and properly hydrated semolina pasta dough to guide you to success.

Too wet The mixture clumps and begins to form a cohesive dough in the mixing chamber, resulting in dough that cannot be extruded properly through the channel in the extruder.

Too dry The mixture remains floury and barely clumps in the mixing chamber, resulting in pasta that is not able to hold its shape after being extruded.

Just right The mixture begins to form crumbles with no dry flour remaining, resulting in pasta that extrudes properly and holds its shape.

too wet

too dry

just right

Whole-Wheat Pasta Dough for an Extruder

Makes about 1 pound
Total Time: 25 minutes

1¾ cups (9⅔ ounces) whole-wheat flour

¾ cup (3¾ ounces) all-purpose flour, plus extra as needed

3 large eggs

2 tablespoons warm water, plus extra as needed

WHY THIS RECIPE WORKS: To adapt our whole-wheat dough for use with an extruder, we increase the amounts of whole-wheat flour and all-purpose flour and add an additional 1 tablespoon water. When properly hydrated, this dough will have more of a coarse-sand appearance than the egg dough or the semolina dough. You can substitute rye, spelt, or farro flour for the whole-wheat flour. Be aware that your extruder may have automatic mixing and extruding settings that will need to be adjusted to match the instructions given in this recipe. If using an extruding attachment for your stand mixer, combine the dough in the mixer bowl on low speed using the paddle attachment, then extrude the dough on low speed using an extruder attachment. For more information on using a pasta extruder, see pages 38–39. See suggestions for flavoring your pasta dough on pages 28–29.

1 Attach desired pasta die to pasta extruder. Whisk whole-wheat flour and all-purpose flour together in bowl, then add to mixing chamber. Whisk eggs and water together in now-empty bowl. Select mixing setting, slowly add egg mixture to flour, and mix until no dry flour remains and mixture begins to form crumbles, about 3 minutes. (Mixture should not form cohesive dough.) Pause extruder and let dough rest for 10 minutes.

2 Lightly dust rimmed baking sheet with flour. Select extruding setting and allow about 3 inches of pasta to extrude through die; pause extruder. Cut off pasta, crumble into small pieces, and return to mixing chamber. Resume extruding, cutting pasta into desired lengths and transferring to prepared sheet. (If extruded pasta does not hold its shape, add up to 1 tablespoon extra water to mixing chamber, 1 teaspoon at a time, and mix for 30 seconds before extruding further.)

VARIATION

Buckwheat Pasta Dough for an Extruder
Substitute ⅔ cup buckwheat flour for whole wheat flour; increase all-purpose flour to 1¾ cups.

Achieving Properly Hydrated Whole-Wheat Pasta Dough

Unlike traditional rolled pasta dough, extruded pasta dough needs to be much less hydrated and mixed in order to form shapes properly. Here are visual examples of over-hydrated, under-hydrated, and properly hydrated whole-wheat pasta dough to help guide you to success.

Too wet   The mixture clumps and begins to form a cohesive dough in the mixing chamber, resulting in dough that cannot be extruded properly through the extruder channel.

Too dry   The mixture remains floury and barely clumps in the mixing chamber, resulting in pasta that is not able to hold its shape after being extruded.

Just right   The mixture begins to form crumbles with no dry flour remaining, resulting in pasta that extrudes properly and holds its shape.

too wet

too dry

just right

Gluten-Free Pasta Dough for an Extruder

Makes about 1 pound
Total Time: 25 minutes

WHY THIS RECIPE WORKS: Here again we adjust the proportion of the ingredients to adapt our gluten-free dough for use with an extruder, increasing the amount of brown rice flour and tapioca starch, decreasing the eggs from four to three, and using warm water instead of olive oil. Be aware that your extruder may have automatic mixing and extruding settings that will need to be adjusted to match the instructions given in this recipe. If using an extruding attachment for your stand mixer, combine the dough in the mixer bowl on low speed using the paddle attachment, then extrude the dough on low speed using an extruder attachment. For more information on using a pasta extruder, see pages 38–39. See suggestions for flavoring your pasta dough on pages 28–29.

2   cups (9 ounces) brown rice flour

¾   cup (3 ounces) tapioca starch

1   tablespoon xanthan gum

3   large eggs

2   tablespoons warm water, plus extra as needed

1   Attach desired pasta die to pasta extruder. Whisk rice flour, tapioca starch, and xanthan gum together in bowl, then add to mixing chamber. Whisk eggs and water together in now-empty bowl. Select mixing setting, slowly add egg mixture to flour mixture, and mix until no dry flour remains and mixture begins to form crumbles, about 3 minutes. (Mixture should not form cohesive dough.) Pause extruder and let dough rest for 10 minutes.

2   Lightly dust rimmed baking sheet with rice flour. Select extruding setting and allow about 3 inches of pasta to extrude through die; pause extruder. Cut off pasta, crumble into small pieces, and return to mixing chamber. Resume extruding, cutting pasta into desired lengths and transferring to prepared sheet. (If extruded pasta does not hold its shape, add up to 1 tablespoon extra water to mixing chamber, 1 teaspoon at a time, and mix for 30 seconds before extruding further.)

Achieving Properly Hydrated Gluten-Free Pasta Dough

Unlike traditional rolled pasta dough, extruded pasta dough needs to be much less hydrated and mixed in order to form shapes properly. Here are visual examples of over-hydrated, under-hydrated, and properly hydrated gluten-free pasta dough to guide you to success.

Too wet The mixture clumps and begins to form a cohesive dough in the mixing chamber, resulting in dough that cannot be extruded properly through the extruder chamber.

Too dry The mixture remains floury and barely clumps in the mixing chamber, resulting in pasta that is not able to hold its shape after being extruded.

Just right The mixture begins to form crumbles with no dry flour remaining, resulting in pasta that extrudes properly and holds its shape.

too wet

too dry

just right

Test Kitchen Tips for Success Using Pasta Extruders

MACHINE PURCHASE AND CARE

- While testing various machines, we learned that more expensive extruders tended to have heavier-duty, better-quality moving parts, often made of metal instead of plastic. With pasta extruders, you do get what you pay for.

- On the flip side, however, the more bells and whistles your machine has (one model we tested also had a bread dough function, for example), the greater the likelihood that you will at some point end up with a confounding error message while using it. In general, we preferred the simpler, single-purpose machines.

- Different brands of extruders come with different pasta dies, and additional dies can be purchased. Feel free to adapt the recipes in this book according to the shapes you are able to extrude using your machine.

- Whatever machine you do have, allow for a learning curve when first using it. Read the manual and allow time for practicing before making a full recipe to serve.

- Always clean your machine relatively soon after each use. Soft pasta is easier to remove from the small nooks and crannies than dried-out pasta.

- If the dough is sticking to the extruding die when you are cleaning it, let the dough dry for just a couple of minutes in the die. This may help you more easily extract the small bits.

- After removing all the bits of dough, rinse all the moving parts of the machine thoroughly and arrange them on a rimmed sheet pan to air-dry before storing them.

MIXING DOUGH

- In general, the formulation for extruded pasta dough is much dryer than the formulation for rolling dough by hand or with a pasta machine. You want to create a dough that just begins to form crumbles.

- Slowly adding the liquid ingredients to the mixing chamber evenly across the top opening helps to ensure even hydration of the dough.

- If you're planning to add flavoring ingredients to your dough, it's important to remember that you may need to reduce hydration elsewhere. See pages 38–39 for specific guidance.

- Be prepared to pause the machine during the mixing cycle to scrape down the sides of the chamber and the mixing arms completely to ensure a fully combined and hydrated dough.

- If you accidentally hit the "extrude" button during the mixing process (don't beat yourself up—we've done it), you may need to clear out the chamber, auger, and extruding die before proceeding.

- After mixing, let the dough rest for about 10 minutes before beginning to extrude it. This resting period further allows for proper dough hydration. Most extruders don't have a rest function, so you will need to hit the "pause" button. (Don't turn the machine off.)

- If your dough gets over-hydrated and won't cut properly, don't despair! Dump out the dough, add a little flour, knead it by hand, and then roll and cut it by hand.

EXTRUDING DOUGH

○ Inevitably the first few inches of pasta will be ragged. Cut off the first 3 inches and return them to the mixing chamber. If you get overeager with your cutting, you can also return too-short pieces to the mixing chamber.

○ Toward the end of extruding, there is typically dough that doesn't get pulled into the auger. Pause the machine and either push the dough toward the auger or manually add the dough pieces to the auger opening.

○ Sometimes the machine will self-pause while extruding (especially with weaker machines). Clearing the auger chamber or hitting the "pause" button and then trying to extrude again will usually solve the problem. This especially happens with firmer doughs like our semolina and whole-wheat doughs.

○ If the dough is fraying as it extrudes, it is too dry. You may need to mix in a small amount of liquid before attempting to extrude again. Sometimes if the dough if fraying (particularly with tube shapes), there may be a piece of dried pasta or other object blocking the opening. Pause the machine to check.

○ You will always have some dough left at the very end that just doesn't make it through the extruder. Our dough recipes take into account the normal yield loss that happens through the extruding process so that you will end up with 1 pound of fresh pasta.

○ Extruders either come with a cutting tool or have a built-in cutter. In addition to the cutting tools provided, we had success making clean cuts using a paring knife or a bench scraper. We did not get clean cuts using wire, string, or dental floss.

○ You will have the best success and get the cleanest edges using decisive, swift cutting motions. Position your cutting tool tightly against the surface of the die.

○ If the ends of tube shapes are sticking together while cutting, either your dough is over-hydrated or you're not cutting swiftly enough or with a thin-enough blade.

○ You can't make angled cuts when using an extruder, so expect your penne to have straight edges.

○ It's important to support long-strand pasta as it extrudes to prevent tearing or excess stretching.

○ Be sure to position a lightly floured rimmed baking sheet below the die to catch your extruded pasta.

USING A KITCHENAID EXTRUDING ATTACHMENT

○ Feed small clumps of dough into the hopper slowly. Adding the dough all at once or in large pieces tends to clog the hopper.

○ Since the KitchenAid extrudes pasta down toward the counter rather than straight out, make sure to prepare enough space between the extruding die and the counter surface to support and cut the extruding pasta, especially if making long strands.

Which Dough Should I Use?

We developed our fresh pasta doughs to be as versatile as possible. You really can use just about any dough for any pasta shape. The exception is hand-shaped pastas such as orecchiette, cavatelli, and fileja. In order for these to keep their shape when you cook them, you need a higher-gluten, malleable dough made from semolina or whole wheat.

	EGG PASTA DOUGH	SEMOLINA PASTA DOUGH	WHOLE-WHEAT PASTA DOUGH	GLUTEN-FREE PASTA DOUGH
ROLLED, CUT, AND SHAPED PASTA				
SHEETS FOR LASAGNA AND FILLED PASTA	✓	✓	✓	✓
STRAND PASTA	✓	✓	✓	✓
HAND-CUT PASTA (maltagliati, garganelli, farfalle)	✓	✓	✓	✓
HAND-SHAPED PASTA (orecchiette, fileja, trofie, busiate, cavatelli, malloreddus)		✓	✓	
EXTRUDED PASTA				
STRAND PASTA	✓	✓	✓	✓
EXTRUDED SHAPES (spaghetti, bucatini, penne, rigatoni, shells, tubetti, etc.)	✓	✓	✓	✓

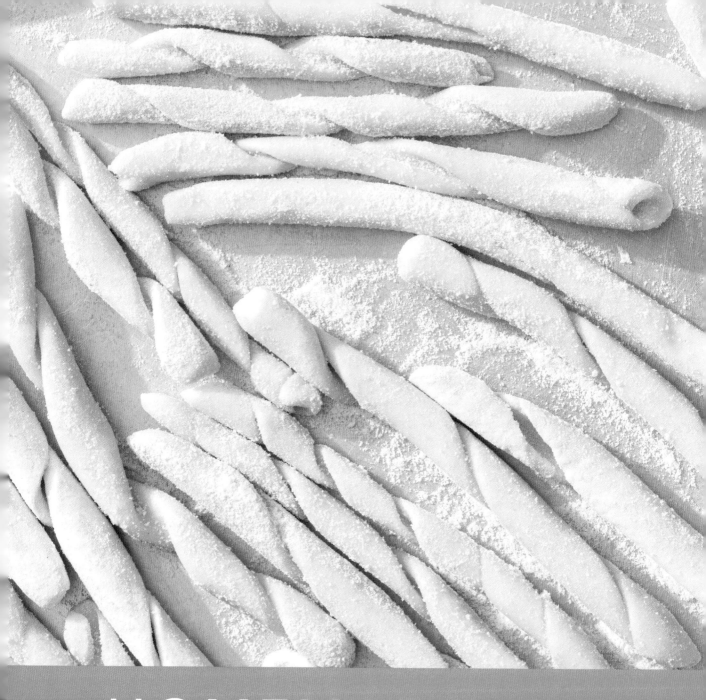

HOMEMADE PASTA SHAPES

Chapter 2

Pasta Fillings

Rolling Dough into Sheets with a Machine

A manual pasta machine greatly speeds up the work of turning any ball of pasta dough into long, delicate sheets of pasta ready to be cut into strands or shapes. It's also easier to use less added flour than if rolling the dough out by hand, though you may need to dust the dough with a little flour as you roll. Letting the sheets of pasta air-dry for about 15 minutes after rolling them slightly "cures" them, making them less likely to tear when you start cutting them.

1 Divide the dough into 6 pieces (for strand pasta and filled pasta shapes) or 10 pieces (for lasagna sheets) and cover with plastic wrap. Flatten 1 piece of dough into a ½-inch-thick disk. Using a pasta machine with the rollers set to the widest position, feed the dough through the rollers twice.

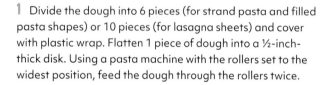

2 Bring the tapered ends of the dough toward the middle and press to seal. Feed the dough seam side up through the rollers again. Repeat feeding the dough, tapered end first, through the rollers set at the widest position, without folding, until the dough is smooth. (If the dough sticks to your fingers or the rollers, lightly dust it with flour and roll again.)

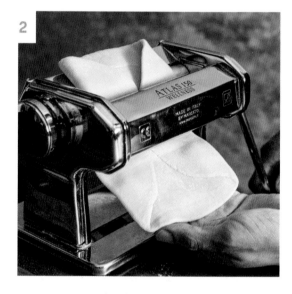

3 Narrow the rollers to the next setting and feed the dough through the rollers twice. Continue to progressively narrow the rollers, feeding the dough through each setting twice, until the desired thickness is achieved. (If the dough becomes too long to manage, halve crosswise.) For strand pasta, cut pasta shapes, and lasagna sheets, transfer the dough sheets to clean dish towel(s) and let air-dry for about 15 minutes. For filled pasta shapes, stack the dough sheets between sheets of liberally floured parchment paper and cover with a damp kitchen towel. Repeat rolling with the remaining dough pieces.

Rolling Dough into Sheets by Hand

Our Egg Pasta Dough for Rolling and Cutting (page 20) is tender enough to roll out by hand, if you like. When rolling by hand, you will likely use a bit more flour than if using a machine. You need to dust the dough with enough flour so that it's not too sticky to work with, but a little cling is okay. If you use too much flour, it won't get incorporated into the dough, but instead will end up turning the surface of your cooked pasta gummy.

1 Divide the dough into 6 pieces (for strand pasta and filled pasta shapes) or 10 pieces (for lasagna sheets); cover with plastic wrap.

2 Working with 1 piece of dough at a time, dust both sides with flour, then press the cut side down into a 3-inch square. With a rolling pin, roll it into a 6-inch square, then dust both sides again with flour.

3 Roll the dough to 12 by 6 inches, rolling from the center of the dough 1 way at a time, then dust with flour. Continue rolling the dough to 20 by 6 inches, lifting it frequently to release it from the work surface. For strand pasta, cut pasta shapes, and lasagna sheets, transfer the dough sheets to clean dish towel(s) and air-dry for about 15 minutes. For filled pasta shapes, stack the dough sheets between sheets of liberally floured parchment paper and cover with a damp kitchen towel. Repeat rolling with the remaining dough pieces.

Cutting Strand Pasta
with a Machine

Manual pasta makers often come with a couple of different cutters, and you can also purchase a wide array of additional cutters. Before cutting strands, we recommend rolling the pasta dough into sheets that are thin but still sturdy, typically at setting 5 or 6 on a standard pasta machine. Cut the rolled-out and air-dried pasta sheets in half crosswise to make 10-inch lengths before feeding the sheets through the machine. After cutting, liberally toss the strands with flour and transfer them to a lightly floured rimmed baking sheet. Repeat with the remaining pasta sheets.

You can use any of the doughs in Chapter 1 to make strand pasta.

Thin but still sturdy   setting 5 or 6 (strand pasta, lasagna sheets)

Thin and semi-transparent   setting 6 or 7 (filled pasta shapes)

Cutting Strand Pasta by Hand

1 Cut 1 air-dried pasta sheet in half crosswise. Starting with the short end, gently fold each half-sheet at 2-inch intervals to create flat, rectangular roll.

2 Using a sharp knife, slice the pasta rolls crosswise to the desired width. Use your fingers to unfurl the pasta, then liberally dust the strands with flour and transfer them to a lightly floured rimmed baking sheet. Repeat with the remaining pasta sheets.

Linguine about ⅛ inch wide

Fettuccine about ¼ inch wide

Tagliatelle about ½ inch wide

Pappardelle about 1 inch wide

Lasagna Noodles

If you've only had lasagna made using dried or no-boil lasagna noodles, you're in for a treat. Whether you roll out pasta dough sheets using a machine or by hand, you need to trim them before cutting them into evenly sized lasagna noodles. From 1 pound of fresh pasta dough, you will get twenty 10 by 3-inch lasagna sheets. For each of the lasagna recipes in Chapter 5, you will need 10 lasagna sheets. Before cutting lasagna noodles, we recommend rolling the pasta dough into sheets that are thin but still sturdy.

You can use any of the doughs in Chapter 1 to make lasagna sheets.

1 Using a sharp knife or pizza cutter, trim and square off the corners of 1 air-dried pasta sheet, then cut the trimmed pasta sheet crosswise into two 10-inch-long pieces.

2 Cut each piece lengthwise into 3-inch-wide lasagna noodles. Let the lasagna noodles sit uncovered on the counter while cutting the remaining pasta sheets (do not overlap the noodles, as they may stick together).

Maltagliati

Maltagliati means "badly cut," and part of the charm of this easy pasta shape is its irregularity. It was born out of frugality—cooks didn't want to discard the trimmings from rolled-out pasta dough. Before cutting this shape, we recommend rolling the pasta dough into sheets that are thin but still sturdy.

You can use any of the doughs in Chapter 1 to make maltagliati.

1 Using a sharp knife or pizza cutter, cut 1 air-dried pasta sheet lengthwise into rough 1½-inch-wide strips.

2 Cut the pasta strips at a 45-degree angle at rough 1½-inch intervals. Transfer the maltagliati to a lightly floured rimmed baking sheet. Repeat with the remaining pasta sheets.

Garganelli

Garganelli, which resemble pointed quills, originated in Emilia-Romagna. A ridged pattern (or no pattern) is the most common, but dedicated garganelli boards can also have beautiful geometric patterns on them. Before cutting this shape, we recommend rolling the pasta dough into sheets that are thin but still sturdy.

Egg pasta dough is traditional, but you can use any of the doughs in Chapter 1 to make garganelli.

1 Using a sharp knife or pizza cutter, cut 1 air-dried pasta sheet into 1½-inch squares; discard the scraps. Lay 1 square of pasta diagonally on the counter or, to create ridges in the pasta, on top of a garganelli or gnocchi board, inverted fork, or wire rack.

2 Wrap 1 corner of the pasta square around a ⅜-inch dowel (or pencil), and with gentle pressure roll away from you until the pasta is completely wrapped around the dowel and the seam is sealed. Slide the shaped pasta off the dowel onto a lightly floured rimmed baking sheet and repeat with the remaining pasta squares and sheets.

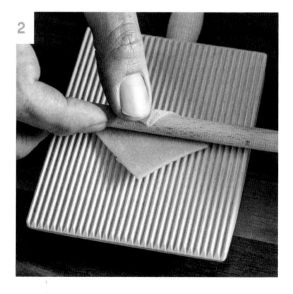

Farfalle

These pretty shapes are also known as bowties, but *farfalle* translates as "butterflies." They are surprisingly easy to shape by hand. Before cutting this shape, we recommend rolling the pasta dough into sheets that are thin but still sturdy.

Egg pasta dough is traditional, but you can use any of the doughs in Chapter 1 to make farfalle.

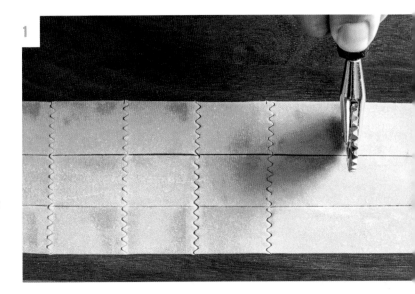

1 Using a sharp knife or pizza cutter, cut 1 air-dried pasta sheet into 1-inch-wide strips. Using a fluted cutter, cut the strips at 1½-inch intervals to make rectangles; discard the scraps.

2 Using your thumb and index fingers, crimp the long sides of a pasta rectangle until they reach the center and firmly pinch to seal. Transfer the farfalle to a lightly floured rimmed baking sheet and repeat with the remaining pasta squares and sheets.

Orecchiette

These "little ears" originated in Puglia, the heel of the Italian boot. Their bowl shape encourages chunky sauces to nestle inside.

Semolina dough is traditional, and we recommend that you use semolina or whole-wheat dough to make orecchiette. Other doughs will not hold the shape.

1 Divide the dough into 8 pieces and cover with plastic wrap. Stretch and roll 1 piece of dough into a ½-inch-thick rope, then cut the rope into ½-inch nuggets.

2 Working with 1 dough nugget at a time, arrange it cut side down on the counter. Using continuous motion, gently press the tip of a butter knife into dough, serrated side down, and drag toward you to form a curled pasta shape.

3 Using lightly floured fingers, place the smooth side of the curled pasta over the tip of your thumb and gently pull on the sides to form an even cup shape. Transfer the orecchiette to a lightly floured rimmed baking sheet. Repeat rolling, cutting, and shaping the remaining dough pieces.

Fileja

From the toe of the Italian boot, Calabria, comes this ancient pasta shape, which is rustically coiled to form a satisfyingly substantial mouthful of pasta.

Semolina dough is traditional, and we recommend that you use semolina or whole-wheat dough to make fileja. Other doughs will not hold the shape.

1 Divide the dough into 16 pieces and cover with plastic wrap. Stretch and roll 1 piece of dough into a ¼-inch-thick rope, then cut the rope into 5-inch lengths.

2 Working with 1 dough length at a time, position it at a 45-degree angle to the counter edge. Place a thin wooden skewer at the top edge of the dough, parallel to the counter edge. Arrange the palms of your hands at the ends of the skewer, apply even pressure against the dough, and roll the skewer toward you in a fluid motion. (Anchor one end of the rope with your palm to help the dough coil around the skewer.)

3 Continue to roll and stretch the dough around the skewer into a 6-inch-long hollow spiraled tube. Slide the fileja off the skewer onto a lightly floured rimmed baking sheet. Dust the skewer with flour as needed if the dough begins to stick. Repeat rolling, cutting, and shaping with the remaining dough pieces.

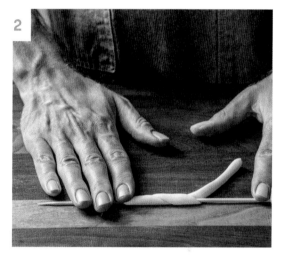

Trofie

Trofie is a short, twisted, rope-like pasta from Liguria that resembles an elongated screw, with thinner ends and a slightly thicker central part.

Semolina dough is traditional, and we recommend that you use semolina or whole-wheat dough to make trofie. Other doughs will not hold the shape.

1 Divide the dough into 8 pieces and cover with plastic wrap. Stretch and roll 1 piece of dough into a ½-inch-thick rope, then cut the rope into ½-inch nuggets.

2 Working with a few nuggets at a time, roll into ¼-inch-thick ropes with tapered ends.

3 Position a rope at a 45-degree angle to the counter edge. Place the edge of a bench scraper at the top of the rope, parallel to the counter edge, and angle the scraper toward you with the surface nearly parallel to the counter surface. While applying even pressure against the dough, pull the scraper toward you in a fluid motion to create a twisted shape. (Lightly mist the trofie with water if there is not enough traction to form a twist.) Transfer the trofie to a lightly floured rimmed baking sheet. Repeat rolling, cutting, and shaping the remaining dough pieces.

Busiate

This pasta shape is often prepared in Sicily and Calabria and resembles an old-fashioned, tightly curled telephone cord, making it extra-fun to eat.

Semolina dough is traditional, and we recommend that you use semolina or whole-wheat dough to make busiate. Other doughs will not hold the shape.

1 Divide the dough into 16 pieces and cover with plastic wrap. Stretch and roll 1 piece of dough into a ¼-inch-thick rope, then cut the rope into 3-inch lengths.

2 Working with 1 dough length at a time, position it at a 45-degree angle to the counter edge. Place a thin wooden skewer at the top edge of the dough, parallel to the counter edge. Arrange the palms of your hands at the ends of the skewer, apply even pressure against the dough, and roll the skewer toward you in a fluid motion to create a tightly coiled rope. (Anchor one end of the rope with your palm to help the dough coil around the skewer.)

3 Slide the busiate off the skewer onto a lightly floured rimmed baking sheet. Dust the skewer with flour as needed if the dough begins to stick. Repeat rolling, cutting, and shaping with the remaining dough pieces.

Cavatelli

These "little hollows" are a small, shell-shaped pasta that's popular throughout southern Italy, with slightly different variations in shape.

Semolina dough is traditional, and we recommend that you use semolina or whole-wheat dough to make cavatelli. Other doughs will not hold the shape.

1 Divide the dough into 8 pieces and cover with plastic wrap. Stretch and roll 1 piece of dough into a ½-inch-thick rope, then cut the rope into ½-inch nuggets.

2 Working with 1 dough nugget at a time, place it cut side down on the counter. Using a continuous motion, gently press the tip of your thumb into the dough and away from you to form a curled pasta shape. Transfer the pasta to a lightly floured rimmed baking sheet. Repeat rolling, cutting, and shaping the remaining dough pieces.

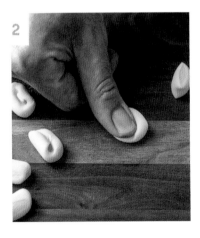

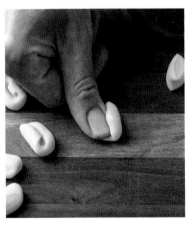

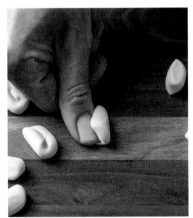

Malloreddus

Also known as gnocchetti sardi, this Sardinian shape resembles cavatelli, but they are ridged and are traditionally made using a shaping board rather than just your hands. In Sardinia, the semolina dough for malloreddus is often flavored with saffron (see page 4).

Semolina dough is traditional, and we recommend that you use semolina or whole-wheat dough to make malloreddus. Other doughs will not hold the shape.

1 Divide the dough into 8 pieces and cover with plastic wrap. Stretch and roll 1 piece of dough into a ½-inch-thick rope, then cut the rope into ½-inch nuggets.

2 Working with 1 dough nugget at a time, place it cut side down on a malloreddus board (or a gnocchi board). Using a continuous motion, gently press the tip of your thumb into the dough and toward the work surface to form a curled pasta shape with ridges on the exterior. Transfer the pasta to a lightly floured rimmed baking sheet. Repeat rolling, cutting, and shaping the remaining dough pieces.

Ravioli

This most famous of filled pastas can be stuffed and sauced in hundreds of different ways. Before cutting this shape, we recommend rolling the pasta dough into thin, semi-transparent sheets that are at least 20 by 5 inches. If your pasta sheets are shorter, you will need to adjust the number of mounds in step 2. To get 1½ pounds of ravioli (about 36), you will need 1 pound pasta dough and about 2½ cups filling.

Egg dough is traditional, but you can use any of the doughs in Chapter 1 to make ravioli.

1 Lay 1 pasta sheet on the counter with the long side parallel to the edge. Using a sharp knife or pizza cutter, trim and square off the corners. Lightly brush the bottom half with egg white.

2 Starting 1½ inches from the left edge of the dough and 1 inch from the bottom, evenly space six 1-tablespoon mounds of filling. Cut the sheet at the center points between the filling mounds.

3 Lift the top edge of the dough and pull it over the filling to line up with bottom edge. Keeping the top edge of the dough suspended over the filling with your thumbs, use your fingers to press the dough layers together, working around each mound of filling from back to front, pressing out as much air as possible before sealing completely.

4A To make square ravioli Using a fluted cutter, pizza wheel, or sharp knife, cut away the excess dough, leaving a ¼- to ½-inch border around each mound of filling. Place the ravioli on a parchment paper–lined rimmed baking sheet. Repeat with the remaining pasta sheets and filling. Let the ravioli sit uncovered until dry to the touch and slightly stiffened, about 30 minutes.

4B To make round ravioli Use a 2½-inch round ravioli stamp or cookie cutter to cut out circles around the filling. Place the ravioli on a parchment paper–lined rimmed baking sheet. Repeat with the remaining pasta sheets and filling. Let the ravioli sit uncovered until dry to the touch and slightly stiffened, about 30 minutes.

Mezzelune

Ravioli's first cousin is shaped like a half-moon. Before cutting this shape, we recommend rolling the pasta dough into sheets that are thin and semi-transparent. To get 1½ pounds of mezzelune (about 42), you will need 1 pound pasta dough and about 1½ cups filling.

Egg dough is traditional, but you can use any of the doughs in Chapter 1 to make mezzelune.

1 Lay 1 pasta sheet on the counter with the long side parallel to the edge. Using a 3-inch round cookie cutter, cut the pasta into rounds; discard the scraps. Place 1½ teaspoons filling in the center of each round.

2 Working with 1 pasta round at a time, lightly brush the edges with egg white. Lift the top edge of the dough over the filling to line up with bottom edge to form half-moon shape. Keeping the top edge of the dough suspended over the filling with your thumbs, use your fingers to press the dough layers together, working around each mound of filling from back to front, pressing out as much air as possible before sealing completely. Place the mezzelune on a parchment paper–lined rimmed baking sheet. Repeat with the remaining pasta sheets and filling. Let the mezzelune sit uncovered until dry to the touch and slightly stiffened, about 30 minutes.

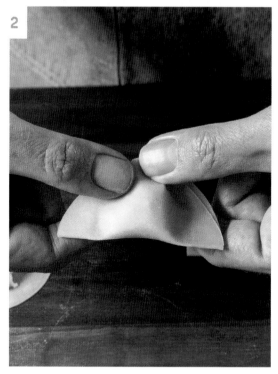

Agnolotti

Agnolotti traditionally contain a meat filling, though you can try others in this Piedmontese specialty. Before cutting this shape, we recommend rolling the pasta dough into thin, semi-transparent sheets that are at least 20 by 5 inches. If your pasta sheets are shorter, you will need to adjust the number of pinched sections in step 3. Instead of a pastry bag, you can use a 1-gallon zipper-lock bag; snip off a corner to create a ¾-inch opening. To get 1½ pounds of agnolotti (about 60), you will need 1 pound pasta dough and about 3 cups filling.

Egg dough is traditional, but you can use any of the doughs in Chapter 1 to make agnolotti.

1 Lay 1 pasta sheet on the counter with the long side parallel to the edge. Using a sharp knife or pizza cutter, trim the pasta into a 4-inch-wide sheet. Place the filling in a pastry bag fitted with ¾-inch round tip. Pipe the filling lengthwise down the center of the sheet, leaving a 1-inch border at each end.

2 Lightly brush the edges with egg white. Fold the bottom edge of the pasta over the filling until it is flush with the top edge. Gently press to seal the long edge of the pasta flush to the filling; leave the narrow edges unsealed.

3 With the index finger and thumb of both your hands facing downward, pinch the filled portion of pasta together at 1-inch increments to create 15 individual sections.

4 Using a fluted cutter or sharp knife, cut away the excess dough from the edges, leaving a ¼- to ½-inch border. Starting at the bottom edge of the strip, roll the cutter away from you between the pinched sections to fold and seal the dough and separate the agnolotti. Pinch the edges of each agnolotto to reinforce the seal. Place the agnolotti on a parchment paper–lined rimmed baking sheet. Repeat with the remaining pasta sheets and filling. Let the agnolotti sit uncovered until dry to the touch and slightly stiffened, about 30 minutes.

Tortellini

Near Bologna, where they're from, tortellini are nearly always served in broth, though you can certainly serve these navel-shaped dumplings with sauce instead. Before cutting this shape, we recommend rolling the pasta dough into sheets that are thin and semi-transparent. To get 1½ pounds of tortellini (about 96), you will need 1 pound pasta dough and about 1 cup filling.

Egg dough is traditional, but you can use any of the doughs in Chapter 1 to make tortellini.

1 Lay 1 pasta sheet on the counter with the long side parallel to the edge. Using a 2½-inch round cookie cutter, cut pasta into rounds; discard the scraps. Place ½ teaspoon filling in the center of each round.

2 Working with 1 pasta round at a time, lightly brush the edges with egg white. Lift the top edge of the dough over the filling to line up with the bottom edge to form a half-moon shape. Keeping the top edge of the dough suspended over the filling with your thumbs, use your fingers to press the dough layers together, working around each mound of filling from back to front, pressing out as much air as possible before sealing completely.

3 Pull the folded corners together below the filling until slightly overlapped to create a tortellino with a cupped outer edge and a dimpled center. Press to seal the overlapping edges and transfer to a parchment paper–lined rimmed baking sheet. Repeat with the remaining pasta sheets and filling. Let the tortellini sit uncovered until dry to the touch and slightly stiffened, about 30 minutes.

Cappelletti

Cappelletti use a dough square instead of a dough round, and so they resemble "little hats" more than they do belly buttons. They are sometimes formed larger than tortellini as well. Before cutting this shape, we recommend rolling the pasta dough into thin, semi-transparent sheets that are 5 inches wide. If your sheets are narrower, fold them in half crosswise and roll again. To get 1½ pounds of cappelletti (about 96), you will need 1 pound pasta dough and about 1 cup filling.

Egg dough is traditional, but you can use any of the doughs in Chapter 1 to make cappelletti.

1 Lay 1 pasta sheet on the counter with the long side parallel to the edge. Using a sharp knife or pizza cutter, cut pasta into 2½-inch squares; discard the scraps. Place ½ teaspoon filling in the center of each square.

2 With one corner of a pasta square facing you, lift the top corner of the dough over the filling to line up with the bottom corner. Keeping the top edge of the dough suspended over the filling with your thumbs, use your fingers to press the dough layers together, working around each mound of filling from back to front, pressing out as much air as possible before sealing completely.

3 Pull the folded corners together below the filling until slightly overlapped to create a cappelletto with a cupped outer edge and a dimpled center. Press to seal the overlapping edges and transfer to a parchment paper–lined rimmed baking sheet. Repeat with the remaining pasta sheets and filling. Let the cappelletti sit uncovered until dry to the touch and slightly stiffened, about 30 minutes.

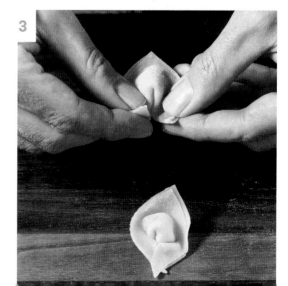

Cappellacci

Where cappelletti are "little hats," dramatic-looking cappellacci are "big hats." Made from squares of pasta dough that are twice as large as their siblings, they enclose lots more filling. Before cutting this shape, we recommend rolling the pasta dough into sheets that are thin and semi-transparent. To get 1½ pounds of cappellacci (about 24), you will need 1 pound pasta dough and about 1½ cups filling.

Egg dough is traditional, but you can use any of the doughs in Chapter 1 to make cappellacci.

1 Working with 1 pasta sheet at a time, cut it into 5-inch squares on a lightly floured counter; discard the scraps. Place rounded 1 tablespoon filling in the center of each square.

2 Working with 1 pasta square at a time, lightly brush the edges with egg white. With one corner of a pasta square facing you, lift the top corner of pasta over the filling and extend it so that it lines up with bottom corner. Keeping the top corner of the dough suspended over the filling with your thumbs, use your fingers to press the dough layers together, working around each mound of filling from back to front, pressing out as much air as possible before sealing completely.

3 Pull the corners together below the filling until slightly overlapped to create a cappellaccio with a cupped outer edge and a dimpled center. Press to seal the overlapping edges and transfer to a parchment paper–lined rimmed baking sheet. Repeat with the remaining pasta sheets and filling.

Pansotti

Pansotti ("pot-bellied") are filled and folded so that their bellies bulge. Despite their homespun name, this Ligurian specialty is an elegant filled pasta similar to cappelletti or tortellini. Before cutting this shape, we recommend rolling the pasta dough into sheets that are thin and semi-transparent. To get 1½ pounds of pansotti (about 96), you will need 1 pound pasta dough and about 1½ cups filling.

Egg dough is traditional, but you can use any of the doughs in Chapter 1 to make pansotti.

1 Working with 1 pasta sheet at a time, cut it into 2½-inch squares on a lightly floured counter; discard the scraps. Place rounded ½ teaspoon filling in the center of each square.

2 Working with 1 pasta square at a time, lightly brush the edges with egg white. With one corner of the pasta square facing you, lift the top corner of the dough over the filling to line up with the bottom corner. Keeping the top edge of the dough suspended over the filling with your thumbs, use your fingers to press the dough layers together, working around each mound of filling from back to front, pressing out as much air as possible before sealing completely.

3 Pull the edges closest to the filling toward each other below the filling until they are just overlapping to create a pansotto with a collared outer edge and a dimpled center. Press to seal the edges and transfer to a parchment paper–lined rimmed baking sheet. Repeat with the remaining pasta sheets and filling.

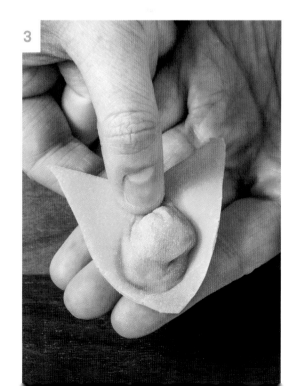

Potato Gnocchi

WHY THIS RECIPE WORKS: For potato flavor with personality, we use russets, parcooking them in the microwave and finishing them in the oven before mashing them. Russets are lower in moisture than other potatoes, which is essential to creating light gnocchi. Peeling and processing the spuds as soon as they come out of the oven allows the maximum amount of steam to escape, so don't be temped to let them cool. To avoid lumps, which can cause gnocchi to break apart during boiling, we use a potato ricer. Using an exact amount of flour based on the ratio of potato to flour (rather than a range) means minimal mixing, which also keeps the gnocchi light. Although the egg isn't traditional, it tenderizes them. After processing the cooked potatoes, you may have slightly more than the 3 cups (16 ounces) of potatoes required; reserve the remainder.

Makes
1½ pounds
(enough to
serve 4 to 6)
Total Time:
1½ hours

2   pounds russet potatoes

1   large egg, lightly beaten

¾   cup plus 1 tablespoon
     (4 ounces) all-purpose flour,
     plus extra for the work
     surface

1   teaspoon table salt

1   Adjust oven rack to middle and heat oven to 450 degrees. Poke each potato 8 times with paring knife over entire surface. Place potatoes on plate and microwave until slightly softened at ends, about 10 minutes, flipping potatoes halfway through cooking. Transfer potatoes directly to oven rack and bake 18 to 20 minutes, until skewer glides easily through flesh and potatoes yield to gentle pressure.

2   Hold potato with pot holder or kitchen towel and peel with paring knife. Process potato through a ricer or food mill onto a rimmed baking sheet. Repeat with remaining potatoes. Gently spread riced potatoes into even layer and cool for 5 minutes.

3   Transfer 3 cups (16 ounces) warm potatoes to a large bowl. Using fork, gently stir in egg until just combined. Sprinkle flour and salt over potato mixture. Using fork, gently combine until no pockets of dry flour remain. Press mixture into rough dough, transfer to lightly floured work surface, and gently knead until smooth but still slightly sticky, about 1 minute, lightly dusting work surface with flour as needed to prevent sticking.

4   Line 2 rimmed baking sheets with parchment paper and dust liberally with flour. Lightly dust work surface with flour. Cut dough into 8 pieces and cover with plastic wrap. Gently roll 1 piece of dough into ½-inch-thick rope, dusting with flour to prevent sticking. Cut rope into ¾-inch lengths.

5   Place 1 length of dough cut side down on gnocchi board or on tines of inverted fork. Using continuous motion, gently press and stretch dough away from you to roll into curled shape with ridges on exterior. Transfer formed gnocchi to prepared sheet and repeat with remaining dough.

1 Divide the dough into 8 pieces and cover with plastic wrap. Stretch and roll 1 piece of dough into a ½-inch-thick rope, dusting it with flour to prevent sticking. Cut the rope into ¾-inch lengths.

2 Working with 1 dough nugget at a time, place it cut side down on a gnocchi board (or the tines of an inverted fork). Using a continuous motion, gently press and stretch the dough down toward counter to roll it into a curled shape with ridges on the exterior. Transfer the formed gnocchi to a parchment paper–lined baking sheet and repeat with the remaining dough.

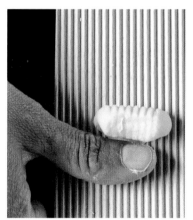

Ricotta Filling

Makes about 1 cup

Ricotta-based pasta fillings are universal crowd-pleasers and can be jazzed up in many different ways. Here are six of our favorites, including versions made with other cheeses, herbs, vegetables, and meat, which are all classics for ravioli and which work in any variety of filled pasta. This filling can be easily doubled or tripled.

- 8 ounces (1 cup) whole-milk ricotta cheese
- 1 ounce Parmesan cheese, grated (½ cup)
- 1 large egg yolk
- ¼ teaspoon pepper
- ⅛ teaspoon table salt
- 2 tablespoons chopped fresh parsley or basil (optional)

Process ricotta, Parmesan, egg, pepper, and salt in food processor until smooth paste forms, 25 to 30 seconds, scraping down sides of bowl as needed. Stir in parsley, if using. (Filling can be refrigerated for up to 24 hours.)

Three-Cheese Filling
Reduce ricotta to 4 ounces. Add 2 ounces Italian fontina cheese, cut into ¼-inch pieces, and pinch ground nutmeg to processor with ricotta.

Spinach and Ricotta Filling
Omit parsley. Reduce ricotta to 4 ounces. Add 5 ounces frozen chopped spinach, thawed and squeezed dry, to processor with ricotta.

Pesto and Ricotta Filling
Omit parsley. Reduce ricotta to 4 ounces. Add 1 cup fresh basil leaves, 2 tablespoons extra-virgin olive oil, 2 tablespoons toasted pine nuts, and 1 minced small garlic clove to processor with ricotta.

Artichoke and Lemon Ricotta Filling
Omit parsley. Reduce ricotta to 4 ounces. Add ¾ cup jarred marinated artichoke hearts, drained and squeezed dry, ¼ teaspoon grated lemon zest, and ½ teaspoon lemon juice to processor with ricotta.

Meat and Ricotta Filling
Heat 1 tablespoon extra-virgin olive oil in 12-inch skillet over medium-high heat until shimmering. Add 4 ounces ground beef, pork, or veal (singly or combined) and cook, breaking up meat with wooden spoon, until no longer pink, about 5 minutes. Off heat, stir in 1 minced garlic clove and let cool completely. Omit parsley. Reduce ricotta to 4 ounces and stir cooled meat mixture into ricotta mixture.

Braised Short Rib Filling

Makes about 3 cups

This filling was inspired by an agnolotti recipe traditional to the Piedmont region of Italy (see page 146 for our version of it), but you can certainly use it in other filled pastas such as ravioli and cappelletti. You can find Grana Padano at most well-stocked cheese counters; if not, you can substitute Parmesan.

1½	pounds boneless beef short ribs, trimmed and cut into 1½-inch pieces
½	teaspoon table salt
¼	teaspoon pepper
2	tablespoons unsalted butter
2	cups chopped savoy cabbage
1	onion, chopped
3	garlic cloves, minced
2	teaspoons minced fresh rosemary
½	cup dry red wine
2	cups beef broth
1	ounce Grana Padano cheese, grated (½ cup)
1	large egg
⅛	teaspoon ground nutmeg

1 Pat beef dry with paper towels and sprinkle with salt and pepper. Melt butter in Dutch oven over medium-high heat. Brown beef on all sides, 7 to 10 minutes; transfer to plate.

2 Add cabbage and onion to fat left in pot and cook over medium heat until softened, about 3 minutes. Stir in garlic and rosemary and cook until fragrant, about 30 seconds. Stir in wine, scraping up any browned bits, then stir in broth. Return beef and any accumulated juices to pot and bring to simmer. Reduce heat to medium-low, cover, and simmer until beef is tender, about 1 hour.

3 Drain beef mixture in fine-mesh strainer set over bowl. Reserve ¼ cup cooking liquid; discard remaining liquid. Transfer beef mixture and liquid to food processor; process until finely ground, about 1 minute, scraping down sides of bowl as needed. Add Grana Padano, egg, and nutmeg and process until combined, about 30 seconds. Transfer filling to bowl; refrigerate for 30 minutes. (Filling can be refrigerated for up to 24 hours or frozen for up to 1 month.)

Ground Pork Filling

Makes about 1 cup

This all-purpose pasta filling is anything but ordinary. The simple panade made from sandwich bread keeps the ground pork tender and moist, and garlic, fennel, and lemon zest add classic Italian flavors. This filling can be easily doubled or tripled.

1	slice hearty white sandwich bread, torn into small pieces
1	ounce Parmesan cheese, grated (½ cup)
2	tablespoons chicken or vegetable broth
1	large egg yolk
1	tablespoon minced fresh parsley
1	garlic clove, minced
½	teaspoon table salt
½	teaspoon ground fennel seeds
¼	teaspoon grated lemon zest
¼	teaspoon pepper
¼	teaspoon dry mustard
6	ounces ground pork

Process bread, Parmesan, broth, egg yolk, parsley, garlic, salt, fennel, lemon zest, pepper, and mustard in food processor until paste forms, 10 to 15 seconds, scraping down sides of bowl as needed. Add pork and pulse until mixture is well combined, about 5 pulses. Transfer filling to bowl, cover with plastic wrap, and refrigerate until needed. (Filling can be refrigerated for up to 24 hours.)

Squash, Prosciutto, and Parmesan Filling

Makes about 1 cup

The light sweetness of roasted acorn squash combines with salty prosciutto and Parmesan and herbal sage in this hearty, versatile pasta filling. An egg yolk makes it silky, and a touch of nutmeg enhances the flavor of the squash. This filling can be easily doubled or tripled.

½   acorn squash (12 ounces), seeded

2   ounces thinly sliced prosciutto, chopped fine

1   ounce Parmesan cheese, grated (½ cup)

1   large egg yolk

1   teaspoon minced fresh sage

     Pinch ground nutmeg

1   Adjust oven rack to middle position and heat oven to 400 degrees. Place squash, cut side down, on rimmed baking sheet and bake until tender, about 35 minutes.

2   Let squash cool slightly, then scoop out flesh and transfer to food processor. Process until squash is smooth, about 20 seconds, scraping down sides of bowl as needed. Transfer squash to bowl and stir in prosciutto, Parmesan, egg yolk, sage, and nutmeg. Cover and refrigerate mixture until cool, about 30 minutes. (Filling can be refrigerated for up to 24 hours.)

Wild Mushroom Filling

Makes about 1 cup

Fresh mushrooms bolstered by dried porcini make a pasta filling with earthy, autumnal flavors. A good amount of minced parsley is just the right herbal complement. We love to use a combination of mushrooms, but a single variety will also work well. White, cremini, portobello, oyster, maitake, fresh porcini, and/or shiitake are all great choices. This filling can be easily doubled or tripled.

½   ounce dried porcini mushrooms, rinsed

1   tablespoon extra-virgin olive oil

1   garlic clove, minced

5   ounces fresh mushrooms, trimmed and chopped fine

4   ounces (½ cup) whole-milk ricotta cheese

¼   cup grated Parmesan cheese

2   tablespoons minced fresh parsley

1   large egg yolk

1   Microwave ½ cup water and porcini in covered bowl until steaming, about 1 minute. Let sit until softened, about 5 minutes. Lift mushrooms from bowl with fork and chop fine; discard liquid.

2   Heat oil and garlic in 10-inch skillet over medium heat. Cook, stirring often, until garlic turns golden but not brown, about 3 minutes. Add fresh mushrooms and cook until softened, about 5 minutes. Stir in porcini and cook until mushrooms are lightly browned, about 2 minutes. Season with salt and pepper to taste. Transfer mushroom mixture to bowl, let cool slightly, then stir in ricotta, Parmesan, parsley, and egg yolk. Cover and refrigerate mixture until cool, about 30 minutes. (Filling can be refrigerated for up to 24 hours.)

Bitter Greens Filling

Makes about 1 cup

Based on a traditional pasta filling from Liguria called pre-boggion, which highlights local foraged greens including dandelion, nettles, and borage, our bitter greens filling uses more widely available options. We love the pairing of kale with dandelion and fresh herbs. You can substitute Swiss chard, curly spinach, watercress, mustard greens, beet greens, turnip greens, or arugula for the dandelion greens. This filling can be easily doubled or tripled; cook and cool kale and dandelion greens in additional batches.

4	ounces kale, stemmed
⅛	teaspoon table salt, plus salt for cooking greens
8	ounces dandelion greens, stemmed
2	ounces (¼ cup) whole-milk ricotta cheese
¼	cup grated Parmesan cheese
1	tablespoon minced fresh chervil or 1 teaspoon minced fresh tarragon
1	small garlic clove, minced
½	teaspoon minced fresh marjoram or oregano
⅛	teaspoon pepper

1 Bring 4 quarts water to boil in large pot over high heat. Add half of kale and 1 tablespoon salt and cook for 2 minutes. Add half of dandelion greens and cook, stirring frequently, until greens are tender, 2 to 3 minutes. Use tongs or slotted spoon to transfer greens to colander; run under cold water until cool enough to handle. Return water to boil, add remaining kale and dandelion greens, and repeat cooking and draining.

2 Using hands, firmly press cooled greens to release as much liquid as possible. Transfer to food processor and process until finely chopped, about 30 seconds. Transfer to bowl and stir in ricotta, Parmesan, chervil, garlic, marjoram, salt, and pepper until combined. Cover and refrigerate until needed. (Filling can be refrigerated for up to 24 hours.)

Leek Filling

Makes about 1 cup

Simply cooking leeks in butter transforms them into a silky-soft and richly flavorful side dish. But combine those cooked leeks with Parmesan and an egg yolk and you end up with an elegant, melt-in-your-mouth filling for any type of filled pasta. This filling can be easily double or tripled.

2	pounds leeks, white and light-green parts only, halved lengthwise, sliced thin, and washed thoroughly
2	tablespoons unsalted butter
¼	teaspoon table salt
¼	cup grated Parmesan cheese
1	large egg yolk
⅛	teaspoon pepper

1 Combine leeks, ½ cup water, butter, and salt in Dutch oven. Cover and cook over medium heat, stirring occasionally, until leeks are very soft, about 30 minutes. Uncover, increase heat to medium-high, and continue to cook until leeks are golden brown and all of liquid has evaporated, about 5 minutes.

2 Transfer leek mixture to bowl, let cool slightly, then stir in Parmesan, egg yolk, and pepper. Cover and refrigerate mixture until cool, about 30 minutes. (Filling can be refrigerated for up to 24 hours.)

FAVORITE PAIRINGS

Maltagliati with Weeknight Meat Sauce

tagliatelle | spaghetti | orecchiette | rigatoni

WHY THIS RECIPE WORKS: The irregularly shaped, "badly cut" pieces of fresh maltagliati fold and drape to pick up bits of sauce in a delightfully haphazard way. This easy fresh pasta is a great pairing with a quick but complex tomato and meat sauce. To develop layered flavor in the sauce with little effort, we use meatloaf mix, a blend of ground beef, veal, and pork. Many meat sauces aren't weeknight friendly because of their long cooking times, but this sauce takes only 35 minutes of hands-off simmering to develop a rich flavor that's elevated by the addition of chopped pancetta and a good slug of white wine (such as Pinot Grigio). You can substitute an equal amount of 80 percent lean ground beef for meatloaf mix.

Serves 4
Total Time: 1 hour

2   tablespoons extra-virgin olive oil

4   ounces pancetta, chopped fine

½   onion, chopped fine

8   ounces meatloaf mix

3   garlic cloves, minced

1   tablespoon tomato paste

⅛   teaspoon red pepper flakes

¼   cup dry white wine or dry vermouth

1   (28-ounce) can crushed tomatoes

¼   teaspoon table salt, plus salt for cooking pasta

¼   teaspoon pepper

1   pound fresh maltagliati (page 49)
    Grated Parmesan cheese

1   Heat oil in large saucepan over medium-high heat until shimmering. Add pancetta and onion and cook until onion is softened and lightly browned, 5 to 7 minutes. Add meatloaf mix and cook, breaking up meat with wooden spoon, until no longer pink, about 5 minutes. Stir in garlic, tomato paste, and pepper flakes and cook until fragrant, about 1 minute. Stir in wine, scraping up any browned bits, and cook until nearly evaporated, about 2 minutes.

2   Stir in tomatoes, salt, and pepper and bring to simmer. Cover partially, reduce heat to low, and cook until sauce has thickened and flavors have blended, 35 to 40 minutes.

3   Meanwhile, bring 4 quarts water to boil in large pot. Add pasta and 1 tablespoon salt and cook, stirring often, until al dente. Reserve ½ cup cooking water, then drain pasta and return it to pot. Add sauce and toss to combine. Adjust consistency with reserved cooking water as needed. Season with salt and pepper to taste. Serve, passing Parmesan separately.

Fettuccine Alfredo

linguine | tagliatelle | pappardelle | farfalle

WHY THIS RECIPE WORKS: Here's the OG fettuccine Alfredo: Parmigiano-Reggiano cheese, butter, fettuccine, and a pinch of salt. No cream. No eggs. No black pepper. The cheese and butter meld to create a creamy sauce that delicately coats each pasta strand. Like so many great pasta dishes, it has humble origins. In 1914, Roman restaurateur Alfredo di Lelio needed a high-calorie meal to serve his pregnant (and queasy) wife and created this pasta for her. He promptly added it to his restaurant's menu, after which it was brought to America by visiting silent film stars Mary Pickford and Douglas Fairbanks. But because American butter and Parmesan-style cheese weren't as rich and creamy as they are in Italy, the dish began its detour into something di Lelio would not have recognized. The simplest process produces the best results: Toss the cooked pasta with some cooking water (we use less water than usual to get extra-starchy water), grated cheese, butter, and salt. Then—and this step is important—we cover the pot and let the pasta sit for a minute to allow any errant water droplets to be absorbed. Tossing the pasta again after removing the lid ensures that all the cheese is incorporated. It's essential to use real Italian Parmigiano-Reggiano cheese. Grate it on a rasp-style grater for ultrasmall (almost feathery) shreds, which will melt smoothly into the sauce. For the best results, heat ovensafe dinner bowls in a 200-degree oven for 10 minutes prior to serving.

Serves 4
Total Time:
30 minutes

1¼ pounds fresh fettuccine (page 47)

½ teaspoon table salt, plus salt for cooking pasta

4 ounces Parmigiano-Reggiano cheese, grated fine (2 cups), plus extra for serving

5 tablespoons unsalted butter, cut into 5 pieces

1 Bring 3 quarts water to boil in large pot. Add pasta and 1 tablespoon salt and cook, stirring frequently, until al dente. Reserve 1 cup cooking water, then drain pasta and return it to pot.

2 Moving quickly, add Parmigiano-Reggiano, butter, reserved cooking water, and salt to pot. Set pot over low heat and, using tongs, toss and stir pasta to thoroughly combine, about 1 minute. Remove pot from heat, cover, and let pasta sit for 1 minute.

3 Toss pasta once more so sauce thoroughly coats pasta and any cheese clumps are emulsified into sauce, about 30 seconds. (Mixture may look wet at this point, but pasta will continue to absorb excess moisture as it cools slightly.) Season with salt to taste.

4 Transfer pasta to individual bowls. (Use rubber spatula as needed to remove any clumps of cheese stuck to tongs and bottom of pot.) Serve immediately, passing extra Parmigiano-Reggiano separately.

Linguine with Clams

spaghetti | tagliatelle | fileja

WHY THIS RECIPE WORKS: One of the most beloved Neapolitan pastas is pasta alle vongole: linguine or spaghetti lightly tossed with garlic and oil and topped with tiny in-shell clams, which open while cooking in the sauce to release their briny liquor. In trattorias and homes, it can be found with or without tomatoes in the sauce. Here, we add just two minced plum tomatoes for their sweetness and bright acidity as well as a bit of texture. As for the clams themselves, the tiny, sweet vongole veraci aren't available in the United States, and large native clams like cherrystones and quahogs have a different flavor and tougher texture. Littlenecks (the smaller, the better) work well; they have a fresh brininess and cook up tender. Cockles, if you can find them, are also a great choice. To ensure that the small clams don't overcook, we steam them first, stopping when they give up their juice and reserving the juice to build the flavorful sauce. Recombining the clams with the garlicky, winey sauce at the last minute gives them just enough time to finish cooking. We like to make this using linguine flavored with fresh herbs (see pages 28–29).

Serves 4 to 6
Total Time:
30 minutes

4   pounds littleneck clams or cockles, scrubbed

½   cup dry white wine

     Pinch cayenne pepper

¼   cup extra-virgin olive oil

2   garlic cloves, minced

2   plum tomatoes, peeled, seeded, and chopped fine

1   pound fresh linguine (page 47)

     Table salt for cooking pasta

¾   cup chopped fresh parsley

1 Bring clams, wine, and cayenne to boil in 12-inch straight-sided sauté pan, cover, and cook, shaking pan occasionally, for 5 minutes. Stir clams thoroughly, cover, and continue to cook until they just begin to open, 2 to 5 minutes longer. Using slotted spoon, transfer partially opened clams to large bowl. Discard any unopened clams.

2 Strain clam steaming liquid through fine-mesh strainer lined with coffee filter, leaving behind any gritty sediment that has settled on bottom of pan. Add water as needed to equal 1 cup and set aside. Wipe out pan with paper towels.

3 Heat oil and garlic in now-empty pan over medium heat. Cook, stirring often, until garlic turns golden but not brown, about 3 minutes. Stir in tomatoes, increase heat to medium-high, and cook until toma-toes soften, about 2 minutes. Stir in clams, cover, and cook until all clams are completely opened, about 2 minutes.

4 Meanwhile, bring 4 quarts water to boil in large pot. Add pasta and 1 tablespoon salt and cook, stirring often, until al dente. Drain pasta and return it to pot. Add clam sauce and reserved steaming liquid to pasta and cook over medium heat, tossing to combine, until flavors meld, about 30 seconds. Stir in parsley and season with salt and pepper to taste. Serve immediately.

Fettuccine with Anchovies and Parsley

pappardelle | garganelli | malloreddus | busiate

WHY THIS RECIPE WORKS: Anchovy fans, this one's for you. While sometimes we add an anchovy or two to a sauce for its umami qualities rather than its actual fishy flavor, in this dish the pungent little fishes are front and center, along with garlic, parsley, and lemon, for a bold rusticity. It's a simple olive oil–based preparation that really showcases your homemade fresh pasta. Adding starchy pasta cooking water to the finished pasta helps emulsify the sauce so that it clings to the noodles in a velvety way. Mincing the anchovies ensures that their potent flavor gets evenly distributed. We especially love the way this sauce cloaks fresh egg pastas, whether plain or flavored.

Serves 4
Total Time:
30 minutes

⅛ teaspoon table salt, plus salt for cooking pasta

1 pound fresh fettuccine (page 47)

⅓ cup extra-virgin olive oil

2 anchovy fillets, minced

2 garlic cloves, minced

½ teaspoon pepper

2 tablespoons chopped fresh parsley

4 teaspoons lemon juice

1 Bring 4 quarts water to boil in large pot. Add pasta and 1 tablespoon salt and cook, stirring often, until al dente. Reserve 1 cup cooking water, then drain pasta and return it to pot.

2 Meanwhile, heat oil in 12-inch skillet over medium-low heat until shimmering. Add anchovies, garlic, pepper, and salt; cook until fragrant, about 30 seconds.

3 Add pasta, ½ cup reserved cooking water, parsley, and lemon juice to sauce; toss to combine, adjusting consistency with remaining reserved cooking water as needed. Season with salt and pepper to taste, and serve.

Fileja with 'Nduja Tomato Sauce

busiate | cavatelli | penne | filled pasta

WHY THIS RECIPE WORKS: So soft it's spreadable, 'nduja is a kind of salumi that traces its 19th-century origins to the small Calabrian town of Spilinga, where they still celebrate it with an annual festival. While thrifty in its composition, it represents a flavor indulgence of the highest order. It's often made from a mix of pork shoulder, belly, and fatback as well as various other cuts; liberally spiced to a fiery brick red with hot Calabrian peppers; and slow-fermented, so it takes on a notable tangy funk. When added to tomato sauce, the salami melts into the sauce, making it piquant and supersavory. We pair the sauce with another Calabrian treasure, fresh fileja. Garnishes of grated Pecorino and chopped basil provide welcome salty and fresh counterpoints to the pungent sauce. You can find 'nduja in most Italian markets or online.

Serves 4
Total Time:
30 minutes

1 (15-ounce) can whole peeled tomatoes

2 tablespoons extra-virgin olive oil

½ onion, chopped fine

½ teaspoon table salt, plus salt for cooking pasta

1 garlic clove, minced

6 ounces 'nduja sausage, casings removed

1 pound fresh fileja (page 53)

2 tablespoons chopped fresh basil
Grated Pecorino Romano cheese

1 Pulse tomatoes and their juice in food processor until mostly smooth, 10 to 12 pulses.

2 Heat oil in large saucepan over medium heat until shimmering. Add onion and ½ teaspoon salt and cook until softened and lightly browned, about 4 minutes. Stir in garlic and cook until fragrant, about 30 seconds. Stir in tomatoes, bring to simmer, and cook, stirring occasionally, until thickened slightly, about 10 minutes. Add 'nduja, breaking up meat with wooden spoon, until fully incorporated. Season with salt and pepper to taste.

3 Meanwhile, bring 4 quarts water to boil in large pot. Add pasta and 1 tablespoon salt and cook, stirring often, until al dente. Reserve ½ cup cooking water, then drain pasta and return it to pot. Add sauce and toss to combine. Adjust consistency with reserved cooking water as needed. Sprinkle with basil and serve, passing Pecorino separately.

Farfalle with Sautéed Mushrooms

orecchiette | trofie | fettuccine

WHY THIS RECIPE WORKS: The intense flavor of sautéed mushrooms combined with a cream sauce infused with garlic and thyme yields this woodsy, autumn-inspired pasta dish. Using spinach-flavored pasta adds dramatic color (see pages 28–29). We combine cremini and shiitake mushrooms for rich, meaty flavor and varying texture. Overloading the skillet with the sliced mushrooms and red onion and cooking them covered until they release their juices jump-starts their cooking and minimizes shrinkage. We then remove the lid to drive off moisture and maximize browning. After transferring the mushrooms and onion to a bowl, we add broth and cream to the skillet to ensure that all the fond from cooking the vegetables adds big flavor to the sauce. A splash of lemon juice and a sprinkling of parsley brighten everything up.

Serves 4
Total Time: 1 hour

4	tablespoons unsalted butter
2	tablespoons extra-virgin olive oil
1	red onion, chopped fine
12	ounces shiitake mushrooms, stemmed and sliced ¼ inch thick
12	ounces cremini mushrooms, trimmed and sliced ¼ inch thick
½	teaspoon table salt, plus salt for cooking pasta
3	garlic cloves, minced
1	tablespoon minced fresh thyme
1	cup vegetable or chicken broth
½	cup heavy cream
1½	tablespoons lemon juice
1	pound fresh farfalle (page 51)
2	ounces Parmesan cheese, grated (1 cup)
¼	cup minced fresh parsley

1 Heat butter and oil in 12-inch skillet over medium heat until butter is melted. Add onion and cook until softened, about 5 minutes. Stir in shiitakes, cremini, and ½ teaspoon salt, cover, and cook until mushrooms have released their liquid, about 8 minutes. Uncover and continue to cook until mushrooms are dry and browned, about 8 minutes. Stir in garlic and thyme and cook until fragrant, about 30 seconds; transfer to bowl and cover to keep warm.

2 Add broth and cream to now-empty skillet and bring to simmer, scraping up browned bits. Off heat, stir in lemon juice and season with salt and pepper to taste.

3 Meanwhile, bring 4 quarts water to boil in large pot. Add pasta and 1 tablespoon salt and cook, stirring often, until al dente. Reserve 1 cup cooking water, then drain pasta and return it to pot.

4 Add mushrooms, sauce, Parmesan, and parsley to pasta and toss to combine. Add reserved cooking water as needed to adjust consistency, and serve.

Tagliatelle with Artichokes, Bread Crumbs, and Parmesan

pappardelle | fettuccine | filled pasta

WHY THIS RECIPE WORKS: In Italian produce markets, trimmed fresh artichoke hearts floating in acidulated water are a common sight, making elegant fresh pasta dishes like this one easy to make at home. To achieve this dish in our kitchens, we start with water-packed artichoke hearts, trimming the outer leaves and giving the leaves a quick soak in water to remove any off flavors. Halving the hearts and patting them dry promotes deep browning when cooked in olive oil. Garlic, anchovies, and oregano bolster the flavors, and then we add white wine and the artichoke leaves and stir in parsley, Parmesan, and lemon zest when combining the cooked pasta and sauce. A bread crumb topping adds a marvelous savory crunch. We prefer jarred artichoke hearts labeled "baby" or "cocktail" that are 1½ inches or less in length; you'll need three 9.9-ounce jars for this recipe. Larger artichoke hearts tend to have fibrous leaves. If you are using larger hearts, trim the top ¼ to ½ inch from the leaves. Do not use marinated or oil-packed artichoke hearts.

Serves 4
Total Time:
1¼ hours

Topping

2	slices hearty white sandwich bread
2	tablespoons extra-virgin olive oil
¼	cup grated Parmesan cheese

Pasta

4	cups jarred whole baby artichoke hearts packed in water
¼	cup extra-virgin olive oil, divided, plus extra for drizzling
⅛	teaspoon table salt, plus salt for cooking pasta
4	garlic cloves, minced
2	anchovy fillets, minced
1	tablespoon minced fresh oregano or 1 teaspoon dried
⅛	teaspoon red pepper flakes
½	cup dry white wine
1	pound fresh tagliatelle (page 47)
1	ounce Parmesan cheese, grated (½ cup), plus extra for serving
¼	cup minced fresh parsley
1½	teaspoons grated lemon zest

1 For the topping Pulse bread in food processor until finely ground, 10 to 15 pulses. Heat oil in 12-inch nonstick skillet over medium heat until shimmering. Add bread crumbs and cook, stirring constantly, until they begin to brown, 3 to 5 minutes. Add Parmesan and continue to cook, stirring constantly, until crumbs are golden, 1 to 2 minutes. Transfer crumbs to bowl and season with salt and pepper to taste.

2 For the pasta Cut leaves from artichoke hearts and place in bowl. Cut hearts in half and pat dry with paper towels. Cover artichoke leaves in bowl with water and let sit for 15 minutes. Drain well.

3 Meanwhile, wipe out skillet and heat 1 tablespoon oil in skillet over medium-high heat until shimmering. Add artichoke hearts and salt and cook, stirring frequently, until spotty brown, 7 to 9 minutes. Stir in garlic, anchovies, oregano, and pepper flakes and cook, stirring constantly, until fragrant, about 30 seconds. Stir in wine and bring to simmer. Off heat, stir in artichoke leaves.

4 Meanwhile, bring 4 quarts water to boil in large pot. Add pasta and 1 tablespoon salt and cook, stirring often, until al dente. Reserve 1½ cups cooking water, then drain pasta and return it to pot. Add 1 cup reserved cooking water, artichoke mixture, Parmesan, parsley, lemon zest, and remaining 3 tablespoons oil and toss to combine. Season with salt and pepper to taste and adjust consistency with remaining reserved cooking water as needed. Serve, sprinkling individual portions with bread crumbs and extra Parmesan and drizzling with extra oil.

Cacio e Pepe

linguine | bucatini | rigatoni | cavatelli

WHY THIS RECIPE WORKS: One of Rome's many famed pasta dishes, cacio e pepe combines spaghetti with salty Pecorino Romano and freshly cracked black pepper in an intensely flavored sauce. In theory, the sauce forms itself when cheese and some cooking water are stirred with the cooked pasta, as the starch in the water prevents the cheese's proteins from clumping together. In practice, however, we find that the cheese still clumps. For a more foolproof route to an ultrasmooth sauce, we cut the usual amount of cooking water in half when boiling the pasta; this ups the starch level in the water, providing a safeguard. In addition, adding a couple spoonfuls of heavy cream further ensures fluidity (the cream contains molecules called lipoproteins that act as a liaison between protein and fat, keeping them emulsified). Don't adjust the amount of water for cooking the pasta; the amount used is critical to the success of the recipe. Draining the pasta water into the serving bowl warms the bowl and helps keep the dish hot until it is served. Letting the dish rest briefly before serving allows the flavors to develop and the sauce to thicken to the right consistency.

Serves 4
Total Time:
30 minutes

6   ounces Pecorino Romano cheese,
     4 ounces grated fine (2 cups) and
     2 ounces grated coarse (1 cup)

1   pound fresh spaghetti
     Table salt for cooking pasta

2   tablespoons heavy cream

2   teaspoons extra-virgin olive oil

1½   teaspoons pepper

1   Place finely grated Pecorino in medium bowl. Set colander in large serving bowl.

2   Meanwhile, bring 2 quarts water to boil in large pot. Add pasta and 1½ teaspoons salt and cook, stirring often, until al dente. Drain pasta in prepared colander, reserving cooking water. Pour 1½ cups cooking water into 2-cup liquid measuring cup and discard remainder. Return pasta to now-empty bowl.

3   Slowly whisk 1 cup reserved cooking water into finely grated Pecorino until smooth, then whisk in cream, oil, and pepper. Gradually pour Pecorino mixture over pasta, tossing to coat. Let pasta rest for 1 to 2 minutes, tossing frequently and adjusting consistency with remaining reserved cooking water as needed. Serve immediately, passing coarsely grated Pecorino separately.

Whole-Wheat Tagliatelle with Oyster Mushrooms and Browned Butter

fettuccine | linguine | gnocchi | filled pasta

WHY THIS RECIPE WORKS: With their fan-shaped caps and connected clusters, oyster mushrooms are as beautiful as they are delicious, and here we make the most of them to adorn fresh whole-wheat pasta in a dish whose deliciousness belies its simplicity. Because oyster mushrooms have less moisture than other varieties, they cook quickly. Here we sauté the mushrooms for 4 to 6 minutes, until they are soft and golden, which enhances their delicate woodsy flavor and gives them a silky texture. But oyster mushrooms also have secret superpowers: If you cook them a bit longer in step 2, 7 to 8 minutes, they will lose even more moisture and transform into chewy-crunchy nuggets that are almost bacon-y. Try them both ways in this dish and see if you can choose a favorite.

Serves 4
Total Time:
30 minutes

1   pound oyster mushrooms, trimmed and chopped

¾   teaspoon kosher salt, plus salt for cooking pasta

2   tablespoons extra-virgin olive oil

6   tablespoons unsalted butter

20   fresh sage leaves, sliced thin

1   pound fresh whole-wheat tagliatelle (page 47)

2   ounces Parmesan cheese, grated (1 cup), divided

1   Toss mushrooms and salt together in bowl and let sit until slightly softened, about 5 minutes.

2   Heat oil in 12-inch skillet over medium-high heat until shimmering. Add mushrooms and cook, stirring often, until softened and beginning to brown at edges, 4 to 6 minutes. Transfer mushrooms to bowl.

3   Add butter and sage to now-empty skillet, reduce heat to medium-low, and cook until butter is dark golden brown and has nutty aroma, 1 to 3 minutes. Return mushrooms to skillet, remove from heat, and cover to keep warm.

4   Meanwhile, bring 4 quarts water to boil in large pot. Add pasta and 2 tablespoons salt and cook, stirring often, until al dente. Reserve 1½ cups cooking water, then drain pasta and return it to pot. Add mushroom sauce, 1 cup reserved cooking water, and ½ cup Parmesan and toss well to combine. Season with salt and pepper to taste. Adjust consistency with remaining reserved cooking water as needed. Serve immediately, passing remaining Parmesan separately.

Farfalle al Limone

linguine | spaghetti | penne | busiate

WHY THIS RECIPE WORKS: If you close your eyes when you take your first bite, you'll be transported to a veranda framed by lemon trees on the Italian island of Capri. Every forkful of this pasta bursts with bright, bracing citrus flavor. In addition to plenty of lemon juice, we stir in a generous dose of grated lemon zest; its fragrant floral notes boost the lemon presence without making this dish mouth-puckering. The sauce uses equal amounts of extra-virgin olive oil and heavy cream: The dairy fat works in tandem with the olive oil to boost the presence of the aromatic oil in the lemon zest, making its fruity and floral notes readily available to your taste buds. The cream also neutralizes some of the acidity of the lemon juice. Nutty Parmesan, chopped fresh herbs, and a final drizzle of olive oil finish this pasta in style. Although the aroma is pretty irresistible, make sure to let the dish rest for those 2 minutes before serving so that the sauce thickens and the flavors blossom.

Serves 4
Total Time:
45 minutes

1 pound fresh farfalle (page 51)

½ teaspoon table salt, plus salt for cooking pasta

¼ cup extra-virgin olive oil, divided, plus extra for drizzling

1 shallot, minced

¼ cup heavy cream

1 ounce Parmesan cheese, grated (½ cup), plus extra for serving

2 teaspoons grated lemon zest plus ¼ cup juice (2 lemons)

½ teaspoon pepper

2 tablespoons chopped fresh basil or parsley

1 Bring 4 quarts water to boil in large pot. Add pasta and 1 tablespoon salt and cook, stirring often, until al dente. Reserve 1¾ cups cooking water, then drain pasta and set aside.

2 Heat 1 tablespoon oil in now-empty pot over medium heat until shimmering. Add shallot and salt and cook until softened, about 2 minutes. Stir in cream and 1½ cups reserved cooking water, bring to simmer, and cook for 2 minutes. Off heat, add pasta, Parmesan, lemon zest and juice, pepper, and remaining 3 tablespoons oil and toss to combine.

3 Cover and let pasta stand for 2 minutes, tossing frequently and adjusting consistency of sauce with remaining reserved cooking water as needed. Stir in basil and season with salt and pepper to taste. Drizzle individual portions with extra oil and serve, passing extra Parmesan separately.

Maccheroni di Fuoco

penne | fileja | busiate

WHY THIS RECIPE WORKS: A fiery infused oil dresses bucatini in this Southern Italian pasta. The essential oils in red chiles are oil-soluble, so blooming chili flakes in extra-virgin olive oil produces infused flavor that permeates the hollow pasta strands inside and out. We gently cook whole cloves of garlic in the oil as well before mincing them. This allows their flavor to become sweeter and rounder than if they were minced before cooking, since cutting raw cloves creates the compound allicin that imparts the harsh flavors associated with garlic. Allowing the oil to steep while we toast bread crumbs (for some crunch) and cook the pasta bolsters its intensity. The addition of cheese is contentious from a traditional standpoint, but we appreciate how it tempers the fire. Cooks in Basilicata, where this dish hails from, use the diavolicchio (little red devil) chile, which boasts a Scoville rating in the five figures and has complex, smoky notes. These are not widely available in the U.S., but Calabrian peperoncini flakes are an excellent substitute available at most Italian markets. If you can't find them, 1½ teaspoons ground dried arbol chiles are the next best alternative. This dish is intended to be quite spicy but can be made milder by using the lesser amount of peperoncini flakes.

Serves 4
Total Time:
45 minutes

½ cup plus 1 tablespoon extra-virgin olive oil, divided

4 garlic cloves, peeled

2–4 teaspoons Calabrian peperoncini flakes

½ cup panko bread crumbs

⅛ teaspoon plus ½ teaspoon table salt, divided, plus salt for cooking pasta

1 pound fresh bucatini

2 tablespoons chopped fresh parsley

Grated Parmesan cheese

1 Cook ¼ cup oil and garlic in 8-inch skillet over medium-low heat, turning occasionally, until garlic begins to brown, 5 to 7 minutes. Stir in peperoncini flakes and cook until slightly darkened in color, about 45 seconds. Immediately transfer oil mixture to bowl and let cool for 5 minutes. Transfer garlic to cutting board, mince to paste, then return to oil mixture. Let sit until flavors meld, about 20 minutes.

2 Meanwhile, wipe skillet clean with paper towels. Cook panko, 1 tablespoon oil, and ⅛ teaspoon salt in now-empty skillet over medium heat, stirring often, until lightly toasted, 3 to 5 minutes. Transfer to clean bowl.

3 Bring 4 quarts water to boil in large pot. Add pasta and 1 tablespoon salt and cook, stirring often, until al dente. Reserve ½ cup cooking water, then drain pasta and return it to pot. Add oil mixture, ¼ cup reserved cooking water, parsley, remaining ½ teaspoon salt, and remaining ¼ cup oil and toss to combine. Adjust consistency with remaining reserved cooking water as needed. Season with salt and pepper to taste. Sprinkle individual portions with bread crumbs and Parmesan before serving.

Linguine with Shrimp

spaghetti | tagliatelle | fileja | farfalle

WHY THIS RECIPE WORKS: The inspiration for this dish comes from a specialty of Venice. Seafood has always been central to Venetian cuisine, thanks to the bounty found in the city's lagoon ecosystem, and schie, a uniquely delicious small local shrimp, are celebrated in many ways. Because shrimp of this size found in the U.S. are often lacking in flavor and quality, we use reliably delicious large shrimp instead in this pasta that manages to capture the sweet, briny flavors of the Venetian version. Purchasing shell-on shrimp and cooking the shrimp shells in extra-virgin olive oil and white wine (such as Pinot Grigio) creates the delicate broth. Shrimp shells are rich in glutamates, which add depth, as well as volatile fatty acids, which generate fresh flavors when cooked. After straining it, we quickly cook the shrimp and garlic in this broth. Using squid ink pasta (see pages 28–29) adds dramatic color and a hit of umami, and stirring in parsley, butter, and lemon zest at the end creates a deeply flavorful fresh pasta dish.

Serves 4 to 6
Total Time:
45 minutes

- ⅓ cup extra-virgin olive oil, divided
- 2 pounds large shrimp (26 to 30 per pound), peeled and deveined, shells reserved
- 1 cup dry white wine
- 5 garlic cloves, minced
- ½ teaspoon table salt, plus salt for cooking pasta
- ¼ cup minced fresh parsley
- 4 tablespoons unsalted butter, cut into 4 pieces
- 1½ teaspoons grated lemon zest, plus lemon wedges for serving
- 1 pound fresh linguine (page 47)

1 Heat ¼ cup oil in 12-inch skillet over high heat until shimmering. Add shrimp shells and cook, stirring frequently, until they begin to turn spotty brown, 2 to 4 minutes. Off heat, carefully add wine. Once bubbling subsides, return skillet to medium heat and simmer for 5 minutes. Strain broth through fine-mesh strainer into large bowl, pressing on solids to extract as much liquid as possible; discard solids. (You should have about ⅔ cup broth.) Wipe skillet clean with paper towels.

2 Heat remaining oil (about 1 tablespoon plus 1 teaspoon) and garlic in now-empty skillet over medium-low heat, stirring occasionally, until garlic is fragrant and just beginning to brown, about 30 seconds. Add reserved broth and ½ teaspoon salt and bring to simmer. Add shrimp, cover, and cook, stirring occasionally, until just opaque, 2 to 4 minutes. Off heat, stir in parsley, butter, and lemon zest.

3 Meanwhile, bring 4 quarts water to boil in large pot. Add pasta and 1 tablespoon salt and cook, stirring often, until al dente. Reserve ½ cup cooking water, then drain pasta and return it to pot. Add sauce and toss to coat. Adjust consistency with reserved cooking water as needed. Season with pepper to taste. Serve with lemon wedges.

Pasta alla Gricia

penne | farfalle | bucatini

WHY THIS RECIPE WORKS: Another of Rome's greatest pasta dishes, less famous than cacio e pepe but every bit as iconic, pasta alla gricia features cured pork, freshly ground black pepper, and Pecorino Romano cheese. The fat from the pork combines with starchy pasta cooking water and cheese to create an emulsified sauce. The traditional method is to let parcooked pasta finish cooking in the sauce, where it releases its starch for body, but this technique works better with dried pasta than with fresh. Here, we cook the pasta to al dente in half the usual amount of water (unsalted, to avoid a too-salty finished dish) and then add the extra-starchy pasta cooking water to the rendered pork fat and reduce the mixture. The boiling action concentrates the starches in the water and emulsifies the mixture before we add the pasta. If you can't find guanciale, use the highest-quality pancetta you can find, and decrease the browning time in step 2 to 8 to 10 minutes. Because we call for cutting the pork to a specified thickness, we recommend having it cut to order at the deli counter; avoid presliced or prediced products.

Serves 4
Total Time:
40 minutes

- 8 ounces guanciale, sliced ¼ inch thick
- 1 tablespoon extra-virgin olive oil
- 1 pound fresh rigatoni
- 1 teaspoon coarsely ground pepper, plus extra for serving
- 2 ounces Pecorino Romano cheese, grated fine (1 cup), plus extra for serving

1 Slice each piece of guanciale into rectangular pieces that measure about ½ inch by 1 inch.

2 Heat guanciale and oil in Dutch oven over medium-low heat, stirring frequently, until fat is rendered and guanciale is deep golden brown but still has slight pinkish hue, 10 to 12 minutes, adjusting heat as necessary to keep it from browning too quickly. Using slotted spoon, transfer guanciale to bowl; set aside. Pour fat from pot into liquid measuring cup. You should have ¼ to ⅓ cup fat; discard any extra. Return fat to Dutch oven and set aside.

3 Bring 2 quarts water to boil in large pot. Add pasta and cook, stirring often, until al dente. Reserve 3 cups cooking water, then drain pasta and return it to pot.

4 Add pepper and 2 cups reserved cooking water to Dutch oven with fat and bring to boil over high heat. Boil mixture rapidly, scraping up any browned bits, until emulsified and reduced to 1½ cups, about 5 minutes. (If you've reduced it too far, add more reserved cooking water to equal 1½ cups.)

5 Reduce heat to low, add pasta and guanciale, and stir to evenly coat. Add Pecorino and toss until cheese is melted and sauce is slightly thickened, about 1 minute. Off heat, adjust sauce consistency with remaining reserved cooking water as needed. Transfer pasta to platter and serve immediately, passing extra pepper and extra Pecorino separately.

Spaghetti alla Carbonara

linguine | rigatoni | gnocchi

WHY THIS RECIPE WORKS: Romans love their Pecorino Romano cheese, and this might be the most famous pasta dish that features it. Its piquant, funky flavor is integral to a luscious carbonara. You can certainly make a great version with Parmesan, but it will be different. The cured pork product of choice is salty, meaty guanciale. We render some of the fat, which serves as the backbone of the sauce. The keys to ensuring silky texture in carbonara are threefold: the eggs, the pasta cooking water, and the tossing. We call for three whole eggs plus two yolks for richness; the raw eggs are tossed into the hot pasta and (just barely) cook from the heat of the noodles. The starches in the reserved cooking water help temper the eggs and emulsify the sauce so that it coats and clings to every strand of pasta (instead of turning into scrambled eggs). And in order for that to happen, you have to toss the sauced pasta for a minute or two right before serving. We also recommend heating your serving bowls or plates; this will help the carbonara stay warm and fluid. You can substitute pancetta for the guanciale; just be sure to buy a 4-ounce chunk and not presliced pancetta. It's best to use freshly ground black pepper here.

Serves 4
Total Time:
45 minutes

3 large eggs plus 2 large yolks

2½ ounces Pecorino Romano cheese, grated (1¼ cups), plus extra for serving

1 teaspoon pepper, plus extra for serving

¼ teaspoon table salt, plus salt for cooking pasta

4 ounces guanciale, cut into ½-inch chunks

2 tablespoons extra-virgin olive oil

1 pound fresh spaghetti

1 Beat eggs and yolks, Pecorino, pepper, and salt together in bowl; set aside. Combine guanciale and oil in 12-inch nonstick skillet and cook over medium heat, stirring frequently, until guanciale begins to brown and is just shy of crisp, about 6 minutes. Remove skillet from heat.

2 Meanwhile, bring 4 quarts water to boil in large pot. Add pasta and 1 tablespoon salt and cook, stirring often, until al dente.

3 Reserve ½ cup cooking water, then drain pasta and immediately return it to pot. Add guanciale and rendered fat from skillet and toss with tongs to coat pasta.

4 Working quickly, whisk ¼ cup reserved cooking water into egg mixture, then add egg mixture to pasta in pot. Toss pasta until sauce begins to thicken and looks creamy, 1 to 2 minutes. Adjust consistency with remaining reserved cooking water as needed. Serve immediately, passing extra Pecorino and pepper separately.

Cacio e Uova

cavatelli | penne | trofie

WHY THIS RECIPE WORKS: Don't call this a meat-free carbonara or you'll risk the wrath of the residents of Naples, where this pasta dish originates. Similar to carbonara, though, cas' e ova (as it's known in Neapolitan dialect) features an egg and cheese–based sauce that relies on the heat of the cooked pasta to come together. The pasta (cooked in half the usual amount of water to create extra-starchy cooking water) is returned to the pot and tossed with garlic-infused fat. The magic happens when a mixture of Pecorino Romano, Parmesan, and beaten eggs is poured into the pot—as the eggs, cheese, and hot pasta are stirred together, the cheese melts, the eggs cook, and the smooth and glossy sauce forms. We use olive oil, but lard (and even butter) are also considered traditional. For balance, we use 1 ounce each of tangy Pecorino Romano and nutty Parmesan and just 2 eggs.

Serves 4 to 6
Total Time:
35 minutes

6   tablespoons extra-virgin olive oil

4   garlic cloves, lightly crushed and peeled

4   large eggs

2   ounces Parmesan cheese, grated (1 cup)

2   ounces Pecorino Romano cheese, grated (1 cup)

¼   cup minced fresh parsley

½   teaspoon table salt, plus salt for cooking pasta

½   teaspoon pepper

1   pound fresh tubetti

1 Heat oil in 8-inch skillet over medium-low heat. Add garlic and cook, swirling skillet and flipping garlic occasionally, until garlic is pale golden brown, 7 to 10 minutes. (Tiny bubbles will surround garlic, but garlic should not actively fry. Reduce heat if necessary.) Turn off heat, but leave skillet on burner. Discard garlic.

2 Meanwhile, bring 2 quarts water to boil in large pot. Beat eggs in medium bowl until very few streaks of white remain. Stir in Parmesan, Pecorino, parsley, salt, and pepper and set aside.

3 Stir pasta and 1½ teaspoons salt into boiling water and cook, stirring often, until pasta is al dente. Reserve ¼ cup cooking water, then drain pasta and return it to pot. Immediately add oil, egg mixture, and 1 tablespoon reserved cooking water to pasta and toss until cheese is fully melted. Adjust consistency with remaining reserved cooking water, 1 tablespoon at a time, as needed. Serve immediately.

Pasta alla Norcina

penne | orecchiette | garganelli

WHY THIS RECIPE WORKS: Farfalle tossed in a creamy, cheesy sauce with fresh seasoned sausage is a cozy and satiating cold-weather meal. The sauce is named for the Umbrian town of Norcia, which is justifiably famous for its pork-focused butchers (and its black truffles, which are sometimes added). In keeping with local tradition, we favor from-scratch sausage over store-bought Italian links; it's surprisingly easy to make. We start by combining ground pork with salt and baking soda and letting it sit for 10 minutes. The baking soda raises the meat's pH, improving its ability to hold on to moisture. Rosemary, nutmeg, and garlic round out its flavor. We form the pork mixture into one big patty, brown it on both sides, and chop it up; the large sausage pieces finish cooking through in the sauce, guaranteeing juicy, tender meat. Mushrooms are a debated addition, but we like how they bolster the dish's earthiness.

Serves 4
Total Time:
1¼ hours

½ teaspoon plus pinch table salt, plus salt for cooking pasta

¼ teaspoon baking soda

4 teaspoons water

8 ounces ground pork

3 garlic cloves, minced, divided

1¼ teaspoons minced fresh rosemary, divided

1¼ teaspoons pepper, divided

⅛ teaspoon ground nutmeg

8 ounces cremini or white mushrooms, trimmed

7 teaspoons extra-virgin olive oil, divided

1 pound fresh farfalle (page 51)

½ cup dry white wine

¾ cup heavy cream

1½ ounces Pecorino Romano cheese, grated (¾ cup)

3 tablespoons minced fresh parsley

1 tablespoon lemon juice

1 Spray large plate with vegetable oil spray. Dissolve ½ teaspoon salt and baking soda in water in medium bowl. Gently fold in pork until combined and let stand for 10 minutes. Add one-third of garlic, ¾ teaspoon rosemary, ¾ teaspoon pepper, and nutmeg and smear with rubber spatula until well combined and tacky, 10 to 15 seconds. Transfer sausage mixture to prepared plate and form into rough 6-inch patty. Pulse mushrooms in food processor until finely chopped, 10 to 12 pulses.

2 Heat 2 teaspoons oil in 12-inch skillet over medium-high heat until just smoking. Add patty and cook, without moving it, until browned, 2 to 3 minutes. Flip and continue to cook until well browned on second side, 2 to 3 minutes longer (very center will be raw). Transfer patty to cutting board and chop into ⅛- to ¼-inch pieces.

3 Bring 4 quarts water to boil in large pot. Add pasta and 1 tablespoon salt and cook, stirring often, until al dente. Reserve 1½ cups cooking water, then drain pasta and return it to pot.

4 Heat 1 tablespoon oil in now-empty skillet over medium heat. Add mushrooms and remaining pinch salt and cook, stirring frequently, until browned, 5 to 7 minutes. Stir in remaining garlic, remaining ½ teaspoon rosemary, remaining ½ teaspoon pepper, and remaining 2 teaspoons oil and cook until fragrant, about 30 seconds. Stir in wine, scraping up any browned bits, and cook until completely evaporated, 1 to 2 minutes. Stir in sausage, cream, and ¾ cup pasta cooking water and simmer until meat is no longer pink, 1 to 3 minutes. Off heat, stir in Pecorino until smooth.

5 Add sauce, parsley, and lemon juice to pasta and toss to coat. Adjust consistency with reserved cooking water as needed. Season with salt and pepper to taste. Serve immediately.

Creamy Corn Bucatini with Ricotta and Basil

fettuccine | busiate | penne

WHY THIS RECIPE WORKS: Turn your fresh pasta into an essence-of-summer meal with this ingenious technique. Fresh corn serves as the base for a creamy pasta sauce that comes together easily. We start by bringing corn kernels and milk to a simmer before blending the mixture to a smooth puree. Corn kernels naturally contain cornstarch, which thickens into a clingy sauce if heated above 150 degrees. Heating also intensifies the characteristic aroma of corn, which is largely due to a compound that is also prominent in the aroma of milk. That means that our puree tastes more like corn, and it also tastes more like milk. Simmering our pasta in this sauce further thickens the sauce to a velvety consistency while ensuring a perfect al dente texture for the pasta. A touch of red pepper flakes brings a subtle kick. Finished with dollops of creamy ricotta and fresh basil, this is a delightful al fresco dinner. Although this is a fantastic use for in-season corn, you can substitute 18 ounces frozen corn for fresh.

Serves 4
Total Time:
45 minutes

4   ears corn, kernels cut from cobs (about 3 cups)

1   cup whole milk

1   pound fresh bucatini

¼   teaspoon table salt, plus salt for cooking pasta

¼   teaspoon red pepper flakes

6   ounces (¾ cup) whole-milk ricotta cheese

¼   cup fresh basil leaves, torn

1 Bring corn and milk to simmer in 12-inch skillet over medium heat. Carefully transfer corn and milk to blender and let cool slightly, about 5 minutes. Process until smooth, about 3 minutes, scraping down sides of blender jar as needed. Strain corn mixture through fine-mesh strainer into now-empty skillet, pressing on solids to extract as much liquid as possible.

2 Meanwhile, bring 4 quarts water to boil in large pot. Add pasta and 1 tablespoon salt and cook, stirring often, until al dente. Reserve 2 cups cooking water, then drain pasta.

3 Stir pasta, 1 cup reserved cooking water, ¼ teaspoon salt, and pepper flakes into corn mixture in skillet. Cook over medium-high heat, stirring constantly, until pasta is well coated with sauce, 1 to 3 minutes. Adjust consistency with remaining reserved cooking water as needed. Season with salt and pepper to taste.

4 Transfer pasta to serving dish, dollop with ricotta, and sprinkle with basil. Serve.

Dill Trofie with Smoked Salmon and Crispy Capers

farfalle | maltagliati | orecchiette | penne

WHY THIS RECIPE WORKS: Flavored pasta always looks so beautiful, and here, assertive and aromatic fresh dill adds its emphatic presence to fresh trofie. To make the most of the dill, we developed this Scandinavian-inspired dish with a nearly no-cook sauce that takes about as long to come together as does boiling the pasta water. Smoked salmon and tangy crème fraîche combine with lemon and caraway seeds, accented by an unexpected but perfectly complementary topping. We use the microwave to quickly create perfect little fried nonpareil capers for intense hits of seasoning to complement the just-warmed smoked salmon. The leftover caper oil makes an excellent vinaigrette, or drizzle it over bruschetta. Toast the caraway in a dry skillet over medium heat until fragrant (about 2 minutes), and then remove from the skillet so that the seeds won't scorch. Sour cream is a suitable alternative for crème fraîche, if necessary. See pages 28–29 for more information on making flavored pasta.

Serves 4
Total Time:
30 minutes

¼   cup capers, rinsed and patted dry

3   tablespoons extra-virgin olive oil

1   pound fresh trofie (page 54) flavored with dill

     Table salt for cooking pasta

¾   cup crème fraîche

1   teaspoon grated lemon zest plus 1 tablespoon juice

1   teaspoon caraway seeds, toasted

4   ounces smoked salmon, cut into ½-inch-wide strips

2   tablespoons dill fronds (optional)

1 Combine oil and capers in medium bowl (capers should be mostly submerged). Microwave until capers are darkened in color and have shrunk, 3 to 5 minutes, stirring halfway through microwaving. Using slotted spoon, transfer capers to paper towel–lined plate (they will continue to crisp as they cool); set aside. Reserve caper oil for another use.

2 Meanwhile, bring 4 quarts water to boil in large pot. Add pasta and 1 tablespoon salt and cook, stirring often, until al dente. Reserve ½ cup cooking water, then drain pasta and return it to pot. Stir in crème fraîche, lemon zest and juice, and caraway seeds and toss to combine. Adjust consistency with reserved cooking water as needed. Gently stir in smoked salmon. Sprinkle with capers and dill fronds, if using, before serving.

Pasta alla Norma

rigatoni | penne | fileja | maltagliati

WHY THIS RECIPE WORKS: Named in honor of the title character in Vincenzo Bellini's opera, this pasta dish originated in the Sicilian city of Catania—as did Bellini himself. With its lively combination of tender fried eggplant, robust tomato sauce, al dente pasta, and salty ricotta salata, pasta alla Norma truly does sing with each bite. To prepare it, we microwave eggplant pieces to remove excess moisture, toss them with a little olive oil and kosher salt (which clings better to the eggplant than table salt), and sauté them in a skillet until well browned. Leaving the skin on prevents the eggplant from breaking up while cooking. We remove the eggplant and then build the tomato sauce in the skillet, adding the eggplant back at the end. A secret ingredient, anchovies, contributes deep savor without adding any fishy flavors. The finished pasta is topped with a generous amount of ricotta salata, a slightly aged, tangy sheep's-milk cheese that bears little resemblance to the moist fresh ricotta cheese sold in tubs. Since ricotta salata is a semihard cheese, we shave it or shred it on the large holes of a box grater. If using table salt instead of kosher salt, reduce salt amounts by half.

Serves 4
Total Time: 50 minutes

1½ pounds eggplant, cut into ½-inch pieces

1 teaspoon kosher salt, plus salt for cooking pasta

¼ cup extra-virgin olive oil, divided

4 garlic cloves, minced

2 anchovy fillets, minced

¼–½ teaspoon red pepper flakes

1 (28-ounce) can crushed tomatoes

6 tablespoons chopped fresh basil

1 pound fresh ziti

3 ounces ricotta salata, shredded (1 cup)

1 Toss eggplant with salt in large bowl. Line large plate with double layer of coffee filters and lightly spray with vegetable oil spray. Spread eggplant in even layer over coffee filters; wipe out bowl with paper towels and set aside. Microwave eggplant until dry to touch and slightly shriveled, about 10 minutes, tossing halfway through cooking. Let cool slightly.

2 Transfer eggplant to now-empty bowl, drizzle with 1 tablespoon oil, and toss gently to coat; discard coffee filters and reserve plate. Heat 1 tablespoon oil in 12-inch nonstick skillet over medium-high heat until shimmering. Add eggplant and cook, stirring every 1½ to 2 minutes (more frequent stirring may cause eggplant pieces to break apart), until well browned and fully tender, about 10 minutes. Transfer eggplant to now-empty plate and set aside. Let skillet cool slightly, about 3 minutes.

3 Heat 1 tablespoon oil, garlic, anchovies, and pepper flakes in now-empty skillet over medium heat. Cook, stirring often, until garlic turns golden but not brown, about 3 minutes. Stir in tomatoes, bring to simmer, and cook, stirring occasionally, until slightly thickened, 8 to 10 minutes. Add eggplant and continue to cook, stirring occasionally, until eggplant is heated through and flavors meld, 3 to 5 minutes. Stir in basil and remaining 1 tablespoon oil and season with salt to taste.

4 Meanwhile, bring 4 quarts water to boil in large pot. Add pasta and 2 tablespoons salt and cook, stirring often, until al dente. Reserve ½ cup cooking water, then drain pasta and return it to pot. Add sauce to pasta and toss to combine. Adjust consistency with reserved cooking water as needed. Sprinkle with ricotta salata and serve.

Spaghetti al Tonno

busiate | maltagliati | farfalle

WHY THIS RECIPE WORKS: Most Italian families have their own routine for making a simple tomato sauce, folding in good-quality canned or jarred tuna, and combining it with a tangle of pasta. Our rendition is tuna forward and accented by tomato, rather than the inverse. We wholeheartedly recommend using olive oil–packed tuna: In both flavor and texture, it easily beats the water-packed kind. If budget and availability allow, a high-end brand will really elevate this dish. (Having said that, if water-packed is what you have on hand, don't let that stop you.) Since cooking tinned fish risks drying it out, we wait until the end to add it. Lots of garlic is essential. For layered garlicky goodness, we add it in two stages, sizzling some in olive oil for nutty sweetness and just warming some through in the hot pasta for an assertive edge. Red pepper flakes heat things up, while minced anchovies strengthen the umami backbone.

Serves 4
Total Time:
30 minutes

- 2 (5- to 7-ounce) jars or cans olive oil–packed tuna, drained
- 1 tablespoon lemon juice
- 1 teaspoon table salt, divided, plus salt for cooking pasta
- ½ teaspoon pepper, divided
- ¼ cup extra-virgin olive oil, divided, plus extra for drizzling
- 1½ tablespoons minced garlic, divided
- 3 anchovy fillets, minced
- ¼–½ teaspoon red pepper flakes
- 1 (14.5-ounce) can whole peeled tomatoes, drained with juice reserved and crushed by hand
- 1 pound fresh spaghetti
- 6 tablespoons chopped fresh parsley, divided

1 Gently stir tuna, lemon juice, ¼ teaspoon salt, and ¼ teaspoon pepper together in small bowl.

2 Heat 2 tablespoons oil, 1 tablespoon garlic, anchovies, and pepper flakes in saucepan over medium heat, stirring occasionally, until oil sizzles gently and anchovies break down, 1½ to 2 minutes. Stir in tomatoes and their juice and ½ teaspoon salt. Increase heat to high and bring to strong simmer. Adjust heat to maintain gentle simmer and cook, stirring occasionally, until slightly thickened, 6 to 7 minutes. Cover and keep warm over low heat.

3 Meanwhile, bring 4 quarts water to boil in large pot. Add pasta and 1 tablespoon salt and cook, stirring often, until barely al dente. Reserve ½ cup cooking water, then drain pasta and return it to pot. Off heat, add sauce, remaining ¼ teaspoon salt, remaining ¼ teaspoon pepper, and remaining 1½ teaspoons garlic and toss until pasta is well coated. Add tuna mixture and toss gently. Cover and set aside for 3 minutes so flavors can meld and pasta can finish cooking.

4 Adjust consistency of sauce with reserved cooking water as needed. Add ¼ cup parsley and remaining 2 tablespoons oil and toss to combine. Season with salt and pepper to taste. Distribute among pasta bowls. Drizzle each portion with extra oil. Sprinkle with remaining 2 tablespoons parsley and serve.

Garganelli with Tomatoes, Crispy Prosciutto, and Peas

farfalle | orecchiette | cavatelli | penne

WHY THIS RECIPE WORKS: Thanks to the convenience and quality of frozen peas, this colorful pasta dinner can be a year-round favorite. The fat rendered from cut-up prosciutto adds meaty depth to the sauce when used to sauté the onion and garlic. Then in go canned whole tomatoes to simmer, crushed by hand into irregular pieces. The addition of quick-cooking frozen peas gives the sauce a bright, sweet, textured finish. Since the peas get added just at the end of the cooking time to preserve their texture, be sure to thaw them first so that they will warm through quickly when tossed with the hot pasta, sauce, and grated Parmesan. The final garnish of the crisped-up prosciutto pieces and the chopped basil finish this off in style. If you would like to use fresh peas, cook them in a large skillet over medium-high heat with ¼ cup water until tender, 5 to 7 minutes, before adding them to the pot in step 3. We love this with tomato pasta (see pages 28–29).

Serves 4
Total Time:
40 minutes

---

2 tablespoons extra-virgin olive oil, plus extra for drizzling

6 ounces thinly sliced prosciutto, cut into ½-inch pieces

1 onion, chopped

½ teaspoon pepper

¼ teaspoon red pepper flakes

⅛ teaspoon table salt, plus salt for cooking pasta

3 garlic cloves, minced

1 (28-ounce) can whole peeled tomatoes, drained and crushed by hand

1 pound fresh garganelli (page 50)

1½ cups frozen peas, thawed

2 ounces Parmesan cheese, grated (1 cup), divided

2 tablespoons chopped fresh basil

1 Heat oil in 12-inch skillet over medium heat until shimmering. Add prosciutto and cook until crispy, about 10 minutes. Using slotted spoon, transfer prosciutto to paper towel–lined plate. Return skillet to medium heat; to fat left in skillet, add onion, pepper, pepper flakes, and salt. Cook until onion is softened, about 5 minutes. Add garlic and cook until fragrant, about 30 seconds. Add tomatoes and cook, stirring occasionally, until sauce is thickened, about 10 minutes.

2 Meanwhile, bring 4 quarts water to boil in large pot. Add pasta and 1 tablespoon salt and cook, stirring often, until al dente. Reserve ½ cup cooking water, then drain pasta and return it to pot.

3 Add peas, ¾ cup Parmesan, sauce, and ¼ cup reserved cooking water to pasta and toss to combine. Adjust consistency with remaining reserved cooking water as needed. Serve, sprinkled with prosciutto, basil, and remaining ¼ cup Parmesan and drizzled with extra oil.

Shells with Burst Cherry Tomato Sauce and Fried Caper Crumbs

penne | orecchiette | garganelli | trofie

WHY THIS RECIPE WORKS: Savory-sweet, juicy cherry tomatoes are a fabulous choice for this elegant dish. Toss these gems into the pan without any prep, and thanks to their high levels of glutamates and pectin, they quickly thicken into a superflavorful sauce. To ensure that some of the tomatoes stay intact so that they can pop in the mouth with a bright flood of juices, we cook them for just 10 minutes in a covered saucepan, where only the ones in direct contact with the bottom of the pan burst and those on top steam gently. Slivered garlic, red pepper flakes, a touch of sugar, and a couple of anchovies melt into the tomatoes, and stirring in some butter brings a light creaminess. We finish the pasta with a topping of fried bread crumbs and capers, transforming this into something special. Don't use grape tomatoes; they are less juicy and will produce a drier sauce.

Serves 4
Total Time: 50 minutes

Topping

- 2 tablespoons extra-virgin olive oil
- ¼ cup capers, rinsed and patted dry
- 1 anchovy fillet, minced
- ½ cup panko bread crumbs
- ⅛ teaspoon table salt
- ⅛ teaspoon pepper
- ¼ cup minced fresh parsley
- 1 teaspoon grated lemon zest

Pasta

- ¼ cup extra-virgin olive oil
- 2 garlic cloves, sliced thin
- 2 anchovy fillets
- 2 pounds cherry tomatoes
- 1½ teaspoons table salt, plus salt for cooking pasta
- ¼ teaspoon sugar
- ⅛–¼ teaspoon red pepper flakes
- 1 pound fresh shells
- 2 tablespoons unsalted butter, cut into 2 pieces and chilled
- 1 cup fresh basil leaves, torn if large

1 For the topping Heat oil in 10-inch skillet over medium heat until shimmering. Add capers and anchovy and cook, stirring frequently, until capers have darkened and shrunk, 3 to 4 minutes. Using slotted spoon, transfer caper mixture to paper towel–lined plate; set aside. Leave oil in skillet and return skillet to medium heat. Add panko, salt, and pepper to skillet and cook, stirring constantly, until panko is golden brown, 4 to 5 minutes. Transfer panko to medium bowl. Stir in parsley, lemon zest, and reserved caper mixture.

2 For the pasta Heat oil, garlic, and anchovies in large saucepan over medium heat. Cook, stirring occasionally, until anchovies break down and garlic is lightly browned, 4 to 5 minutes. Add tomatoes, salt, sugar, and pepper flakes to saucepan and stir to combine. Cover and increase heat to medium-high. Cook, without stirring, for 10 minutes.

3 Meanwhile, bring 4 quarts water to boil in large pot. Add pasta and 1 tablespoon salt and cook, stirring often, until al dente. Reserve ½ cup cooking water, then drain pasta and return it to pot. Off heat, add butter and tomato mixture to pasta and stir gently until oil, butter, and tomato juices combine to form light sauce, about 15 seconds. Adjust consistency with reserved cooking water as needed, adding 2 tablespoons at a time. Stir in basil and season with salt to taste. Serve, passing topping separately.

Malloreddus with Fava Beans and Mint

cavatelli | trofie | rigatoni | gnocchi

WHY THIS RECIPE WORKS: Sardinia's signature pasta is served with a wide range of sauces and other complements, from hearty meat ragùs and sausages to briny clams and other seafood to simple tomato sauces and vegetables. It's often prepared for holidays, festivals, and weddings where, traditionally, a Sardinian bride prepares a batch of malloreddus on her wedding night to share with her new husband. To make our fresh malloreddus shine, we use saffron in the dough, as is traditional (see pages 28–29), and pair it with a classic spring combination of tender fresh fava beans (prized in Sardinia for their nutrition and meaty flavor), tangy Pecorino cheese, and fresh mint. We use readily available Pecorino Romano, but if you happen to find Pecorino Sardo, use that instead. You will need to blanch the favas and then remove their waxy sheaths before using them. If you can't find fresh fava beans, you can substitute 2 cups thawed frozen fava beans; skip the blanching and peeling step.

Serves 4
Total Time: 1 hour

2 pounds fava beans, shelled (2 cups)

Table salt for cooking beans and pasta

3 tablespoons extra-virgin olive oil, divided

½ onion, chopped fine

2 garlic cloves, minced

Pinch red pepper flakes

1 pound fresh malloreddus (page 57) flavored with saffron

1 ounce Pecorino Romano cheese, grated (½ cup), plus extra for serving

½ cup chopped fresh mint

1 Bring 4 quarts water to boil in large pot. Fill large bowl halfway with ice and water. Add beans and 1 tablespoon salt to boiling water and cook for 1 minute. Using slotted spoon, transfer beans to ice water and let sit until chilled, about 2 minutes; drain well. Using paring knife, make small cut along edge of each bean through waxy sheath, then gently squeeze sheath to release bean; discard sheath. Set aside.

2 Meanwhile, return water to boil, add pasta, and cook, stirring often, until al dente. Reserve 1½ cups cooking water, then drain pasta in colander. Toss pasta with 1 tablespoon oil in colander and set aside.

3 Heat remaining 2 tablespoons oil in 12-inch skillet over medium heat until shimmering. Add onion and cook until softened and lightly browned, 5 to 7 minutes. Stir in garlic and pepper flakes and cook until fragrant, about 30 seconds. Stir in beans and ½ cup reserved cooking water and cook until beans are tender and liquid has mostly evaporated, 3 to 4 minutes.

4 Stir in pasta, ½ cup reserved cooking water, and Pecorino and cook, stirring often, until cheese has melted and sauce has thickened slightly, 1 to 2 minutes. Adjust consistency with remaining reserved cooking water as needed. Sprinkle with mint and serve, passing extra Pecorino separately.

Linguine allo Scoglio

spaghetti | fettuccine | farfalle | busiate

WHY THIS RECIPE WORKS: Versions of briny-sweet pasta allo scoglio are found all over coastal Italy, containing different shellfish according to what's local ("scoglio" refers to the rocky shores where the shellfish for the dish are caught). The technique in this recipe lies primarily in ensuring that all the seafood turns plump and tender at the same time, so we cook the varieties in a careful sequence, also layering in cherry tomatoes, clam juice, lots of garlic, fresh herbs, and lemon. Then at the end we add cooked fresh pasta and toss to combine. For a simpler version, you can omit the clams and squid and increase the amounts of mussels and shrimp to 1½ pounds each; increase the amount of salt in step 2 to ¾ teaspoon. You may use frozen squid instead of fresh, if needed.

Serves 4 to 6
Total Time: 1 hour

6	tablespoons extra-virgin olive oil, divided
12	garlic cloves, minced
¼	teaspoon red pepper flakes
1	pound littleneck or cherrystone clams, scrubbed
1	pound mussels, scrubbed and debearded
1¼	pounds cherry tomatoes (half of tomatoes halved, remaining tomatoes left whole), divided
1	(8-ounce) bottle clam juice
1	cup dry white wine
1	cup minced fresh parsley, divided
1	tablespoon tomato paste
4	anchovy fillets, minced
1	teaspoon minced fresh thyme
½	teaspoon table salt, plus salt for cooking pasta
1	pound extra-large shrimp (21 to 25 per pound), peeled and deveined
8	ounces squid, sliced crosswise into ½-inch-thick rings
2	teaspoons grated lemon zest, plus lemon wedges for serving
1	pound fresh linguine (page 47)

1 Heat ¼ cup oil in large Dutch oven over medium-high heat until shimmering. Add garlic and pepper flakes and cook until fragrant, about 1 minute. Add clams, cover, and cook, shaking pot occasionally, for 4 minutes. Add mussels, cover, and continue to cook, shaking pot occasionally, until clams and mussels have opened, 3 to 4 minutes. Transfer clams and mussels to bowl, discarding any that haven't opened, and cover to keep warm; leave any broth in pot.

2 Add whole tomatoes, clam juice, wine, ½ cup parsley, tomato paste, anchovies, thyme, and salt to pot and bring to simmer over medium-high heat. Reduce heat to medium and cook, stirring occasionally, until tomatoes have started to break down and sauce is reduced by one-third, about 10 minutes.

3 Reduce heat to medium-low, stir in shrimp, cover, and cook for 4 minutes. Stir in squid, lemon zest, halved tomatoes, and remaining ½ cup parsley; cover and continue to cook until shrimp and squid are just cooked through, about 2 minutes. Gently stir in clams and mussels. Remove pot from heat, cover, and let stand until clams and mussels are warmed through, about 2 minutes.

4 Meanwhile, bring 4 quarts water to boil in large pot. Add pasta and 1 tablespoon salt and cook, stirring often, until al dente. Reserve ½ cup cooking water, then drain pasta and add to Dutch oven with sauce; toss to combine. Adjust consistency with reserved cooking water as needed. Season with salt and pepper to taste. Transfer to large serving dish, drizzle with remaining 2 tablespoons oil, and serve, passing lemon wedges separately.

Maccheroni alla Chitarra with Lamb Ragù

spaghetti | pappardelle | fileja | gnocchi

WHY THIS RECIPE WORKS: Lamb ragùs perfumed with mountain herbs and saffron are favorites in Italy's Abruzzo region, classically paired with a unique pasta known as maccheroni alla chitarra—egg dough rolled into thick sheets and cut into squared-off strands. Traditionally, a cutter called a chitarra ("guitar" in Italian) is used to cut the pasta by hand, although many pasta machines and extruders also now come with chitarra attachments. For the ragù, we braise large chunks of boneless lamb shoulder for meltingly tender meat in a rich, tomatoey sauce. If it's difficult to chop the guanciale, put it in the freezer for 15 minutes to firm up. You can roll the pasta dough either with a machine or by hand (see pages 44–45); roll until it is about ⅛ inch thick. If your chitarra has more than one set of strings, choose the set spaced ⅛ inch apart.

1½ pounds boneless lamb shoulder, trimmed and cut into 3-inch pieces

½ teaspoon table salt, plus salt for cooking pasta

½ teaspoon pepper

1 tablespoon extra-virgin olive oil

2 ounces guanciale, chopped fine

1 onion, chopped fine

1 carrot, peeled and chopped fine

1 celery rib, minced

3 garlic cloves, minced

1 tablespoon tomato paste

2 teaspoons minced fresh rosemary

½ teaspoon saffron threads, crumbled

¼ teaspoon red pepper flakes

½ cup dry white wine

1 (28-ounce) can whole peeled tomatoes

1 pound Egg Pasta Dough (page 20), rolled into sheets

   Grated Pecorino Romano cheese

1 Adjust oven rack to lower-middle position and heat oven to 300 degrees. Pat lamb dry with paper towels and sprinkle with salt and pepper. Heat oil in Dutch oven over medium-high heat until just smoking. Brown lamb on all sides, about 8 minutes; transfer to plate. Pour off all but 1 tablespoon fat from pot and let pot cool slightly.

2 Add guanciale to fat left in pot and cook over medium-low heat until fat is rendered, about 2 minutes. Stir in onion, carrot, and celery, increase heat to medium, and cook until softened and lightly browned, 6 to 8 minutes. Stir in garlic, tomato paste, rosemary, saffron, and pepper flakes and cook until fragrant, about 30 seconds.

3 Stir in wine, scraping up any browned bits, and cook until reduced by half, about 3 minutes. Stir in tomatoes and their juice, breaking up tomatoes into rough 1-inch pieces with wooden spoon, and bring to simmer. Nestle lamb into pot along with any accumulated juices and return to simmer. Cover, transfer pot to oven, and cook until lamb is very tender, 2 to 2½ hours, turning lamb halfway through cooking.

4 Meanwhile, liberally dust 1 pasta sheet with flour and cut into lengths approximately 2 inches shorter than length of chitarra strings. Lay pasta sheet on top of strings and firmly roll floured rolling pin over pasta to cut into strands. Dust pasta with flour and arrange in small bundles on rimmed baking sheet. Repeat with remaining sheets.

5 Remove pot from oven. Transfer lamb to cutting board, let cool slightly, then shred into bite-size pieces using 2 forks; discard excess fat. Stir lamb and any accumulated juices into sauce, cover, and let sit until heated through, about 5 minutes. Season with salt and pepper to taste. Cover to keep warm. (Ragù can be refrigerated for up to 3 days; gently reheat before using.)

6 Bring 4 quarts water to boil in large pot. Add pasta and 1 tablespoon salt and cook, stirring often, until al dente. Reserve ½ cup cooking water, then drain pasta and return it to pot. Add lamb ragù and toss to combine. Adjust consistency with reserved cooking water as needed. Season with salt and pepper to taste. Serve with Pecorino.

Pappardelle with Duck and Chestnut Ragù

tagliatelle | maltagliati | rigatoni

WHY THIS RECIPE WORKS: We found inspiration in the Veneto area of Italy for our robust ragù that pairs duck with sweet, creamy chestnuts. Slowly browning duck legs produces plenty of flavorful fat for cooking aromatics. Assertive rosemary and acidic red wine cut through the duck's richness to make a flavorful, lustrous sauce that clings beautifully to wide noodles such as pappardelle. Chestnuts not only thicken the sauce but also appear in the crispy bread crumb topping. You can find fresh chestnuts seasonally in markets, but they must be roasted before use and are difficult to peel. We prefer to purchase the roasted peeled chestnuts that are sold jarred or vacuum-packed in many supermarkets near other nuts. Don't substitute water chestnuts, which belong to an entirely different plant family.

2   cups (9 ounces) peeled cooked chestnuts, divided

1   large onion, chopped coarse

1   carrot, peeled and chopped coarse

1   celery rib, chopped coarse

2   (12- to 14-ounce) duck leg quarters, trimmed

1   teaspoon table salt, plus salt for cooking pasta

1½ teaspoons minced fresh rosemary, divided

1   cup dry red wine

2½ cups chicken broth

¼   cup panko bread crumbs

1   teaspoon red wine vinegar

1   pound fresh pappardelle (page 47)

1 Adjust oven rack to middle position and heat oven to 300 degrees. Pulse chestnuts in food processor until finely chopped, 10 to 12 pulses, scraping down sides of bowl as needed; transfer to bowl. Pulse onion, carrot, and celery in now-empty processor until finely chopped, 10 to 12 pulses; set aside.

2 Using metal skewer, poke 15 to 20 holes in skin of each duck leg quarter, then pat dry with paper towels. Place duck skin side down in Dutch oven and cook over medium heat until well browned on first side and fat has rendered, 15 to 20 minutes. Flip duck and continue to cook until well browned on second side, about 3 minutes; transfer to plate. Pour off and reserve all but 2 tablespoons fat from pot.

3 Add vegetable mixture and salt to fat left in pot and cook over medium heat until vegetables are softened, 5 to 7 minutes. Stir in 1 teaspoon rosemary and cook until fragrant, about 30 seconds. Stir in wine, scraping up any browned bits, and cook until reduced slightly, about 1 minute.

4 Stir in broth and half of chestnuts. Nestle duck into pot with any accumulated juices and bring to simmer. Cover, transfer pot to oven, and cook until duck is very tender and falling off bones, about 2 hours.

5 While duck cooks, heat 1 tablespoon reserved fat in 10-inch skillet over medium heat until shimmering (discard remaining fat or reserve for another use). Add panko and cook, stirring frequently, until light golden brown, 2 to 3 minutes. Stir in remaining chestnuts and remaining ½ teaspoon rosemary and cook until fragrant and deep golden brown, about 2 minutes; set aside.

6 Remove pot from oven. Transfer duck to cutting board, let cool slightly, then shred meat into bite-size pieces using 2 forks; discard skin and bones. Bring sauce to simmer over medium-high heat and cook until thickened slightly, 3 to 5 minutes. Stir in shredded meat and vinegar and season with salt and pepper to taste.

7 Meanwhile, bring 4 quarts water to boil in large pot. Add pasta and 1 tablespoon salt and cook, stirring often, until al dente. Reserve ½ cup cooking water, then drain pasta and return it to pot. Add sauce and toss to combine. Adjust consistency with reserved cooking water as needed. Season with salt and pepper to taste. Sprinkle individual portions with chestnut-panko mixture before serving.

Pizzoccheri with Swiss Chard, Potatoes, and Taleggio

pappardelle | maltagliati | orecchiette

WHY THIS RECIPE WORKS: Short ribbons of fresh buckwheat pasta, pizzoccheri mingle with melted cheese, bitter greens, and soft potatoes in this traditional wintry dish from Valtellina, northeast of Milan. Wheat doesn't grow locally in the mountainous areas of northern Italy, but buckwheat does. Valtellina Casera, the alpine cheese usually used, is hard to find in the U.S., but Taleggio, another local cheese, makes a delicious alternative. It has a fruity, strong flavor that stands up to the assertive buckwheat and maintains a smooth consistency when melted. Swiss chard and savoy cabbage are commonly used in this dish; we love chard's tender leaves for our version. Cutting the potatoes into cubes encourages the starchy edges to melt into and thicken the cheese sauce. You can roll the pasta dough for pizzoccheri either with a machine or by hand (see pages 44–45); roll until it's thin but opaque.

Serves 4 to 6
Total Time:
40 minutes

1 pound Buckwheat Pasta Dough (page 25), rolled into sheets

3 tablespoons unsalted butter

1 tablespoon minced fresh sage

1 garlic clove, minced

2 pounds Swiss chard, stemmed and chopped coarse

8 ounces russet potatoes, peeled and cut into ½-inch pieces

½ teaspoon table salt, plus salt for cooking potatoes and pasta

6 ounces Taleggio cheese, rind removed, cut into ¼-inch pieces

1 Using pizza cutter or sharp knife, cut air-dried pasta sheets into 2 by ¾-inch strips. Toss lightly with flour and transfer to rimmed baking sheet.

2 Melt butter in Dutch oven over medium-high heat. Add sage and garlic and cook until fragrant, about 1 minute. Add chard, one handful at a time, and cook, stirring occasionally, until wilted and most liquid has evaporated, about 8 minutes. Cover and keep warm over low heat.

3 Meanwhile, bring 4 quarts water to boil in large pot. Add potatoes and 1 tablespoon salt and cook until just tender, 5 to 8 minutes. Using slotted spoon, transfer potatoes to bowl. Stir cheese, ¼ cup cooking water, and salt into chard until cheese is melted and sauce is smooth.

4 Return cooking water to boil. Add pasta and cook, stirring often, until al dente. Reserve ¼ cup cooking water, then drain pasta. Add pasta and potatoes to chard mixture and toss gently to combine. Season with salt and pepper to taste. Adjust consistency with reserved cooking water as needed before serving.

Busiate with Spring Vegetables

linguine | spaghetti | farfalle

WHY THIS RECIPE WORKS: Although nonnas have been whipping up similar creations in home kitchens in Italy for centuries, the most famous version of pasta with spring vegetables was born in New York City in 1975, when Chef Sirio Maccioni of the high-end restaurant Le Cirque put "pasta primavera" on his menu. As the dish exploded in popularity, variations proliferated. Our modern rendition focuses on two spring vegetables: asparagus and green peas, which cook quickly and concurrently. Instead of using the traditional cream to create the sauce, we use a versatile summer vegetable: zucchini. Cooking zucchini slices for a long time over gentle heat causes them to break down into a creamy, silky paste. Add some garlic and a heavy dose of olive oil and it becomes a flavorful sauce that's full of body. We cook the peas and asparagus directly in this sauce before tossing it with fresh pasta. Just before serving, we mix in fresh chives, lemon juice, and grated Pecorino Romano. In homage to Maccioni's original dish, we spoon halved cherry tomatoes in a little olive oil over the top. A shower of fresh mint completes the lively spring lilt of this pasta.

Serves 4
Total Time:
40 minutes

---

6 ounces cherry tomatoes, halved

6 tablespoons extra-virgin olive oil, divided, plus extra for drizzling

5 garlic cloves, divided (1 small, minced; 4 sliced thin)

¾ teaspoon table salt, divided, plus salt for cooking pasta

¼ teaspoon pepper

1 zucchini, halved lengthwise and sliced ¼ inch thick

⅛ teaspoon red pepper flakes

1 pound asparagus, trimmed and cut on bias into 1-inch lengths

1 cup frozen peas, thawed

¾ cup water

1 pound fresh busiate (page 55)

¼ cup minced fresh chives

1 tablespoon lemon juice

½ ounce Pecorino Romano cheese, grated (¼ cup), plus extra for serving

2 tablespoons torn fresh mint leaves

1 Toss tomatoes, 1 tablespoon oil, minced garlic, ¼ teaspoon salt, and pepper together in bowl; set aside.

2 Heat 3 tablespoons oil in 12-inch nonstick skillet over medium-low heat until shimmering. Add zucchini, pepper flakes, sliced garlic, and remaining ½ teaspoon salt and cook, covered, until zucchini softens and breaks down, 10 to 15 minutes, stirring occasionally. Add asparagus, peas, and water and bring to simmer over medium-high heat. Cover and cook until asparagus is crisp-tender, about 2 minutes.

3 Meanwhile, bring 4 quarts water to boil in large pot. Add pasta and 1 tablespoon salt and cook, stirring often, until al dente. Drain pasta and return it to pot.

4 Add vegetable mixture, chives, lemon juice, and remaining 2 tablespoons oil to pasta and toss to combine. Transfer to serving bowl, sprinkle with Pecorino, and drizzle with extra oil. Spoon tomatoes and their juices over top and sprinkle with mint. Serve, passing extra Pecorino separately.

Summer Squash Fettuccine with Ricotta and Lemon-Parmesan Bread Crumbs

pappardelle | spaghetti | rigatoni

WHY THIS RECIPE WORKS: Summer squash is front and center in this fresh pasta dish that's begging to be eaten al fresco. Cutting the squash into half-moons encourages excess moisture to cook out while letting the squash retain its structural integrity as it browns in olive oil along with garlic, black pepper, and red pepper flakes. Grated Parmesan adds nutty flavor and makes the dish even more cohesive as it melts when tossed with the cooked pasta, squash, and reserved cooking water. Torn basil offers fresh anise flavor and aroma, and lemon juice adds sunshiny brightness. For dramatic finishing touches, we sprinkle toasted panko (enhanced with lemon zest and Parmesan) over the top for a textural contrast and then dollop each portion with creamy, cool ricotta for a temperature contrast. A final sprinkle of basil reinforces the summery vibes. Choose summer squashes no heavier than 8 ounces each; larger squashes have more seeds and can taste watery.

Serves 4
Total Time: 1 hour

Bread Crumbs

- ¼ cup panko bread crumbs
- 1 tablespoon extra-virgin olive oil
- ¼ teaspoon table salt
- 1 ounce Parmesan cheese, grated (½ cup)
- 1 teaspoon grated lemon zest

Pasta

- 1½ pounds summer squash, halved lengthwise and sliced thin crosswise
- 6 tablespoons extra-virgin olive oil, divided
- 1 teaspoon table salt, plus salt for cooking pasta
- 4 garlic cloves, minced
- ¾ teaspoon red pepper flakes
- ½ teaspoon pepper
- 1 pound fresh fettuccine (page 47)
- 1½ ounces Parmesan cheese, grated (¾ cup)
- ½ cup torn fresh basil, plus extra for sprinkling
- 2½ tablespoons lemon juice
- 8 ounces (1 cup) whole-milk ricotta cheese

1 For the bread crumbs Combine panko, oil, and salt in 12-inch nonstick skillet and cook over medium heat, stirring frequently, until golden brown, 3 to 6 minutes. Transfer to bowl and stir in Parmesan and lemon zest; set aside.

2 For the pasta Combine squash, 3 tablespoons oil, and salt in now-empty skillet. Cook over medium-high heat, stirring occasionally, until squash is fully softened and spotty brown, 15 to 20 minutes. Add garlic, pepper flakes, and pepper and cook until fragrant, about 1 minute. Remove from heat and cover to keep warm.

3 Meanwhile, bring 4 quarts water to boil in large pot. Add pasta and 1 tablespoon salt and cook, stirring often, until al dente. Reserve 2 cups cooking water, then drain pasta and return it to pot.

4 Add squash mixture, 1¼ cups reserved cooking water, Parmesan, basil, lemon juice, and remaining 3 tablespoons oil to pasta and toss to combine. Adjust consistency with remaining reserved cooking water as needed. Season with salt and pepper to taste.

5 Transfer pasta to individual serving bowls. Dollop with ricotta and sprinkle with bread crumbs and extra basil. Serve immediately.

Trofie with Pesto, Potatoes, and Green Beans

penne | busiate | orecchiette

WHY THIS RECIPE WORKS: Known as trofie alla genovese in its Ligurian homeland, this hearty dish features intricate little twisted tubes of fresh pasta (trofie is traditional) that trap basil pesto in their coils, as well as green beans and potatoes. The potatoes might seem like an odd addition if you aren't familiar with this dish, but they perform an integral role, both soaking up the rich pesto flavors and lending body to the sauce. So their treatment is the secret to success. Cutting the potatoes into chunks and then, once cooked, tossing them with the pasta and green beans creates just enough agitation to slough off their corners, which dissolve into the dish and help to pull the pesto and cooking water together to form the creamy sauce.

Serves 4 to 6
Total Time:
50 minutes

12 ounces green beans, trimmed and cut into 1½-inch lengths

Table salt for cooking vegetables and pasta

1 pound red potatoes, peeled and cut into ½-inch pieces

1 pound fresh trofie (page 54)

2 tablespoons unsalted butter, cut into ½-inch pieces and chilled

1 tablespoon lemon juice

¾ cup Classic Basil Pesto (page 194)

½ teaspoon pepper

1 Bring 4 quarts water to boil in large pot. Add green beans and 1 tablespoon salt and cook until tender, 5 to 8 minutes. Using slotted spoon, transfer green beans to rimmed baking sheet.

2 Return water to boil, add potatoes, and cook until they are tender but still hold their shape, 9 to 12 minutes. Using slotted spoon, transfer potatoes to sheet with green beans.

3 Return water to boil, add pasta, and cook, stirring often, until al dente. Reserve 1½ cups cooking water, then drain pasta and return it to pot. Add butter, lemon juice, green beans and potatoes, pesto, pepper, and 1¼ cups reserved cooking water and toss gently until sauce takes on creamy appearance. Adjust consistency with remaining cooking water as needed. Season with salt and pepper to taste. Serve immediately.

Whole-Wheat Busiate with Lentils, Pancetta, and Escarole

linguine | penne | trofie

WHY THIS RECIPE WORKS: "Greens and beans" is an endlessly adaptable recipe template, and pairing them with fresh whole-wheat pasta makes a hearty, soul-satisfying meal full of texture and flavor. What's more, the sauce comes together in a single saucepan while you boil the water for the pasta. Our favored greens to use here are escarole, which we pair with onion, lentils, and savory pancetta. Carrots add a touch of sweetness, and white wine provides a bright punch of acidity. French green lentils, or lentilles du Puy, are our first choice for this recipe, since they retain their firm yet tender texture, but brown, black, or regular green lentils also work (note that cooking times will vary depending on the type used). Pinot Grigio is a good choice for the white wine.

Serves 4
Total Time: 1 hour

¼ cup extra-virgin olive oil, divided

4 ounces pancetta, cut into ¼-inch pieces

1 onion, chopped fine

2 carrots, peeled, halved lengthwise, and sliced ¼-inch-thick

2 garlic cloves, minced

2 cups chicken broth

1½ cups water

¾ cup lentilles du Puy, picked over and rinsed

¼ cup dry white wine

1 head escarole (1 pound), trimmed and sliced ½-inch-thick

1 pound fresh whole-wheat busiate (page 55)

Table salt for cooking pasta

¼ cup chopped fresh parsley

Grated Parmesan cheese

1 Heat 2 tablespoons oil in large saucepan over medium heat until shimmering. Add pancetta and cook, stirring occasionally, until beginning to brown, 3 to 5 minutes. Add onion and carrots and cook until softened, 5 to 7 minutes. Stir in garlic and cook until fragrant, about 30 seconds. Stir in broth, water, and lentils and bring to simmer. Cover, reduce heat to medium-low, and simmer until lentils are fully cooked and tender, 30 to 40 minutes.

2 Stir in wine and simmer, uncovered, for 2 minutes. Stir in escarole, 1 handful at a time, and cook until wilted, about 5 minutes.

3 Meanwhile, bring 4 quarts water to boil in large pot. Add pasta and 1 tablespoon salt and cook, stirring often, until al dente. Reserve ¾ cup cooking water, then drain pasta and return it to pot. Add ½ cup reserved cooking water, lentil mixture, parsley, and remaining 2 tablespoons oil to pasta in pot and toss to combine. Season with salt and pepper to taste and adjust consistency with remaining reserved cooking water as needed. Serve with Parmesan.

Orecchiette with Broccoli Rabe and Sausage

farfalle | rigatoni | maltagliati

WHY THIS RECIPE WORKS: In Puglia, the heel of the Italian boot, broccoli rabe and orecchiette are a popular pairing, often spiked with red chiles. The trick to this pasta dish is cooking the broccoli rabe just right and limiting the number of ingredients so that at the end, you have a moist and flavorful (but not oily) pasta dish. To make this heartier, we include some spicy Italian sausage (another classic pairing with broccoli rabe). We start by browning the sausage in a skillet and then adding the broccoli rabe and chicken broth to absorb the rich, meaty flavors in the pan; covering the pan allows us to steam the rabe with the other sauce ingredients. Besides eliminating the need for a separate pot to blanch the rabe, this cooking method doesn't dilute the pleasingly bitter flavor of this Italian vegetable. Some red pepper flakes amplify the heat from the sausage, and a drizzle of olive oil and grated Parmesan cheese bring the whole dish together. If you prefer a less spicy dish, use sweet Italian sausage.

Serves 4
Total Time:
30 minutes

8   ounces hot Italian sausage, casings removed

6   medium garlic cloves, minced (about 2 tablespoons)

½   teaspoon red pepper flakes

½   teaspoon table salt, plus salt for cooking pasta

1   bunch broccoli rabe (1 pound), trimmed and cut into 1½-inch pieces

½   cup chicken broth

1   pound fresh orecchiette (page 52)

1   tablespoon extra-virgin olive oil

1   ounce Parmesan cheese, grated (½ cup)

1   Cook sausage until browned in 12-inch nonstick skillet over medium-high heat, breaking it into ½-inch pieces with wooden spoon, about 3 minutes. Stir in garlic, pepper flakes, and salt. Cook, stirring constantly, until garlic is fragrant, about 1½ minutes. Add broccoli rabe and chicken broth, cover, and cook until broccoli rabe turns bright green, about 2 minutes. Uncover and cook, stirring frequently, until most of the broth has evaporated and broccoli rabe is tender, 2 to 3 minutes.

2   Meanwhile, bring 4 quarts water to boil in large pot. Add pasta and 1 tablespoon salt and cook, stirring often, until al dente. Reserve ½ cup cooking water, then drain pasta and return it to pot.

3   Add the sausage mixture, oil, and Parmesan to pasta and toss to combine. Adjust consistency with reserved cooking water as needed and serve immediately.

Pasta e Ceci

tubetti | cavatelli | malloreddus

WHY THIS RECIPE WORKS: This classic Italian comfort food originated in Rome but is now found throughout Italy. We start our version by sautéing a soffritto—finely chopped onion, carrot, celery, garlic, and pancetta—in olive oil. We then stir in tomatoes, water, and canned chickpeas along with their aquafaba, which acts as a natural thickener in addition to adding more flavor. Simmering the chickpeas before adding the pasta makes them creamy, and because they break down a bit, they add even more body to the cooking liquid. Ditalini is a popular and traditional pasta choice for its chickpea-like size. We simmer the mixture for about 10 minutes, at which point the pasta turns tender and releases some starch of its own to further thicken the stew. Lemon juice and parsley stirred in at the end add a finishing touch of brightness.

Serves 4
Total Time:
45 minutes

- 2 ounces pancetta, cut into ½-inch pieces
- 1 small carrot, peeled and cut into ½-inch pieces
- 1 small celery rib, cut into ½-inch pieces
- 4 garlic cloves, peeled
- 1 onion, halved and cut into 1-inch pieces
- 1 (14-ounce) can whole peeled tomatoes, drained
- ¼ cup extra-virgin olive oil, plus extra for drizzling
- 2 teaspoons minced fresh rosemary
- 1 anchovy fillet, minced
- ¼ teaspoon red pepper flakes
- 2 (15-ounce) cans chickpeas (shake cans; do not drain)
- 2 cups water
- 1 teaspoon table salt
- 8 ounces fresh ditalini
- 1 tablespoon lemon juice
- 1 tablespoon minced fresh parsley

  Grated Parmesan cheese

1 Process pancetta in food processor until ground to paste, about 30 seconds, scraping down sides of bowl as needed. Add carrot, celery, and garlic and pulse until finely chopped, 8 to 10 pulses. Add onion and pulse until onion is cut into ⅛- to ¼-inch pieces, 8 to 10 pulses. Transfer pancetta mixture to Dutch oven. Pulse tomatoes in now-empty processor until coarsely chopped, 8 to 10 pulses. Set aside.

2 Add oil to pancetta mixture in pot and cook over medium heat, stirring frequently, until fond begins to form on bottom of pot, about 5 minutes. Add rosemary, anchovy, and pepper flakes and cook until fragrant, about 1 minute. Stir in tomatoes, chickpeas and their liquid, water, and salt and bring to boil, scraping up any browned bits. Reduce heat to medium-low and simmer for 10 minutes. Add pasta and cook, stirring frequently, until al dente. Stir in lemon juice and parsley and season with salt and pepper to taste. Serve, passing Parmesan and extra oil separately.

FILLED PASTA, GNOCCHI & GNUDI

Chapter 4

Mushroom Ravioli with Browned Butter, Sage, and Truffle Sauce

WHY THIS RECIPE WORKS: A hearty mixed-mushroom filling (made with your choice of mushrooms) paired with a simple but luxurious truffle-accented sauce elevates fresh ravioli to company-worthy heights. For the sauce, browning butter with fresh sage creates irresistibly nutty flavors and woodsy aromas. Then we add truffle oil. This earthy, pungent oil is made by adding flavor molecules (either fresh or synthetic) to oil (usually olive or safflower). Given that it has such a bold flavor, all that's needed is a mere drizzle to provide maximum impact. To keep the flavor and aroma of the truffle oil pure and intense, we stir it in after the butter has browned, off the heat (cooking truffle oil will dull its flavor). Though you may see both white and black truffle oil, we prefer the flavor of white truffle oil. If you don't have a pot that holds 6 quarts, cook the ravioli in two batches; toss the first batch with sauce in the skillet and cover to keep warm while cooking the remaining ravioli. To make ravioli, see pages 58–59.

Serves 4 to 6
Total Time:
30 minutes

---

8   tablespoons unsalted butter

2   tablespoons minced fresh sage

¼   teaspoon table salt, plus salt for cooking pasta

1   teaspoon white truffle oil

1½   pounds fresh ravioli with Wild Mushroom Filling (page 70)

     Shaved Parmesan cheese

1 Melt butter in 12-inch skillet over medium heat. Add sage and cook, swirling skillet constantly, until sage is crispy and butter is browned and fragrant, about 3 minutes. Off heat, stir in truffle oil.

2 Meanwhile, bring 6 quarts water to boil in large pot. Add ravioli and 1½ tablespoons salt. Cook, maintaining gentle boil, until ravioli are just tender. Using slotted spoon or wire skimmer, transfer ravioli to skillet. Add 2 tablespoons cooking water and toss gently to coat, adjusting consistency with extra cooking water as needed. Serve, topped with Parmesan.

Three-Cheese Ravioli with Pumpkin Cream Sauce

WHY THIS RECIPE WORKS: This showstopper of a dish looks like something you'd order in a restaurant, but it's easily made at home with fresh egg pasta sheets to wow friends and family. Three-cheese ravioli, filled with a fluffy blend of ricotta, fontina, and Parmesan cheeses, is cloaked with a creamy pumpkin sauce and then topped with browned butter infused with hazelnuts and crispy sage leaves for a dish that captures the essence of autumn. The hazelnuts toast right in the butter as the butter browns, making for a deeply flavored finishing drizzle. And the crispy sage leaves are an attractive and elegant garnish. Make sure to purchase unsweetened pumpkin puree, which contains no sweeteners or added spices. If you don't have a pot that holds 6 quarts, cook the ravioli in two batches; toss the first batch with sauce in the skillet and cover to keep warm while cooking the remaining ravioli. To make ravioli, see pages 58–59.

Serves 4 to 6
Total Time:
45 minutes

---

5 tablespoons unsalted butter, divided

¼ cup raw hazelnuts, chopped

12 fresh sage leaves

1 teaspoon sherry vinegar

⅛ plus ½ teaspoon table salt, divided, plus salt for cooking pasta

¼ cup finely chopped shallot

¼ teaspoon ground nutmeg

1 cup heavy cream

½ cup canned unsweetened pumpkin puree

1 ounce Parmesan cheese, grated (½ cup)

1½ pounds fresh ravioli with Three-Cheese Filling (page 68)

1 Melt 4 tablespoons butter in 12-inch nonstick skillet over medium heat. Add hazelnuts and sage and cook, swirling skillet constantly, until sage is crispy, about 3 minutes. Using tongs, transfer sage to paper towel–lined plate; continue to cook butter and hazelnuts until both are browned and fragrant, about 1 minute longer. Transfer to heatproof bowl and stir in vinegar and ⅛ teaspoon salt.

2 Melt remaining 1 tablespoon butter in now-empty skillet over medium heat. Add shallot, nutmeg, and remaining ½ teaspoon salt and cook, stirring occasionally, until shallot is softened, about 3 minutes. Stir in cream and pumpkin and bring to simmer. Cook until thickened, about 5 minutes. Off heat, stir in Parmesan.

3 Meanwhile, bring 6 quarts water to boil in large pot. Add ravioli and 1½ tablespoons salt. Cook, maintaining gentle boil, until ravioli are just tender. Using slotted spoon or wire skimmer, transfer ravioli to skillet. Add 2 tablespoons cooking water and toss gently to coat, adjusting consistency with extra cooking water as needed. Serve, topped with sage and hazelnut butter.

Short Rib Agnolotti with Hazelnuts and Browned Butter

WHY THIS RECIPE WORKS: The specialty filled pastas of Italy vary from region to region, but each one tells a story, since they often contain the prized ingredients of their respective regions. These Piedmontese agnolotti, filled with a comforting, meltingly tender braised beef mixture and tossed in browned butter, are a standout example. Legend has it that after a victorious battle some 700 years ago, a nobleman requested a celebratory meal from his chef. With little food on hand, the chef used leftover braised meat to fill egg pasta. Our modern filling uses boneless beef short ribs for their rich flavor and tender texture, enhanced with savoy cabbage and rosemary. The simple brown butter sauce, made even nuttier by infusing hazelnuts in it, complements the filling without ever competing with it. If you don't have a pot that holds 6 quarts, cook the agnolotti in two batches; toss the first batch with sauce in the skillet and cover to keep warm while cooking the remaining agnolotti. To make agnolotti, see page 61.

Serves 4 to 6
Total Time:
30 minutes

- 8 tablespoons unsalted butter
- ¼ cup hazelnuts, toasted, skinned, and chopped coarse
- 2 teaspoons red wine vinegar
- ¼ teaspoon table salt, plus salt for cooking pasta
- 1½ pounds fresh agnolotti with Braised Short Rib Filling (page 69)
- 2 tablespoons minced fresh parsley

1 Melt butter in 12-inch skillet over medium heat. Add hazelnuts and cook, swirling skillet constantly, until butter and hazelnuts are browned and fragrant, about 3 minutes. Off heat, stir in vinegar and salt.

2 Meanwhile, bring 6 quarts water to boil in large pot. Add agnolotti and 1½ tablespoons salt. Cook, maintaining gentle boil, until agnolotti are just tender. Using slotted spoon or wire skimmer, transfer agnolotti to skillet. Add 2 tablespoons cooking water and toss gently to coat, adjusting consistency with extra cooking water as needed. Sprinkle with parsley and serve immediately.

Cappellacci di Zucca

WHY THIS RECIPE WORKS: Similar in shape to jumbo tortellini but sporting a pointed top, these squash-filled cappellacci are a glorious specialty of the Italian city of Ferrara. The Italian zucca pumpkin is plentiful there, and when combined with Parmesan it serves as a luscious, rich filling. Butternut squash is the best domestic substitute for the sweet-fleshed zucca. (Do not use frozen squash.) Variations on the filling often incorporate mostarda (an assertive, acidic fruit and mustard condiment) or crumbled amaretti cookies. To streamline shopping, we omit these additions, but since we like the brightness that mostarda contributes, we bring a similar flavor note with a drizzle of high-quality balsamic vinegar. If you like, shave some Parmesan over each serving. For more information on rolling pasta sheets and shaping cappellacci, see pages 44–45 and 61.

1½ pounds butternut squash, peeled, seeded, and cut into 1-inch pieces (3½ cups)

2½ ounces Parmesan cheese, grated (1¼ cups)

12 tablespoons unsalted butter

½ teaspoon table salt, plus salt for cooking pasta

⅛ teaspoon pepper

Pinch ground nutmeg

1 recipe Egg Pasta Dough (page 20)

1 large egg white, lightly beaten

6 tablespoons unsalted butter

1 tablespoon minced fresh sage

Balsamic vinegar

1 Microwave squash in covered bowl until very soft and easily pierced with fork, 15 to 18 minutes, stirring halfway through microwaving. Carefully remove cover and drain squash. Process squash, grated Parmesan, 6 tablespoons butter, ¼ teaspoon salt, pepper, and nutmeg in food processor until smooth, about 1 minute, scraping down sides of bowl as needed. Transfer filling to bowl and refrigerate for 30 minutes. (Filling can be refrigerated for up to 24 hours.)

2 Transfer dough to clean counter, divide into 6 pieces, and cover with plastic wrap. Flatten 1 piece of dough into ½-inch-thick disk. Using pasta machine with rollers set to widest position, feed dough through rollers twice. Bring tapered ends of dough toward middle and press to seal. Feed dough seam side first through rollers again. Repeat feeding dough tapered ends first through rollers set at widest position, without folding, until dough is smooth and barely tacky.

3 Narrow rollers to next setting and feed dough through rollers twice. Continue to progressively narrow rollers, feeding dough through each setting twice, until dough is thin and semi-transparent. Transfer pasta sheet to liberally floured sheet of parchment paper. Cover with second sheet of parchment, followed by damp kitchen towel to keep pasta from drying out. Repeat rolling with remaining dough, stacking each pasta sheet between floured parchment.

4 Dust rimmed baking sheet with flour. Using pizza cutter or sharp knife, cut 1 pasta sheet into 5-inch squares on lightly floured counter; discard scraps. Place 1 rounded tablespoon filling in center of each square. Working with 1 pasta square at a time, lightly brush edges with egg white. With one corner of pasta square facing you, lift top corner of pasta over filling and extend it so that it lines up with bottom corner. Keeping top corner of dough suspended over filling with your thumbs, use your fingers to press dough layers together, working around each mound of filling from back to front, pressing out as much air as possible before sealing completely.

5 With folded edge of filled pasta facing you, pull corners together below filling until slightly overlapped to create cappellaccio with cupped outer edge and dimpled center. Press to seal overlapping edges and transfer to prepared baking sheet. Repeat cutting and filling remaining pasta. Let cappellacci sit uncovered until dry to touch and slightly stiffened, about 30 minutes.

6 Melt remaining 6 tablespoons butter in 12-inch skillet over medium heat. Off heat, stir in sage and remaining ¼ teaspoon salt. Bring 4 quarts water to boil in large pot. Add half of cappellacci and 1 tablespoon salt. Cook, maintaining gentle boil, until capellacci are just tender. Using slotted spoon or wire skimmer, transfer cappellacci to skillet, toss gently to coat, and cover to keep warm. Return water to boil and repeat cooking remaining cappellacci; transfer to skillet and toss gently to coat. Drizzle portions with vinegar before serving.

Pansotti al Preboggion con Salsa di Noci

WHY THIS RECIPE WORKS: The traditional filling in Liguria for this elegant filled pasta is preboggion, a blend of foraged wild herbs and greens. Whatever edible plants are in season can be and frequently are used. For our homage, we turn to a combination of trusty kale for its savoriness and texture and dandelion greens for their thrilling and distinctive bitterness. Once these are blanched (preboggion means "preboiled" in the local dialect), the main herbs of Liguria (chervil and marjoram) are added and the filling is bound with ricotta. Pansotti are traditionally served with a walnut pesto, which is regarded by many as the precursor to the better-known basil pesto (which also hails from Liguria). This salsa di noci starts off as a rough paste of walnuts and soaked bread crumbs that emulsifies into a creamy sauce once heated and loosened with some starchy pasta cooking water. You can substitute Swiss chard, curly spinach, watercress, mustard greens, beet greens, turnip greens, or arugula for the dandelion greens. If chervil is unavailable, substitute tarragon. For more information on rolling pasta sheets and shaping pansotti, see pages 44–45 and 65.

Serves 4 to 6
Total Time:
1½ hours

8   ounces Egg Pasta Dough (page 20)

1   recipe Bitter Greens Filling
    (page 71)

1   large egg white, lightly beaten

¼   cup whole milk

2   tablespoons panko bread crumbs

1   cup walnuts, toasted

1   ounce Parmesan cheese, grated
    (½ cup)

2   tablespoons extra-virgin olive oil

1   garlic clove, minced

½   teaspoon minced fresh marjoram or
    oregano

¼   teaspoon table salt, plus salt for
    cooking pasta

¼   teaspoon pepper

1 Transfer dough to clean counter, divide into 3 pieces, and cover with plastic wrap. Flatten 1 piece of dough into ½-inch-thick disk. Using pasta machine with rollers set to widest position, feed dough through rollers twice. Bring tapered ends of dough toward middle and press to seal. Feed dough seam side first through rollers again. Repeat feeding dough tapered ends first through rollers set at widest position, without folding, until dough is smooth and barely tacky.

2 Narrow rollers to next setting and feed dough through rollers twice. Continue to progressively narrow rollers, feeding dough through each setting twice, until dough is thin and semi-transparent. Transfer sheet of pasta to liberally floured sheet of parchment paper. Cover with second sheet of parchment, followed by damp kitchen towel to keep pasta from drying out. Repeat rolling with remaining 2 pieces of dough, stacking pasta sheets between floured layers of parchment.

3 Dust rimmed baking sheet with flour. Using pizza cutter or sharp knife, cut 1 pasta sheet into 2½-inch squares on lightly floured counter; discard scraps. Place rounded ½ teaspoon filling in center of each square (you will have some left over). Working with 1 pasta square at a time, lightly brush edges with egg white. With one corner of pasta square facing you, lift top corner of pasta over filling and extend it so that it lines up with bottom corner. Keeping top corner of dough suspended over filling with your thumbs, use your fingers to press dough layers together, working around each mound of filling from back to front, pressing out as much air as possible before sealing completely.

4 With folded edge of filled pasta facing you, pull edges closest to filling toward each other below filling until they are just overlapping to create pansotto with collared outer edge and dimpled center. Press to seal edges and transfer to prepared baking sheet. Repeat cutting and filling remaining pasta. Let pansotti sit uncovered until dry to touch and slightly stiffened, about 30 minutes.

5 Combine milk and panko in small bowl and let sit until bread crumbs have softened, about 1 minute. Pulse panko mixture, walnuts, Parmesan, oil, garlic, marjoram, salt, and pepper in clean, dry food processor until nearly smooth, about 1 minute, scraping down sides of bowl as needed. (Sauce can be refrigerated for up to 2 days.)

6 Bring 6 quarts water to boil in large pot. Add pansotti and 1½ tablespoons salt. Cook, maintaining gentle boil, until pansotti are just shy of tender.

7 Transfer 1½ cups cooking water to 12-inch skillet. Add walnut pesto and cook over medium heat, stirring constantly, until heated through and smooth, about 2 minutes. Using slotted spoon or wire skimmer, transfer pansotti to skillet and toss gently with sauce to coat. Adjust consistency with extra cooking water as needed. Serve.

Tortellini in Brodo

WHY THIS RECIPE WORKS: This most treasured pasta of Emilia-Romagna can have varied fillings, but the version stuffed with a smooth mixture of pork and chicken that's served in a rich chicken broth is a must-have first course on local tables for Christmas dinner and often New Year's Eve also. For this preparation, the filling is typically ground until very fine and dense. Here, we start with ground chicken because it offers a good balance of fatty and lean meat. In addition, the silky, salty qualities of prosciutto and mortadella help create a smooth, robust filling. Parmesan, parsley, and nutmeg round out the flavors. Given that shaping tortellini is a time-consuming process, we build the brodo using store-bought broth, infusing it with some of our ground chicken, onion, garlic, and more nutmeg for superb flavor. Be sure to use ground chicken, not ground chicken breast (also labeled 99 percent fat-free). For more information on rolling pasta sheets and shaping tortellini, see pages 44–45 and 62.

Broth

8	ounces ground chicken
2	cups chicken broth
½	onion, peeled
3	garlic cloves, peeled and smashed
4	parsley stems
¼	teaspoon table salt
¼	teaspoon ground nutmeg

Tortellini

4	ounces ground chicken
2	ounces mortadella, chopped coarse
1	ounce prosciutto, chopped coarse
2	tablespoons grated Parmesan cheese
2	tablespoons chopped fresh parsley
2	tablespoons extra-virgin olive oil
¼	teaspoon ground nutmeg
8	ounces Egg Pasta Dough (page 20)
1	large egg white, lightly beaten
	Table salt for cooking pasta

1 For the broth Bring all ingredients to simmer in small saucepan. Reduce heat to medium-low, cover, and cook until flavors meld, about 15 minutes. Strain broth through fine-mesh strainer into bowl, pressing on solids to extract as much liquid as possible; discard solids. (Broth can be refrigerated for up to 24 hours.) Return broth to now-empty saucepan, cover, and keep warm over low heat.

2 For the tortellini Process ground chicken, mortadella, prosciutto, Parmesan, parsley, oil, nutmeg, and 1 tablespoon warm broth in food processor until smooth, 30 to 45 seconds, scraping down sides of bowl as needed. Transfer mixture to bowl, cover, and refrigerate until chilled, about 30 minutes.

3 Transfer dough to clean counter, divide into 3 pieces, and cover with plastic wrap. Flatten 1 piece of dough into ½-inch-thick disk. Using pasta machine with rollers set to widest position, feed dough through rollers twice. Bring tapered ends of dough toward middle and press to seal. Feed dough seam side first through rollers again. Repeat feeding dough tapered end first through rollers set at widest position, without folding, until dough is smooth and barely tacky.

4 Narrow rollers to next setting and feed dough through rollers twice. Continue to progressively narrow rollers, feeding dough through each setting twice, until dough is thin and semi-transparent. Transfer sheet of pasta to liberally floured sheet of parchment paper. Cover with second sheet of parchment, followed by damp kitchen towel to keep pasta from drying out. Repeat rolling with remaining 2 pieces of dough, stacking pasta sheets between floured layers of parchment.

5 Dust rimmed baking sheet with flour. Cut 1 pasta sheet into rounds on lightly floured counter using 2½-inch round cookie cutter; discard scraps. Place ½ teaspoon filling in center of each round. Working with 1 pasta round at a time, lightly brush edges with egg white. Lift top edge of pasta over filling and extend it so that it lines up with bottom edge. Keeping top edge of dough suspended over filling with your thumbs, use your fingers to press dough layers together, working around each mound of filling from back to front, pressing out as much air as possible before sealing completely.

6 With folded edge of filled pasta facing you, pull corners together below filling until slightly overlapped to create tortellino with cupped outer edge and dimpled center. Press to seal overlapping edges and transfer to prepared sheet. Repeat cutting and filling remaining pasta. Let tortellini sit uncovered until dry to touch and slightly stiffened, about 30 minutes.

7 Bring 4 quarts water to boil in large pot. Add tortellini and 1 tablespoon salt. Cook, maintaining gentle boil, until tortellini are just tender. Using slotted spoon or wire skimmer, transfer tortellini to individual bowls. Spoon warm broth over top and serve.

Potato Gnocchi with Fontina Sauce

WHY THIS RECIPE WORKS: Potato gnocchi was originally born from frugality—just humble potatoes and flour added up to a meal. While a multitude of variations (made from other vegetables or flours, bread, or cheese, to name a few) exist across Italy, in the mountainous northern region of Valle d'Aosta you'll most likely find hearty potato gnocchi dressed with rich fontina cheese and butter, where it goes by the affectionate nickname of gnocchi alla bava—"drooling gnocchi." While some recipes bind the potatoes with buckwheat flour, all-purpose flour is equally traditional, and we like how it lets the flavor of the fontina shine. At their simplest, recipes for gnocchi alla bava call for tossing chunks of butter and fontina with the hot gnocchi, but whisking melted butter, fontina, and a bit of the gnocchi cooking water together prior to tossing results in a creamier, smoother sauce.

Serves 4 to 6
Total Time:
30 minutes

1½   pounds Potato Gnocchi (page 66)
        Table salt for cooking gnocchi

3   tablespoons unsalted butter

4   ounces Italian fontina cheese,
        shredded (1 cup)

⅛   teaspoon grated nutmeg

1 Bring 6 quarts water to boil in large pot. Add half of gnocchi and 1½ tablespoons salt and simmer gently, stirring occasionally, until firm and just cooked through, about 90 seconds (gnocchi should float to surface after about 1 minute). Using slotted spoon or wire skimmer, transfer gnocchi to bowl and cover to keep warm. Return cooking water to boil and repeat cooking remaining gnocchi.

2 Meanwhile, melt butter in 12-inch skillet over medium heat. Whisk in ¼ cup of cooking water, fontina, and nutmeg until cheese is melted and smooth. Using slotted spoon or wire skimmer, transfer gnocchi to skillet and toss gently to coat. Adjust consistency with extra cooking water as needed. Serve immediately.

Ricotta Gnocchi with Garlicky Cherry Tomato Sauce and Arugula

WHY THIS RECIPE WORKS: Making ricotta-based gnocchi is super-simple and weeknight friendly from start to finish: Stir together a dough until you can form a ball, cut and roll the ball into ropes, and cut those ropes into nuggets. Then let the saucing fun begin. We love these cheesy pasta pillows paired with a sophisticated fresh tomato sauce and plenty of greens. After browning some garlic in extra-virgin olive oil, we toss halved cherry tomatoes into the skillet to soften and then stir in some red wine vinegar and brown sugar to create a sort of agrodolce effect. After tossing the gnocchi and tomatoes together, we fold in peppery fresh arugula and shower everything with grated Parmesan. If you don't have a pot that holds 6 quarts, cook the gnocchi in two batches; toss the first batch with sauce in the skillet and cover to keep warm while cooking the remaining gnocchi.

Serves 4
Total Time:
30 minutes

Gnocchi

- 1   pound (2 cups) whole-milk ricotta cheese
- 1   large egg
- ¼   cup grated Parmesan cheese
- 1   teaspoon table salt, plus salt for cooking gnocchi
- ½   teaspoon pepper
- ⅛   teaspoon ground nutmeg
- 1   cup plus 2 tablespoons (5⅔ ounces) all-purpose flour

Sauce

- 2   tablespoons extra-virgin olive oil
- 5   garlic cloves, minced
- 1   pound cherry tomatoes, halved
- ½   teaspoon table salt
- 1½   teaspoons red wine vinegar
- 1½   teaspoons packed light brown sugar
- 3   ounces (3 cups) baby arugula
- ½   cup chopped fresh basil
- ¼   cup grated Parmesan cheese

1 For the gnocchi Whisk ricotta, egg, Parmesan, salt, pepper, and nutmeg in large bowl until thoroughly combined. Stir in flour with rubber spatula until thoroughly combined. Form dough into rough ball and transfer to well-floured counter. Adding extra flour to hands and dough as needed to prevent sticking, gently knead dough into smooth ball.

2 Line rimmed baking sheet with parchment paper and dust liberally with flour. Using floured bench scraper or chef's knife, cut dough into 8 pieces. Dust cut ends of each piece of dough with more flour to coat. On lightly floured counter, working with 1 piece of dough at a time, gently roll dough into ½-inch-thick rope, sprinkling with more flour as needed if dough begins to stick to counter. Cut rope into ¾-inch lengths. Transfer gnocchi to prepared sheet; set aside. (Gnocchi can be wrapped with plastic wrap and refrigerated for up to 24 hours or chilled in freezer until firm, then transferred to zipper-lock bag and frozen for up to 1 month. If frozen, do not thaw before cooking.)

3 For the sauce Heat oil in 12-inch skillet over medium heat until shimmering. Add garlic and cook until fragrant and lightly browned, about 1 minute. Stir in tomatoes and salt and cook, stirring frequently, until tomatoes have softened and released their juices, about 3 minutes. Off heat, stir in vinegar and sugar. Transfer to large serving bowl and cover to keep warm.

4 Bring 6 quarts water to boil in large pot. Using parchment paper as sling, add gnocchi and 1½ tablespoons salt and simmer gently, stirring occasionally, until firm and just cooked through, about 90 seconds (gnocchi should float to surface after about 1 minute). Using slotted spoon or wire skimmer, transfer gnocchi to skillet and toss gently to coat. Fold in arugula and basil and season with salt and pepper to taste. Sprinkle with Parmesan and serve immediately.

Spinach and Ricotta Gnudi with Tomato-Butter Sauce

WHY THIS RECIPE WORKS: Counterintuitively, the appeal of these delicate dumplings actually comes from the absence of pasta dough. "Gnudi" means "nudes," and these are like ravioli filling without the wrappers, sauced and served just like pasta. We make our gnudi from seasoned ricotta and greens. Both elements are loaded with moisture, which needs to be controlled lest the dough require so much binder that the dumplings are leaden. Draining the cheese on a paper towel–lined baking sheet is fast and efficient. Frozen spinach readily gives up its water as it thaws and becomes easy to squeeze dry. A combination of egg whites, flour, and panko binds the mixture into a tender dough that we scoop and roll into rounds and then simmer gently. Taking inspiration from two traditional sauces—bright tomato sugo and rich browned butter—we make a hybrid by toasting garlic in butter and adding cherry tomatoes, which spill their bright juices into the rich backdrop. Ricotta without stabilizers such as locust bean, guar, and xanthan gums drains better. Frozen whole-leaf spinach is easiest to squeeze dry, but frozen chopped spinach will work. Squeezing the spinach should remove ½ to ⅔ cup liquid; you should have ⅔ cup finely chopped spinach.

Gnudi

12	ounces (1½ cups) whole-milk or part-skim ricotta cheese
½	cup all-purpose flour
1	ounce Parmesan cheese, grated (½ cup), plus extra for garnishing
1	tablespoon panko bread crumbs
¾	teaspoon table salt, plus salt for cooking gnudi
½	teaspoon pepper
¼	teaspoon grated lemon zest
10	ounces frozen whole-leaf spinach, thawed and squeezed dry
2	large egg whites, lightly beaten

Sauce

4	tablespoons unsalted butter
3	garlic cloves, sliced thin
12	ounces cherry or grape tomatoes, halved
2	teaspoons cider vinegar
¼	teaspoon table salt
¼	teaspoon pepper
2	tablespoons shredded fresh basil

1 For the gnudi Line rimmed baking sheet with double layer of paper towels. Spread ricotta in even layer over towels; set aside and let sit for 10 minutes. Place flour, Parmesan, panko, salt, pepper, and lemon zest in large bowl and stir to combine. Process spinach in food processor until finely chopped, about 30 seconds, scraping down sides of bowl as needed. Transfer spinach to bowl with flour mixture. Grasp paper towels and fold ricotta in half; peel back towels. Rotate sheet 90 degrees and repeat folding and peeling 2 more times to consolidate ricotta into smaller mass. Using paper towels as sling, transfer ricotta to bowl with spinach mixture. Discard paper towels but do not wash baking sheet. Add egg whites to bowl and mix gently until well combined.

2 Transfer heaping teaspoons of dough to now-empty sheet (you should have 45 to 50 portions). Using your dry hands, gently roll each portion into 1-inch ball. Set aside.

3 For the sauce Melt butter in small saucepan over medium heat. Add garlic and cook, swirling saucepan occasionally, until butter is very foamy and garlic is pale golden brown, 2 to 3 minutes. Off heat, add tomatoes and vinegar; cover and set aside.

4 Meanwhile, bring 1 quart water to boil in large pot. Add 1½ teaspoons salt. Using slotted spoon or wire skimmer, transfer all gnudi to water. Return water to gentle simmer. Cook, adjusting heat to maintain gentle simmer, for 5 minutes, starting timer once water has returned to simmer (to confirm doneness, cut 1 dumpling in half; center should be firm).

5 While gnudi simmer, add salt and pepper to sauce and cook over medium-high heat, stirring occasionally, until tomatoes are warmed through and slightly softened, about 2 minutes. Divide sauce evenly among 4 bowls. Using slotted spoon or wire skimmer, remove gnudi from pot, drain well, and transfer to bowls with sauce. Garnish with basil and extra Parmesan. Serve immediately.

BAKED PASTA

Chapter 5

Three-Cheese Manicotti with Tomato Sauce

WHY THIS RECIPE WORKS: Manicotti means "sleeves"—which is just what these homey tubes of stuffed fresh pasta resemble. They are the Italian American sibling to Italian cannelloni, which are found throughout Italy but especially in the Marche, Campania, and Emilia-Romagna regions. (Cannelloni means "large reeds.") Any filling used in ravioli also may be used in manicotti, but we especially love this classic version stuffed with a three-cheese blend of ricotta, mozzarella, and Parmesan cheese and cloaked with a simple tomato sauce spiced with garlic, red pepper flakes, and fresh basil. After baking the manicotti, we broil the dish for a few minutes to give it a nicely bronzed crown, so make sure that your baking dish is broiler safe.

Sauce

2   tablespoons extra-virgin olive oil

3   garlic cloves, minced

½   teaspoon red pepper flakes (optional)

2   (28-ounce) cans crushed tomatoes

2   tablespoons chopped fresh basil

Pasta Sheets

1   pound Egg Pasta Dough (page 20)

    Table salt for cooking pasta

4   teaspoons extra-virgin olive oil, divided

Manicotti

1½   pounds (3 cups) whole-milk or part-skim ricotta cheese

8   ounces whole-milk mozzarella cheese, shredded (2 cups)

4   ounces Parmesan cheese, grated (2 cups), divided

2   large eggs, lightly beaten

2   tablespoons minced fresh parsley

2   tablespoons chopped fresh basil

¾   teaspoon table salt

½   teaspoon pepper

1 For the sauce Cook oil, garlic, and pepper flakes, if using, in large saucepan over medium heat until fragrant but not brown, about 2 minutes. Stir in tomatoes, bring to simmer, and cook until thickened slightly, about 15 minutes. Off heat, stir in basil and season with salt and pepper to taste. Set aside.

2 For the pasta sheets Transfer dough to clean counter, divide into 8 pieces, and cover with plastic. Flatten 1 piece of dough into ½-inch-thick disk. Using pasta machine with rollers set to widest position, feed dough through rollers twice. Bring tapered ends of dough toward middle and press to seal. Feed dough seam side first through rollers again. Repeat feeding dough tapered end first through rollers set at widest position, without folding, until dough is smooth. (If dough sticks to fingers or rollers, lightly dust with flour and roll again.)

3 Narrow rollers to next setting and feed dough through rollers twice. Continue to progressively narrow rollers, feeding dough through each setting twice, until dough is thin but still sturdy; transfer to lightly floured counter. Using pizza cutter or sharp knife, trim pasta sheet into 12 by 4-inch rectangle, then cut sheet in half crosswise into two 6 by 4-inch manicotti noodles; discard scraps. Let noodles sit uncovered on counter while rolling remaining 7 pieces of dough (do not overlap noodles, as they may stick together).

4 Bring 4 quarts water to boil in large pot. Add 4 noodles and 1 tablespoon salt. Cook, maintaining gentle boil, until noodles are just shy of al dente. Using slotted spoon or wire skimmer, transfer noodles to large bowl and toss with 1 teaspoon oil. Lay noodles flat on 2 greased rimmed baking sheets, overlapping as needed, and let cool slightly. Repeat cooking remaining noodles in 3 batches and tossing each in 1 teaspoon oil.

5 For the manicotti Adjust oven rack to middle position and heat oven to 400 degrees. Combine ricotta, mozzarella, 1 cup Parmesan, eggs, parsley, basil, salt, and pepper in bowl. Spread 1½ cups sauce over bottom of 13 by 9-inch broiler-safe baking dish. Arrange several noodles with short sides facing you on counter. Spread ¼ cup ricotta mixture evenly over bottom three-quarters of each noodle. Roll noodles up around filling, then arrange seam side down in dish (two columns of 8 manicotti will fit neatly across length of dish). Spread remaining sauce over manicotti.

6 Sprinkle manicotti with remaining 1 cup Parmesan. Spray sheet of aluminum foil with vegetable oil spray, cover dish tightly, and place on foil-lined rimmed baking sheet. Bake until bubbling, about 40 minutes. Remove baking dish from oven. Adjust oven rack 6 inches from broiler element and heat broiler. Uncover dish and broil until Parmesan is spotty brown, 4 to 6 minutes. Let cool for 10 minutes before serving.

Cheese and Tomato Lasagna

WHY THIS RECIPE WORKS: There are so many expressions of lasagna, from extravagant dishes layered with plenty of ground meats to "white" versions with mushrooms, spinach, or zucchini. This southern Italian lasagne di magro (literally "skinny lasagna," meaning without meat) pares things down to three foundational components: noodles, cheese (typically a trio of ricotta, mozzarella, and Parmesan), and tomato sauce. To amp up these elements, we add tomato paste and anchovies to deepen the umami qualities of the tomato sauce, along with a small can of diced tomatoes to add texture to the crushed tomatoes. (Diced tomatoes are treated with calcium chloride, which prevents them from breaking down during cooking.) Since ricotta and mozzarella are naturally mild, we replace them with tangier cottage cheese and Italian fontina cheese (which melts just as wonderfully as mozzarella does), and we swap Parmesan for stronger-tasting Pecorino Romano. For a vegetarian version, omit the anchovies. To make the fontina easier to shred, you can freeze it for 30 minutes to firm it up.

Cheese Sauce

4   ounces Pecorino Romano cheese, grated (2 cups)

8   ounces (1 cup) whole-milk or part-skim cottage cheese

½   cup heavy cream

2   garlic cloves, minced

1   teaspoon cornstarch

¼   teaspoon table salt

¼   teaspoon pepper

Tomato Sauce

¼   cup extra-virgin olive oil

1   onion, chopped fine

1½   teaspoons sugar

½   teaspoon red pepper flakes

½   teaspoon dried oregano

½   teaspoon table salt

4   garlic cloves, minced

8   anchovy fillets, rinsed, patted dry, and minced

1   (28-ounce) can crushed tomatoes

1   (14.5-ounce) can diced tomatoes, drained

1   ounce Pecorino Romano cheese, grated (½ cup)

¼   cup tomato paste

Lasagna

10   fresh lasagna noodles (page 48)

     Table salt for cooking pasta

2   teaspoons extra-virgin olive oil, divided

8   ounces Italian fontina cheese, shredded (2 cups)

⅛   teaspoon cornstarch

¼   cup grated Pecorino Romano cheese

3   tablespoons chopped fresh basil

1 For the cheese sauce Whisk all ingredients in bowl until homogeneous.

2 For the tomato sauce Heat oil in large saucepan over medium heat. Add onion, sugar, pepper flakes, oregano, and salt and cook, stirring frequently, until onions are softened, about 10 minutes. Add garlic and anchovies and cook until fragrant, about 2 minutes. Stir in crushed tomatoes, diced tomatoes, Pecorino, and tomato paste and bring to simmer. Reduce heat to medium-low and simmer until slightly thickened, about 20 minutes.

3 For the lasagna Adjust oven rack to middle position and heat oven to 425 degrees. Bring 4 quarts water to boil in large pot. Add 5 noodles and 1 tablespoon salt. Cook, maintaining gentle boil, until noodles are just shy of al dente. Using slotted spoon or wire skimmer, transfer noodles to large bowl and toss with 1 teaspoon oil. Lay noodles flat on 2 greased rimmed baking sheets, overlapping as needed, and let cool slightly. Repeat cooking remaining noodles and tossing with remaining 1 teaspoon oil.

4 Spread 1 cup tomato sauce in bottom of greased 13 by 9-inch baking dish. Lay 2 noodles lengthwise in dish, trimming edges as needed to fit. Spread 1 cup cheese sauce over noodles, followed by ½ cup fontina. Repeat layering of noodles. Spread 1 cup tomato sauce over second layer of noodles, followed by ½ cup fontina. Create third layer of noodles and top with 1 cup tomato sauce. Create fourth layer of noodles and top with remaining cheese sauce, and ½ cup fontina.

5 Lay remaining 2 noodles over fontina. Spread remaining tomato sauce over noodles. Toss remaining ½ cup fontina with cornstarch, then sprinkle over tomato sauce, followed by Pecorino.

6 Spray sheet of aluminum foil with vegetable oil spray and cover lasagna. (Lasagna can be refrigerated for up to 24 hours; increase covered baking time to 40 minutes.) Bake until bubbling around edges, about 30 minutes. Remove foil and continue to bake until top is spotty brown, about 15 minutes. Let cool for 20 minutes. Sprinkle with basil, cut into pieces, and serve.

Mushroom Lasagna

WHY THIS RECIPE WORKS: Here's a truly spectacular vegetarian mushroom lasagna. Brought to the table steaming hot and bursting with savory, earthy, meaty depth, it holds its own against any other lasagna (or any other special-occasion main dish, for that matter). We build our version with hearty roasted portobellos for concentrated mushroom flavor, daintier white mushrooms, and dried porcini mushrooms for complexity and a subtle woodsiness, layering everything with melty, irresistibly gooey fontina cheese. The creamy, very loose béchamel sauce hydrates the fresh lasagna noodles. If you prefer, you can substitute whole-milk mozzarella for the fontina cheese. To make it easier to shred, you can freeze the cheese for 30 minutes to firm it up.

Serves 8 to 10
Total Time: 3 hours

2   pounds portobello mushroom caps, gills removed, halved and sliced crosswise ¼ inch thick

¼   cup plus 2 teaspoons extra-virgin olive oil, divided

1¾ teaspoons table salt, divided, plus salt for cooking pasta

1¾ teaspoons pepper, divided

4   red onions, chopped

8   ounces white mushrooms, trimmed and halved if small or quartered if large

½   ounce dried porcini mushrooms, rinsed and minced

4   garlic cloves, minced, divided

½   cup dry vermouth

3   tablespoons unsalted butter

3   tablespoons all-purpose flour

3½ cups whole milk

¼   teaspoon ground nutmeg

¼   cup plus 2 tablespoons chopped fresh basil, divided

¼   cup minced fresh parsley, divided

10 fresh lasagna noodles (page 48)

8   ounces Italian fontina cheese, shredded (2 cups)

1½ ounces Parmesan cheese, grated (¾ cup)

½   teaspoon grated lemon zest

1   Adjust oven rack to middle position and heat oven to 425 degrees. Toss portobello mushrooms with 2 tablespoons oil, ½ teaspoon salt, and ¾ teaspoon pepper and spread onto rimmed baking sheet. Roast until shriveled, about 30 minutes, stirring halfway through roasting; transfer to bowl and let cool.

2   Heat 1 tablespoon oil in 12-inch nonstick skillet over medium heat until shimmering. Add onions and ¼ teaspoon salt and cook, stirring occasionally, until onions are softened and lightly browned, 8 to 10 minutes; transfer to bowl with roasted portobellos.

3   Pulse white mushrooms in food processor until coarsely chopped, about 6 pulses. Heat 1 tablespoon oil in now-empty skillet over medium-high heat until shimmering. Add white mushrooms and porcini and cook, stirring occasionally, until browned and all moisture has evaporated, 6 to 8 minutes. Stir in 1 tablespoon garlic, remaining 1 teaspoon salt, and remaining 1 teaspoon pepper; reduce heat to medium and cook, stirring often, until garlic is fragrant, about 30 seconds. Stir in vermouth and cook until liquid has evaporated, 2 to 3 minutes.

4   Add butter and cook until melted. Add flour and cook, stirring constantly, for 1 minute. Stir in 1 cup water, scraping up any browned bits and smoothing out any lumps. Stir in milk and nutmeg and simmer until sauce has thickened and measures 4 cups, 10 to 15 minutes. Off heat, stir in ¼ cup basil and 2 tablespoons parsley.

5   Bring 4 quarts water to boil in large pot. Add 5 noodles and 1 tablespoon salt. Cook, maintaining gentle boil, until noodles are just shy of al dente. Using slotted spoon or wire skimmer, transfer noodles to large bowl and toss with 1 teaspoon oil. Lay noodles flat on 2 greased rimmed baking sheets, overlapping as needed, and let cool slightly. Repeat cooking remaining noodles and tossing with remaining 1 teaspoon oil.

6   Combine fontina and Parmesan in bowl. Spread 1 cup mushroom sauce evenly over bottom of greased 13 by 9-inch baking dish. Lay 2 noodles lengthwise in dish, trimming edges as needed to fit. Spread ½ cup sauce evenly over noodles, then sprinkle with 1½ cups mushroom-onion mixture and ½ cup cheese mixture. Repeat layering of noodles, sauce, mushroom-onion mixture, and cheese mixture 3 more times. Arrange remaining 2 noodles on top, cover with remaining sauce, and sprinkle with remaining cheese.

7   Spray sheet of aluminum foil with vegetable oil spray and cover lasagna. (Lasagna can be refrigerated for up to 24 hours; increase covered baking time to 40 minutes.) Bake until bubbling around edges, about 30 minutes. Remove foil and continue to bake until top is spotty brown, about 15 minutes.

8   Combine remaining garlic, remaining 2 tablespoons basil, remaining 2 tablespoons parsley, and lemon zest together and sprinkle over lasagna. Let cool for 20 minutes. Cut into pieces and serve.

Spinach Lasagna

WHY THIS RECIPE WORKS: Fresh, emerald-green spinach highlighted by a delicate, savory white sauce; tender fresh lasagna noodles; and mild, creamy cheese make this vegetarian spinach lasagna a spectacular success. As we usually do with lasagna, we prefer cottage cheese over ricotta here, for the extra tang and creaminess it lends to the dish. Regular curly-leaf spinach has plenty of texture and an assertive spinach flavor, which we love here; we blanch it and then wring all the excess water from it so that it doesn't end up sogging out the noodles. You can substitute 2 pounds of flat-leaf spinach for the curly-leaf spinach, but don't use baby spinach, because it is much too delicate. Be sure to set up the ice water bath before cooking the spinach, as plunging it into the cold water immediately after blanching retains its bright green color and ensures that it doesn't overcook. If you prefer, you can substitute whole-milk mozzarella for the fontina. To make the cheese easier to shred, you can freeze it for 30 minutes to firm it up.

Serves 8 to 10
Total time: 2 hours

Sauce

1¼   pounds curly-leaf spinach, stemmed

½   teaspoon table salt, plus salt for blanching spinach

5   tablespoons unsalted butter

6   shallots, minced

4   garlic cloves, minced

¼   cup all-purpose flour

3½   cups whole milk

2   bay leaves

½   teaspoon ground nutmeg

¼   teaspoon pepper

1   ounce Parmesan cheese, grated (½ cup)

Lasagna

12   ounces (1½ cups) whole-milk or part-skim cottage cheese

1   large egg

¼   teaspoon table salt

10   fresh lasagna noodles (page 48)

2   ounces Parmesan cheese, grated (1 cup)

2   teaspoons extra-virgin olive oil, divided

8   ounces Italian fontina cheese, shredded (2 cups)

1 For the sauce Bring 4 quarts water to boil in large pot. Fill large bowl halfway with ice and water. Add spinach and 1 tablespoon salt to boiling water and cook until just wilted, about 5 seconds. Using slotted spoon or wire skimmer, transfer spinach to ice water, and let sit until cool, about 1 minute. Drain spinach and transfer to clean dish towel. Wrap towel tightly around spinach to form ball and wring until dry. Chop spinach and set aside.

2 Melt butter in medium saucepan over medium heat. Stir in shallots and garlic and cook until softened, about 4 minutes. Add flour and cook, stirring constantly, until thoroughly combined, about 1½ minutes (mixture should not brown). Gradually whisk in milk, scraping up any browned bits and smoothing out any lumps. Bring to boil, whisking often, then stir in bay leaves, nutmeg, salt, and pepper. Reduce heat to low and simmer, whisking occasionally, for 10 minutes. Discard bay leaves, then whisk in Parmesan until completely melted. Reserve ½ cup sauce in small bowl and press plastic wrap directly against surface; set aside. Transfer remaining sauce to second bowl and stir in spinach, mixing well to break up any clumps, then press plastic directly against surface; set sauce aside.

3 For the lasagna Adjust oven rack to middle position and heat oven to 425 degrees. Process cottage cheese, egg, and salt in food processor until very smooth, about 30 seconds; set aside.

4 Return water to boil. Add 5 noodles and cook, maintaining gentle boil, until noodles are just shy of al dente. Using slotted spoon or wire skimmer, transfer noodles to large bowl and toss with 1 teaspoon oil. Lay noodles flat on 2 greased rimmed baking sheets, overlapping as needed, and let cool slightly. Repeat cooking remaining noodles and tossing with remaining 1 teaspoon oil.

5 Spread reserved sauce evenly over bottom of greased 13 by 9-inch baking dish. Lay 2 noodles lengthwise in dish, trimming edges as needed to fit. Spread ¾ cup spinach mixture evenly over noodles, sprinkle remaining Parmesan over spinach mixture, and top cheese with 2 noodles. Spread ¾ cup spinach mixture evenly over noodles, followed by half of cheese filling, then top with 2 noodles. Repeat with ¾ cup spinach mixture, remaining cheese filling, and 2 noodles. For final layer, spread 1 cup spinach mixture evenly over noodles, sprinkle 1 cup fontina over spinach mixture, and top with 2 noodles. Cover noodles with remaining spinach mixture and sprinkle with remaining 1 cup fontina.

6 Spray sheet of aluminum foil with vegetable oil spray and cover lasagna. (Lasagna can be refrigerated for up to 24 hours; increase covered baking time to 40 minutes.) Bake until bubbling around edges, about 30 minutes. Remove foil and continue to bake until top is spotty brown, about 15 minutes. Let cool for 20 minutes before serving.

Lasagna Verde alla Bolognese

WHY THIS RECIPE WORKS: Possibly the quintessential Italian lasagna, the celebrated and celebratory lasagne verdi alla Bolognese is served at holidays or other special occasions. This showstopper is a decadent combination of meaty Ragù alla Bolognese (page 230); velvety, creamy béchamel sauce; and lots of Parmesan cheese, all layered between thin sheets of vibrant green spinach pasta. Knowing our rich, flavorful meat sauce is a bit of a project (albeit worthwhile), we simplify the béchamel. Instead of cooking milk, butter, and flour, we turn to our favorite unorthodox lasagna option: tangy, creamy cottage cheese. Whisking it with cream, Parmesan, and a touch of cornstarch (to prevent curdling) makes for a lush no-cook béchamel alternative. We finish the lasagna with a sprinkling of Parmesan over a final layer of cream sauce, which bakes into a gooey, crisp-edged, golden-brown top. You will need half of the Ragù alla Bolognese recipe for this dish, so plan on freezing the rest or reserving it for another use. See pages 28–29 for more information on making flavored pasta.

Serves 8 to 10
Total Time:
1½ hours

10   fresh lasagna noodles (page 28) made with spinach

¼   teaspoon table salt, plus salt for cooking pasta

2   teaspoons extra-virgin olive oil, divided

6½   ounces Parmesan cheese, grated (3¼ cups), divided

8   ounces (1 cup) whole-milk or part-skim cottage cheese

1   cup heavy cream

1   tablespoon cornstarch

2   garlic cloves, minced

½   teaspoon pepper

3   cups Ragù alla Bolognese (page 230), room temperature

1 Adjust oven rack to middle position and heat oven to 425 degrees. Bring 4 quarts water to boil in large pot. Add 5 noodles and 1 table-spoon salt. Cook, maintaining gentle boil, until noodles are just shy of al dente. Using slotted spoon or wire skimmer, transfer noodles to large bowl and toss with 1 teaspoon oil. Lay noodles flat on 2 greased rimmed baking sheets, overlapping as needed, and let cool slightly. Repeat cooking remaining noodles and tossing with remaining 1 teaspoon oil.

2 Meanwhile, stir 3 cups Parmesan, cottage cheese, cream, cornstarch, garlic, pepper, and salt together in bowl.

3 Spread 1 cup ragù in bottom of greased 13 by 9-inch baking dish. Lay 2 noodles lengthwise in dish, trimming edges as needed to fit. Spread 1 cup cheese sauce over top, followed by second layer of noodles. Spread 1 cup ragù over top, followed by third layer of noodles. Repeat layering of cream sauce, noodles, and ragù, ending with fifth layer of noodles. Spread remaining cream sauce over top and sprinkle with remaining ¼ cup Parmesan.

4 Spray sheet of aluminum foil with vegetable oil spray and cover lasagna. (Lasagna can be refrigerated for up to 24 hours; increase covered baking time to 40 minutes.) Bake until bubbling around edges, about 30 minutes. Remove foil and continue to bake until top is spotty brown, about 15 minutes. Let cool for 20 minutes before serving.

Lasagna with Hearty Tomato-Meat Sauce

WHY THIS RECIPE WORKS: Fans of "old school" lasagna made hearty with ground meat, tomato sauce, and ricotta cheese, look no further. Our rendition of this comfort classic hits all the high points and then some, since it's elevated with homemade lasagna noodles. The meaty sauce for this style of lasagna can take a long time to cook, but we speed it up by simmering onion, garlic, and meatloaf mix (a combination of ground beef, pork, and veal) together for about 15 minutes. Adding some heavy cream creates a richer, more cohesive sauce; we also stir in a combo of pureed and diced tomatoes for a luxurious, soft sauce with nice chunks of tomato. For a classic cheese layer, we combine ricotta, Parmesan, fresh basil, and an egg, which helps thicken and bind the mixture; a layer of shredded mozzarella ups the creaminess and cheesiness of the filling. You can substitute equal amounts of 80 percent lean ground beef, ground veal, and ground pork for the meatloaf mix (the total amount of meat should be 1 pound).

Serves 8 to 10
Total Time: 2 hours

Tomato-Meat Sauce

- 1 tablespoon extra-virgin olive oil
- 1 onion, minced
- 6 garlic cloves, minced (2 tablespoons)
- 1 pound meatloaf mix
- ½ teaspoon table salt
- ½ teaspoon pepper
- ¼ cup heavy cream
- 1 (28-ounce) can tomato puree
- 1 (28-ounce) can diced tomatoes, drained

Lasagna

- 1¾ cups whole-milk or part-skim ricotta cheese
- 2½ ounces Parmesan cheese, grated (1¼ cups)
- ½ cup chopped fresh basil
- 1 large egg, lightly beaten
- ½ teaspoon table salt
- ½ teaspoon pepper
- 10 fresh lasagna noodles (page 48)
- 2 teaspoons extra-virgin olive oil, divided
- 1 pound whole-milk mozzarella cheese, shredded (4 cups)

1 For the tomato-meat sauce Heat oil in large Dutch oven over medium heat until shimmering. Add onion and cook, stirring occasionally, until softened but not browned, about 2 minutes. Add garlic and cook until fragrant, about 2 minutes. Increase heat to medium-high and add meatloaf mix, salt, and pepper; cook, breaking the meat into small pieces with wooden spoon, until meat loses its raw color but has not browned, about 4 minutes. Add cream and simmer, stirring occasionally, until liquid evaporates and only rendered fat remains, about 4 minutes. Add tomato puree and diced tomatoes and bring to simmer; reduce heat to low and simmer until flavors have blended, about 3 minutes. Set aside. (Cooled sauce can be refrigerated for up to 2 days; reheat before assembling lasagna.)

2 For the lasagna Adjust oven rack to middle position and heat oven to 425 degrees. Combine ricotta, 1 cup Parmesan, basil, egg, salt, and pepper in medium bowl; set aside.

3 Bring 4 quarts water to boil in large pot. Add 5 noodles and 1 tablespoon salt. Cook, maintaining gentle boil, until noodles are just shy of al dente. Using slotted spoon or wire skimmer, transfer noodles to large bowl and toss with 1 teaspoon oil. Lay noodles flat on 2 greased rimmed baking sheets, overlapping as needed, and let cool slightly. Repeat cooking remaining noodles and tossing with remaining 1 teaspoon oil.

4 Spread bottom of greased 13 by 9-inch baking dish evenly with ¼ cup meat sauce (avoiding large chunks of meat). Lay 2 noodles lengthwise in dish, trimming edges as needed to fit. Spread each noodle evenly with rounded 2 tablespoons ricotta mixture and sprinkle entire layer evenly with ¾ cup mozzarella. Spread the cheese evenly with 1 cup meat sauce. Repeat layering of noodles, ricotta, mozzarella, and sauce three more times. Place remaining 2 noodles on top of sauce, spread evenly with remaining sauce, sprinkle with remaining 1 cup mozzarella, then sprinkle with remaining ¼ cup Parmesan.

5 Spray sheet of aluminum foil with vegetable oil spray and cover lasagna. (Lasagna can be refrigerated for up to 24 hours; increase covered baking time to 40 minutes.) Bake until bubbling around edges, about 30 minutes. Remove foil and continue to bake until top is spotty brown, about 15 minutes. Let cool for 20 minutes before serving.

Baked Ziti

WHY THIS RECIPE WORKS: Baked ziti is intended to be a simpler dish than lasagna—pasta and a robust tomato sauce baked under a cover of bubbling cheese—but that's no reason to be lazy about it. To get this baked ziti with perfectly al dente pasta, a rich and flavorful sauce, and melted cheese in every bite, we part from convention in several ways. As with our lasagna recipes, we substitute cottage cheese for ricotta because the larger cheese curds bake up moister and more pillowy. Adding cream and eggs to the tomato sauce makes it lush and creamy without sacrificing any of its brightness. We cook the fresh pasta only partway and then add extra sauce to the dish so that the pasta can finish cooking in it in the oven. Finally, we cut the mozzarella into small cubes rather than shredding it, so it melts into distinct, delectable little pockets of cheese rather than congealing into one unappetizing mass. We prefer heavy cream in this recipe, but you can substitute whole milk; increase the amount of cornstarch to 2 teaspoons and increase the cooking time in step 3 by 1 to 2 minutes.

Serves 6 to 8
Total Time:
2¼ hours

---

1 pound fresh ziti or penne

Table salt for cooking pasta

1 pound (2 cups) whole-milk or part-skim cottage cheese

3 ounces Parmesan cheese, grated (1½ cups), divided

2 large eggs

2 tablespoons extra-virgin olive oil

5 garlic cloves, minced

1 (28-ounce) can tomato sauce

1 (14.5-ounce) can diced tomatoes

1 teaspoon dried oregano

½ cup plus 2 tablespoons chopped fresh basil, divided

1 teaspoon sugar

1 cup heavy cream

¾ teaspoon cornstarch

8 ounces whole-milk or part-skim mozzarella cheese, cut into ¼-inch pieces (1½ cups), divided

1 Adjust oven rack to middle position and heat oven to 350 degrees. Bring 4 quarts water to boil in large pot. Add pasta and 1 tablespoon salt and cook, stirring often, until just shy of al dente. Drain and leave in colander.

2 Meanwhile, whisk cottage cheese, 1 cup Parmesan, and eggs together in medium bowl; set aside. Heat oil and garlic in 12-inch skillet over medium heat. Cook, stirring often, until garlic turns golden but not brown, about 3 minutes. Stir in tomato sauce, diced tomatoes and their juice, and oregano; bring to simmer and cook until thickened, about 10 minutes. Off heat, stir in ½ cup basil and sugar and season with salt and pepper to taste.

3 Stir cream and cornstarch together in small bowl; transfer to now-empty pasta pot and set over medium heat. Bring to simmer and cook until thickened, 3 to 4 minutes. Off heat, stir in cottage cheese mixture, 1 cup tomato sauce, and ¾ cup mozzarella. Add pasta to pot and toss to combine.

4 Transfer pasta mixture to 13 by 9-inch baking dish and spread remaining tomato sauce evenly over top. Sprinkle with remaining ¾ cup mozzarella and remaining ½ cup Parmesan. Spray sheet of aluminum foil with vegetable oil spray, cover dish tightly, and bake for 30 minutes. Remove foil and continue to bake until cheese is bubbling and beginning to brown, about 30 minutes. Let cool for 10 minutes. Sprinkle with remaining 2 tablespoons basil and serve.

Baked Ziti with Creamy Leeks, Kale, and Sun-Dried Tomatoes

WHY THIS RECIPE WORKS: This fresh take on baked ziti is gratifyingly vegetable-forward. It turns out that the often underestimated leek is a shape-shifter, so here we use it to create a creamy, aromatic sauce. We sauté 2 pounds of sliced leeks until they begin to caramelize, add some thyme, deglaze with a splash of wine, and then simmer the mixture in vegetable broth until the leeks are meltingly soft and ready to be blended into a smooth, velvety sauce. Meanwhile, in the pot we use to parcook our pasta, we sauté baby kale and sun-dried tomatoes with a generous dose of garlic plus red pepper flakes, mix in the sauce and cooked pasta, and then bake it all so that the pasta can finish cooking while absorbing some of the flavorful leek sauce. For a crispy topping, we combine panko with Parmesan, plus a bit of fragrant lemon zest, and broil it to golden perfection. You can substitute 8 ounces kale, stemmed and chopped, for the baby kale, if necessary.

Serves 6 to 8
Total Time: 1 hour

½ cup panko bread crumbs

¼ cup grated Parmesan cheese

¼ cup extra-virgin olive oil, divided

½ teaspoon grated lemon zest, plus lemon wedges for serving

2 pounds leeks, white and light green parts only, halved lengthwise, sliced thin, and washed thoroughly

¾ teaspoon table salt, divided, plus salt for cooking pasta

⅛ teaspoon pepper

2 teaspoons minced fresh thyme or ¾ teaspoon dried

½ cup dry white wine

2 cups vegetable broth

1 pound fresh ziti or penne

6 garlic cloves, minced

¼ teaspoon red pepper flakes

6 cups (6 ounces) baby kale

¼ cup oil-packed sun-dried tomatoes, chopped coarse

2 tablespoons chopped fresh parsley

1 Adjust oven rack to upper-middle position and heat oven to 450 degrees. Combine panko, Parmesan, 1 tablespoon oil, and lemon zest in bowl; set aside.

2 Heat 2 tablespoons oil in Dutch oven over medium heat until shimmering. Stir in leeks, ½ teaspoon salt, and pepper and cook until softened and lightly browned, 8 to 12 minutes. Stir in thyme and cook until fragrant, about 30 seconds. Stir in wine, scraping up any browned bits, and cook until evaporated, about 2 minutes. Stir in broth and bring to boil. Reduce heat to low, cover, and simmer until leeks are very tender, about 8 minutes. Process leek mixture in blender on high speed until very smooth, about 2 minutes. Season with salt and pepper to taste.

3 Meanwhile, bring 4 quarts water to boil in large pot. Add pasta and 1 tablespoon salt and cook, stirring often, until just shy of al dente. Reserve 1½ cups cooking water, then drain pasta. Cook remaining 1 tablespoon oil, garlic, and pepper flakes in now-empty pot over medium heat until fragrant, about 1 minute. Stir in kale, sun-dried tomatoes, and remaining ¼ teaspoon salt and cook, stirring occasionally, until kale is wilted and tomatoes are softened, about 3 minutes. Off heat, stir in cooked pasta, leek mixture, and 1 cup reserved cooking water; season with salt and pepper to taste. Adjust consistency with remaining ½ cup cooking water as needed (sauce should be thick but still creamy).

4 Transfer pasta mixture to 13 by 9-inch broiler-safe baking dish, smoothing top with spatula. Cover tightly with aluminum foil and bake until sauce is bubbling, 10 to 12 minutes. Remove baking dish from oven and heat broiler. Remove foil and sprinkle panko mixture evenly over pasta. Broil until panko mixture is golden brown, about 2 minutes. Let cool for 10 minutes. Sprinkle with parsley and serve.

Baked Four-Cheese Penne with Prosciutto and Peas

WHY THIS RECIPE WORKS: Silky-smooth and sophisticated, this is a grown-up version of macaroni and cheese, with Italian flavors. Tubular pasta shapes, such as the fresh penne here, are ideal for any sort of macaroni and cheese because the clingy sauce coats the pasta inside and out. For the sauce, we use a base of creamy Italian fontina, revving it up with more assertive Gorgonzola, Pecorino Romano, and Parmesan. Recipes often start with a béchamel sauce; the flour in the sauce acts as a binder and prevents the cheese and cream from separating or curdling when added to the hot pasta, but the flour can also mute the cheese flavor. This sauce contains less flour than usual, so the cheeses remain the stars. Adding the cheeses at the last minute, tossing them with the hot pasta and hot béchamel, melts them without cooking them, further preserving their flavor. Prosciutto brings a salty, meaty quality, and peas add pops of color and texture. The browned, crispy bread crumb topping contrasts nicely with the creamy pasta.

Bread Crumb Topping

4	slices hearty white sandwich bread, torn into quarters
¼	cup grated Parmesan cheese
¼	teaspoon table salt
⅛	teaspoon pepper

Pasta and Cheese

	Table salt for cooking pasta
1	pound fresh penne
2	teaspoons unsalted butter
2	teaspoons all-purpose flour
1½	cups heavy cream
¼	teaspoon pepper
4	ounces fontina cheese, shredded (1 cup)
3	ounces Gorgonzola cheese, crumbled (¾ cup)
1	ounce Pecorino Romano cheese, grated (½ cup)
¼	cup grated Parmesan cheese
4	ounces prosciutto, chopped
1	cup frozen peas

1 For the bread crumb topping Pulse bread in food processor to coarse crumbs, about 10 pulses (you should have about 1½ cups). Transfer to small bowl and stir in Parmesan, salt, and pepper.

2 For the pasta and cheese Adjust oven rack to middle position and heat oven to 500 degrees. Bring 4 quarts water to boil in large pot. Add pasta and 1 tablespoon salt and cook, stirring often, until just shy of al dente. Drain pasta in colander, leaving pasta slightly wet, and set aside.

3 Wipe pot dry with paper towels, add butter, and melt over medium-low heat. Add flour and cook, stirring constantly, until golden and no lumps remain, about 1 minute. Slowly whisk in cream and pepper until smooth and bring to gentle simmer.

4 Off heat, gradually add fontina, Gorgonzola, Pecorino, and Parmesan and whisk until melted and smooth. Stir in pasta, breaking up any clumps. Stir in prosciutto and peas. Transfer pasta mixture to 13 by 9-inch baking dish.

5 Sprinkle bread crumb topping evenly over pasta mixture. Bake until golden and bubbling around edges, 25 to 35 minutes. Let cool for 10 minutes before serving.

VARIATION

Baked Four-Cheese Penne with Tomatoes and Basil

Add one 14.5-ounce can diced tomatoes, drained, along with fontina, Gorgonzola, Pecorino, and Parmesan in step 5. Stir ¼ cup coarsely chopped fresh basil into pasta mixture just before transferring to baking dish.

Baked Penne with Chicken, Broccoli, and Mushrooms

WHY THIS RECIPE WORKS: Penne with chicken and broccoli is a well-loved Italian American classic, here transformed into a crowd-pleasing casserole with fresh pasta. To lighten up the cream sauce usually used in this baked dish, we replace some of the heavy cream with chicken broth and white wine. To make sure that the sauce is still thick enough to properly coat the pasta, chicken, and vegetables, we incorporate a bit of flour. Asiago cheese, onion, garlic, and fresh thyme round out the sauce's flavor. Just a minute in boiling water takes the raw edge off the broccoli (we use the same water to cook both the broccoli and the pasta). To infuse the chicken with flavor and keep it tender and juicy, we partially poach it right in the sauce, and then let it finish cooking through in the oven. To add earthy depth to our baked penne, we introduce two kinds of mushrooms: sautéed cremini and some dried porcini. After sprinkling on a cheesy panko topping, it takes less than 15 minutes in the oven for this baked pasta to emerge bubbling to perfection.

Serves 6 to 8
Total Time: 2 hours

¾ cup panko bread crumbs

3 ounces Asiago cheese, grated
(1½ cups), divided

3 tablespoons extra-virgin olive oil,
divided

1 teaspoon table salt, divided, plus
salt for cooking broccoli and pasta

½ teaspoon pepper, divided

1½ pounds broccoli (1 large bunch),
stems discarded, florets cut into
1-inch pieces

12 ounces fresh penne

1 onion, minced

1¼ pounds cremini mushrooms,
trimmed and sliced ¼ inch thick

¼ ounce dried porcini mushrooms,
rinsed and minced

8 garlic cloves, minced (8 teaspoons)

1 tablespoon minced fresh thyme

5 tablespoons unbleached
all-purpose flour

1 cup dry white wine

2 cups chicken broth

1 cup heavy cream

1½ pounds boneless, skinless
chicken breasts, trimmed and
sliced ¼ inch thick

1 Adjust oven rack to middle position and heat oven to 450 degrees. In large bowl, toss panko with ½ cup Asiago, 1 tablespoon oil, ¼ teaspoon salt, and ¼ teaspoon pepper.

2 Bring 4 quarts water to boil in large large pot over high heat. Stir in broccoli and 1 tablespoon salt and cook until broccoli is bright green, about 1 minute. Using slotted spoon or wire skimmer, transfer broccoli to a rimmed baking sheet; set aside. Return water to boil. Add penne and cook, stirring often, until just shy of al dente. Drain pasta and transfer to bowl; set aside.

3 Wipe pot dry, add remaining 2 tablespoons oil, and heat over medium heat until shimmering. Add onion, cremini, porcini, and remaining ¾ teaspoon salt, cover, and cook until mushrooms have released their liquid, about 5 minutes. Uncover, increase heat to medium-high, and continue to cook until mushrooms are dry and beginning to brown, 5 to 10 minutes longer.

4 Stir in garlic and thyme and cook until fragrant, about 30 seconds. Stir in flour and cook for 1 minute. Slowly whisk in wine, scraping up any browned bits, and simmer until nearly evaporated, about 1 minute. Gradually whisk in broth and cream, smoothing out any lumps, and bring to simmer. Add chicken and cook, stirring occasionally, just until no longer pink, about 4 minutes.

5 Off heat, stir in remaining 1 cup Asiago and remaining ¼ teaspoon pepper until cheese has melted. Stir in cooked pasta and broccoli. Pour mixture into 13 by 9-inch baking dish and sprinkle with panko mixture. Bake until filling is bubbling and topping is browned and crisp, 12 to 15 minutes. Let cool for 10 minutes before serving.

VARIATION

Baked Penne with Chicken, Broccoli, and Sun-Dried Tomatoes

Omit cremini and dried porcini mushrooms; cook onion and salt as directed in step 3 until softened, 5 to 7 minutes, before adding garlic and thyme in step 4. Substitute 1¼ cups shredded smoked mozzarella for Asiago; toss ½ cup of the cheese with panko in step 1, and stir remaining ¾ cup cheese into sauce in step 4. Add 1 cup oil-packed sun-dried tomatoes, rinsed, patted dry, and cut into thin strips, to sauce with cheese in step 5.

Creamy Baked Tortellini with Radicchio, Peas, and Bacon

WHY THIS RECIPE WORKS: Assertive, burgundy radicchio and sweet green peas turn this into an elevated take on baked tortellini. Best of all, both of these ingredients can simply be tossed with the parcooked tortellini and sauce before baking. After cooking the tortellini to al dente, we drain it and then start building the sauce in the same pot by cooking a few slices of bacon, using the rendered fat to sauté onion, garlic, and thyme. A little flour helps to thicken it, and then we deglaze the pot with white wine and whisk in chicken broth and heavy cream, followed by grated Parmesan, to create a rich yet balanced sauce. After adding the tortellini, radicchio, and frozen peas (no need to thaw them), we transfer the mixture to a baking dish, add a topping, and bake briefly until golden. Instead of using grated cheese in the bread-crumb topping, here we use walnuts; their bittersweet flavor nicely complements the pleasing bitterness of the radicchio. To fill the tortellini for this recipe, we prefer our Ricotta Filling (page 68) or Three-Cheese Filling (page 68).

Serves 6 to 8
Total Time:
1¼ hours

½ cup walnuts

4 slices hearty white sandwich bread, torn into quarters

2 tablespoons unsalted butter, melted

1½ pounds fresh tortellini (page 62)
Table salt for cooking pasta

1 tablespoon extra-virgin olive oil

4 slices bacon, chopped fine

1 onion, chopped fine

6 garlic cloves, minced

2 teaspoons minced fresh thyme

¼ cup all-purpose flour

1 cup dry white wine

2 cups chicken broth

1 cup heavy cream

2 ounces Parmesan cheese, grated (1 cup)

1 head radicchio (10 ounces), cored and chopped

1 cup frozen peas

1 Adjust oven rack to middle position and heat oven to 400 degrees. Process walnuts in food processor until coarsely chopped, about 5 seconds. Add bread and melted butter and continue to process to create uniformly coarse crumbs, about 6 pulses. Set aside.

2 Bring 4 quarts water to boil in large pot over high heat. Add half of tortellini and 1 tablespoon salt. Cook, maintaining gentle boil, until tortellini are just shy of al dente. Using slotted spoon or wire skimmer, transfer tortellini to large bowl and toss gently with oil. Repeat with remaining tortellini.

3 Wipe now-empty pot dry, add bacon, and cook over medium heat until brown and crispy, about 5 minutes. Stir in onion and cook until softened, 5 to 7 minutes. Stir in garlic and thyme and cook until fragrant, about 30 seconds. Stir in flour and cook for 1 minute.

4 Slowly whisk in wine, scraping up any browned bits, and cook until nearly evaporated, about 1 minute. Gradually whisk in broth and cream, smoothing out any lumps, and bring to simmer.

5 Off heat, stir in Parmesan and season with salt and pepper to taste. Stir in tortellini, radicchio, and peas. Pour into 13 by 9-inch baking dish and sprinkle with walnut bread crumbs. Bake until filling is bubbling and topping is brown and crisp, about 15 minutes. Let cool for 10 minutes before serving.

Gnocchi, Cauliflower, and Gorgonzola Gratin

WHY THIS RECIPE WORKS: For this sophisticated take on baked gnocchi, we reach for pungent blue cheese and nutty cauliflower. Gorgonzola is often milder than other blue cheeses, so it won't overshadow your homemade potato gnocchi. The cauliflower provides the perfect contrast in texture, and browning it before building the sauce jump-starts its cooking. Instead of reserving some cheese for the bread-crumb topping, as we usually do for baked pasta dishes, we add it all to the sauce (along with chicken broth and cream) and use only bread crumbs and butter for the topping. Fresh thyme and sherry add depth, while a little cornstarch gives the sauce body without adding any cooking time. For a bright note to offset the rich flavors, we stir in handfuls of baby spinach at the end (which preserves its green hue and fresh, delicate texture). If you don't have a pot that holds 6 quarts, cook the gnocchi in two batches; toss the first batch with sauce in the skillet and cover to keep warm while cooking the remaining gnocchi.

Serves 6 to 8
Total Time: 1 hour

---

4 tablespoons unsalted butter, divided

2 slices hearty white sandwich bread, torn into quarters

¼ teaspoon table salt, plus salt for cooking gnocchi

⅛ teaspoon pepper

½ large head cauliflower (1½ pounds), cored and cut into 1-inch florets

1½ cups chicken broth

2 ounces Gorgonzola cheese, crumbled (½ cup)

4 teaspoons dry sherry

1 tablespoon minced fresh thyme

½ cup heavy cream

1 tablespoon cornstarch

2 ounces (2 cups) baby spinach

1 pound Potato Gnocchi (page 66)

1 Adjust oven rack 6 inches from broiler element and heat broiler. Melt 2 tablespoons butter in bowl in microwave. Pulse bread, melted butter, salt, and pepper in food processor to form coarse crumbs, about 6 pulses. Set aside.

2 Melt remaining 2 tablespoons butter in 12-inch skillet over medium-high heat. Add cauliflower and cook until lightly browned, about 7 minutes. Stir in broth, Gorgonzola, sherry, and thyme. Whisk cream and cornstarch together, then stir into skillet and simmer until cheese is melted and sauce is thickened, about 5 minutes. Stir in spinach until wilted, about 2 minutes.

3 Meanwhile, bring 6 quarts water to boil in large pot. Add gnocchi and 1½ tablespoons salt and simmer gently, stirring occasionally, until firm and just cooked through, about 90 seconds (gnocchi should float to surface after about 1 minute). Using slotted spoon or wire skimmer, transfer gnocchi to skillet and toss gently to coat.

4 Transfer mixture to 13 by 9-inch broiler-safe baking dish. Sprinkle bread crumbs evenly over top and broil until lightly browned, about 5 minutes. Let cool for 10 minutes before serving.

Semolina Gnocchi with Browned Butter

WHY THIS RECIPE WORKS: Roman gnocchi is a completely different breed of dumpling from potato gnocchi but is equally comforting and delicious. These plump rounds are made from semolina flour, egg, butter, and cheese and have a creamy, slightly dense texture reminiscent of polenta. To begin, we whisk semolina flour into hot milk with a touch of woodsy nutmeg. Butter and egg are incorporated to increase the dough's richness (the egg also provides structure). Baking powder boosts their lift without compromising on texture. Gruyère adds big flavor but is firm enough that it doesn't make the gnocchi too tender (softer cheeses like mozzarella result in gnocchi that tend to fuse together in the oven). Minced rosemary contributes warm, savory notes. While some traditional recipes call for stamping out the gnocchi rounds like biscuits, we more efficiently use a measuring cup to portion out the stiff dough onto a tray. Chilling the rounds before baking allows the swollen starches in the semolina flour to rebond on the exterior and form a "skin" through a process called retrogradation. This means that the baked dumplings don't fuse together in the oven and are easy to separate and serve.

Serves 4 to 6
Total Time: 2 hours

2½ cups whole milk

¾ teaspoon table salt

Pinch ground nutmeg

1 cup (6 ounces) fine semolina flour

4 tablespoons unsalted butter, divided

2 teaspoons minced fresh sage

1 large egg, lightly beaten

1½ ounces Gruyère cheese, shredded (½ cup)

½ teaspoon baking powder

2 tablespoons grated Parmesan cheese

1 Adjust oven rack to middle position and heat oven to 400 degrees. Heat milk, salt, and nutmeg in medium saucepan over medium-low heat until bubbles form around edges of saucepan. Whisking constantly, slowly add semolina to milk mixture. Reduce heat to low and cook, stirring often with spatula, until mixture forms stiff mass that pulls away from sides when stirring, 3 to 5 minutes. Remove from heat and let cool for 5 minutes.

2 While semolina mixture cools, heat 3 tablespoons butter in small skillet over medium heat; cook, swirling pan constantly, until butter is dark golden brown and has nutty aroma, 1 to 3 minutes. Remove skillet from heat and stir in sage.

3 Stir butter mixture and egg into semolina mixture until incorporated. (Mixture will appear separated at first but will become smooth and glossy.) Stir in Gruyère and baking powder until incorporated.

4 Fill small bowl with water. Moisten ¼-cup flat-bottomed dry measuring cup with water and scoop even portion of semolina mixture. Invert gnocchi onto tray or large plate. Repeat, moistening measuring cup between scoops to prevent sticking. Place tray of gnocchi, uncovered, in refrigerator for 30 minutes. (Gnocchi can be refrigerated, covered, for up to 24 hours.)

5 Grease interior of 8-inch square baking dish with remaining 1 tablespoon butter. Shingle gnocchi in pan, creating 3 rows of 4 gnocchi each. Sprinkle gnocchi with Parmesan. Bake until tops of gnocchi are golden brown, 35 to 40 minutes. Let cool for 15 minutes before serving.

SAUCES TO MIX AND MATCH

Chapter 6

Garlic Oil Sauce with Parsley and Pecorino

tagliatelle | spaghetti | garganelli | cavatelli

WHY THIS RECIPE WORKS: Italian cooks are masters at turning out dishes far greater than the sum of their parts, and this olive oil–based sauce that comes together while you boil the pasta water is a perfect illustration of that talent. Blooming lots of sliced garlic and some spicy red pepper flakes in a generous amount of extra-virgin olive oil creates giant flavor in the blink of an eye. We toast the garlic over low heat just until it turns a sweet and buttery pale gold and then brighten and balance the sauce with lemon juice and a fistful of fresh parsley. The pungency of grated Pecorino Romano sprinkled on top finishes off this sauce in style, but you can also use grated Parmesan. Use the best-quality extra-virgin olive oil you can here. Try this with lemon-pepper pasta (see pages 28–29).

Makes *enough for 1 pound pasta*
Total Time: 10 minutes

⅓ cup extra-virgin olive oil

4 garlic cloves, sliced thin

½ teaspoon table salt

½ teaspoon pepper

¼ teaspoon red pepper flakes

¼ cup chopped fresh parsley

4 teaspoons lemon juice

Grated Pecorino Romano cheese

1 Combine oil, garlic, salt, pepper, and pepper flakes in 12-inch skillet. Cook over medium heat until garlic is pale golden brown, 2 to 4 minutes.

2 Off heat, stir in parsley and lemon juice. Season with salt and pepper to taste. Serve immediately, passing Pecorino separately.

To serve Reserve 1 cup pasta cooking water when draining pasta. Return pasta to pot and toss with sauce, adding cooking water as needed to reach desired consistency.

VARIATIONS

Garlic Oil Sauce with Lemon and Pine Nuts
Increase lemon juice to 2 tablespoons and stir in 2 teaspoons grated lemon zest and ½ cup toasted pine nuts with parsley and lemon juice.

Garlic Oil Sauce with Capers and Currants
Stir in 3 tablespoons minced capers, 3 tablespoons minced raisins or currants, and 2 minced anchovy fillets with parsley and lemon juice.

Garlic Oil Sauce with Green Olives and Almonds
Stir in 1 cup chopped green olives and ½ cup toasted sliced almonds with parsley and lemon juice.

Browned Butter–Sage Sauce

filled pasta | garganelli | fettuccine | gnocchi

WHY THIS RECIPE WORKS: Nutty, toasty, and complex, browned butter is quick to make and is exponentially better than plain melted butter. It's a simple culinary trick that brings sophistication to many types of fresh pasta. When butter is heated, the water in the butter evaporates and the sugars and amino acids in the butter react to turn from white to brown and create new flavor compounds, taking on heavenly aromas and delicious flavors. Fresh sage infuses the browned butter with an earthy herbal complement. This sauce can be easily doubled for more buttery bliss.

Makes *enough for 1 pound pasta*
Total Time: 10 minutes

8   tablespoons unsalted butter, cut into 4 pieces

1   shallot, minced

2   teaspoons minced fresh sage

1   tablespoon lemon juice

¼   teaspoon table salt

1 Melt butter in 12-inch skillet over medium-high heat, swirling constantly, until butter is browned and releases nutty aroma, 3 to 4 minutes.

2 Off heat, stir in shallot and sage and cook using residual heat from skillet until fragrant, about 1 minute. Stir in lemon juice and salt. Serve immediately.

To serve Reserve 1 cup pasta cooking water when draining pasta. Return pasta to pot and toss with sauce, adding cooking water as needed to reach desired consistency.

VARIATIONS

Browned Butter–Truffle Sauce

Omit sage and lemon juice. Stir 4 teaspoons white truffle oil into browned butter–shallot mixture.

Browned Butter–Hazelnut Sauce

Add ⅓ cup hazelnuts, toasted, skinned, and chopped coarse, to skillet with butter. Add 1 tablespoon minced fresh chives with lemon juice.

Browned Butter–Tomato Sauce

Omit shallot, sage, and lemon juice. Process 1 (28-ounce) can whole peeled tomatoes in food processor until smooth, about 30 seconds. Reduce butter to 4 tablespoons and brown as directed. Stir 2 minced garlic cloves into browned butter, then stir in tomatoes, ½ teaspoon sugar, and salt and simmer until sauce is slightly reduced, about 8 minutes. Off heat, whisk in 3 tablespoons chopped fresh basil, 2 teaspoons sherry vinegar, and additional 1 tablespoon butter.

Classic Basil Pesto

trofie | malloreddus | farfalle | filled pasta

WHY THIS RECIPE WORKS: Herb pestos are enjoyed throughout Italy, not only to sauce fresh and dried pasta and gnocchi but also to slather on bread, dollop into bowls of minestrone soup, or spoon onto simply cooked fish fillets. This one is by far the most famous, hailing from Genoa, on the Ligurian coast. It's redolent with the fragrance and flavor of fresh basil and enriched with buttery pine nuts and Parmesan. Toasting the garlic and pine nuts puts them on a level playing field by mellowing the fiery garlic and boosting the delicate flavor of the nuts. The extra-virgin olive oil shines here, too, so use the highest-quality oil you can. Pounding the herbs helps bring out their flavorful oils.

Makes enough for
2 pounds pasta
Total Time:
20 minutes

6	garlic cloves, unpeeled
½	cup pine nuts
4	cups fresh basil leaves
¼	cup fresh parsley leaves
1	cup extra-virgin olive oil
1	ounce Parmesan cheese, grated (½ cup)

1 Toast garlic in 8-inch skillet over medium heat, shaking skillet occasionally, until softened and spotty brown, about 8 minutes. When garlic is cool enough to handle, remove and discard skins and chop coarsely. Meanwhile, toast pine nuts in now-empty skillet over medium heat, stirring often, until golden and fragrant, 4 to 5 minutes.

2 Place basil and parsley in 1-gallon zipper-lock bag. Pound bag with flat side of meat pounder or with rolling pin until all leaves are bruised.

3 Process garlic, pine nuts, and herbs in food processor until finely chopped, about 1 minute, scraping down sides of bowl as needed. With processor running, slowly add oil until incorporated. Transfer pesto to bowl, stir in Parmesan, and season with salt and pepper to taste. (Pesto can be refrigerated for up to 3 days or frozen for up to 3 months. To prevent browning, press plastic wrap flush to surface or top with thin layer of olive oil. Bring to room temperature before using.)

To serve Reserve 1 cup pasta cooking water when draining pasta. Return pasta to pot and toss with pesto, adding cooking water as needed to reach desired consistency.

Toasted Nut and Parsley Pesto

linguine | trofie | farfalle | filled pasta

WHY THIS RECIPE WORKS: Herb pesto isn't just about basil. While our Classic Basil Pesto really shines in the summertime, when fresh basil is plentiful and irresistibly fragrant in the market, this recipe swaps in hardier parsley for a wonderful, albeit nontraditional, year-round pesto for your fresh pasta. And it's super-adaptable in that it works with practically any nut you might happen to have on hand in the pantry. We like the assertive flavors of the ones suggested here, as they hold their own with the stronger flavor of the fresh parsley. As with the basil pesto, toasting the unpeeled garlic in a skillet mellows its flavor. We think this bold pesto is especially delicious with whole-wheat pasta.

Makes *enough for*
1 pound pasta
Total Time:
20 minutes

---

3   garlic cloves, unpeeled

1   cup pecans, walnuts, blanched almonds, skinned hazelnuts, or unsalted pistachios, or any combination thereof

½   cup packed fresh parsley leaves

7   tablespoons extra-virgin olive oil

1   ounce Parmesan cheese, grated (½ cup)

1 Toast garlic in 8-inch skillet over medium heat, shaking skillet occasionally, until softened and spotty brown, about 8 minutes; When garlic is cool enough to handle, remove and discard skins and chop coarsely. Meanwhile, toast nuts in now-empty skillet over medium heat, stirring often, until golden and fragrant, 4 to 5 minutes.

2 Process garlic, nuts, parsley, and oil in food processor until smooth, 1 to 2 minutes, scraping down sides of bowl as needed. Transfer mixture to bowl and stir in Parmesan; season with salt and pepper to taste. (Pesto can be refrigerated for up to 3 days or frozen for up to 3 months. To prevent browning, press plastic wrap flush to surface or top with thin layer of olive oil. Bring to room temperature before using.)

To serve Reserve 1 cup pasta cooking water when draining pasta. Return pasta to pot and toss with pesto, adding cooking water as needed to reach desired consistency.

Sun-Dried Tomato Pesto

farfalle | garganelli | orecchiette | filled pasta

WHY THIS RECIPE WORKS: For an even more pantry-friendly pesto than one made with herbs, turn to sun-dried tomatoes. Their sweet sunniness defines this red pesto. We prefer oil-packed sun-dried tomatoes for their pleasing chewiness and intense flavor. Dry-pack sun-dried tomatoes can often taste bitter or musty, and they tend to be tough before soaking in water and mushy after soaking. Before we toss the tomatoes into the food processor to combine them with the other ingredients, we rinse them of excess marinade, which helps them break down more easily, rather than getting clogged around the blade. As with our other pestos, we toast the garlic in a skillet first to temper its flavor. Pine nuts are too mild to stand up to the bold tomatoes; toasted walnuts bring a fuller flavor and similar smooth texture.

Makes enough for 1 pound pasta
Total Time: 20 minutes

---

3 garlic cloves, unpeeled

¼ cup walnuts

1 cup oil-packed sun-dried tomatoes, rinsed, patted dry, and chopped

½ cup extra-virgin olive oil

1 ounce Parmesan cheese, grated (½ cup)

1 Toast garlic in 8-inch skillet over medium heat, shaking skillet occasionally, until softened and spotty brown, about 8 minutes. When garlic is cool enough to handle, remove and discard skins and chop coarsely. Meanwhile, toast walnuts in now-empty skillet over medium heat, stirring often, until golden and fragrant, 4 to 5 minutes.

2 Process garlic, walnuts, and tomatoes in food processor until finely chopped, about 1 minute, scraping down sides of bowl as needed. With processor running, slowly add oil until incorporated. Transfer pesto to bowl, stir in Parmesan, and season with salt and pepper to taste. (Pesto can be refrigerated for up to 3 days or frozen for up to 3 months. To prevent browning, press plastic wrap flush to surface or top with thin layer of olive oil. Bring to room temperature before using.)

To serve Reserve 1 cup pasta cooking water when draining pasta. Return pasta to pot and toss with pesto, adding cooking water as needed to reach desired consistency.

Pesto Trapanese

busiate | linguine | fileja | penne

WHY THIS RECIPE WORKS: Almost every region of Italy lays claim to its own version of pesto. In this one, from the Sicilian port town of Trapani, fresh tomatoes take center stage, with basil and a single garlic clove playing supporting roles. Ground almonds thicken and enrich the sauce. This pesto is often made by the families of fishermen, tossed with pasta, and topped with leftover pieces of the fishermen's tiny, unwanted catches to stretch a small amount of fish. Sometimes this pesto features a bit of heat, which we like, so we add some minced peperoncini and an optional pinch of red pepper flakes for a welcome zing. Pecorino Romano is an equally assertive finishing touch. Try this with tomato pasta (see pages 28–29).

Makes enough for
1 pound pasta
Total Time:
15 minutes

¼ cup slivered almonds

12 ounces cherry or grape tomatoes

½ cup fresh basil leaves

1 tablespoon stemmed, patted dry, and minced peperoncini

1 garlic clove, chopped

1 teaspoon table salt

Pinch red pepper flakes (optional)

⅓ cup extra-virgin olive oil

1 ounce Pecorino Romano cheese, grated (½ cup)

1 Toast almonds in 8-inch skillet over medium heat, stirring often, until golden and fragrant, 2 to 3 minutes.

2 Process tomatoes, basil, almonds, peperoncini, garlic, salt, and pepper flakes, if using, in food processor until smooth, about 1 minute, scraping down sides of bowl as needed. With processor running, slowly add oil until incorporated. Transfer pesto to bowl, stir in Pecorino, and season with pepper to taste. (Pesto can be refrigerated for up to 3 days. To prevent browning, press plastic wrap flush to surface or top with thin layer of olive oil. Bring to room temperature before using.)

To serve Reserve 1 cup pasta cooking water when draining pasta. Return pasta to pot and toss with pesto, adding cooking water as needed to reach desired consistency.

Kale and Sunflower Seed Pesto

linguine | orecchiette | penne | farfalle

WHY THIS RECIPE WORKS: Perennially popular kale makes a hearty, thick sauce for fresh pasta. A handful of basil added to the mix brightens and freshens the earthy kale, and pounding them together both tenderizes the sturdy kale and helps to bring out the basil's flavor oils. For a twist on the nut choice, we turn to seeds: Distinctively flavored sunflower seeds complement the kale and have a smooth texture similar to pine nuts. We toast them for extra nuttiness, and we toast the garlic cloves as well. An optional teaspoon of red pepper flakes brings some heat. To prepare the kale, it is necessary to remove the tough center stalks from the leaves. Start by cutting away the leafy portion from either side of the stalk using a chef's knife. Stack several leaves on top of one another and chop.

Makes *enough for 2 pounds pasta*
Total Time: 30 minutes

2 garlic cloves, unpeeled

½ cup raw sunflower seeds

4 ounces kale, stemmed and chopped (2 cups)

1 cup fresh basil leaves

1 teaspoon red pepper flakes (optional)

½ cup extra-virgin olive oil

1½ ounces Parmesan cheese, grated (¾ cup)

1 Toast garlic in 8-inch skillet over medium heat, shaking skillet occasionally, until softened and spotty brown, about 8 minutes. When garlic is cool enough to handle, remove and discard skins and chop coarsely. Meanwhile, toast sunflower seeds in now-empty skillet over medium heat, stirring often, until golden and fragrant, 4 to 5 minutes.

2 Place kale and basil in 1-gallon zipper-lock bag. Pound bag with flat side of meat pounder or with rolling pin until all leaves are bruised.

3 Process garlic, sunflower seeds, kale, basil, and pepper flakes, if using, in food processor until finely chopped, about 1 minute, scraping down sides of bowl as needed. With processor running, slowly add oil until incorporated. Transfer pesto to bowl, stir in Parmesan, and season with salt and pepper to taste. (Pesto can be refrigerated for up to 3 days or frozen for up to 3 months. To prevent browning, press plastic wrap flush to surface or top with thin layer of olive oil. Bring to room temperature before using.)

To serve Reserve 1 cup pasta cooking water when draining pasta. Return pasta to pot and toss with pesto, adding cooking water as needed to reach desired consistency.

Pesto Calabrese

fileja | orecchiette | penne | rigatoni

WHY THIS RECIPE WORKS: Calabria's namesake coral-colored pasta sauce is sweetly spicy and creamy, with a base of red bell peppers, ricotta and Parmesan cheeses, and chiles. Some versions also include tomato, onion or shallot, garlic, or basil. In a departure from most forms of pesto, some of the components are cooked before the mixture is pureed. To coax the most sweetness from the bell peppers, we start them in a covered skillet to soften before finishing uncovered to develop browning. Adding onion, garlic, tomato, and basil during the uncovered phase builds complexity. Calabrian chiles are the traditional heat source, but they aren't readily available in domestic supermarkets, so red pepper flakes make a reasonable substitute. A rasp-style grater makes quick work of turning the garlic into a paste.

Makes *enough for 1 pound pasta*
Total Time: 45 minutes

- 3 red bell peppers, stemmed, seeded, and cut into ¼-inch-wide strips (5 cups), divided
- 3 tablespoons extra-virgin olive oil, divided
- 1 teaspoon table salt, divided
- 1 small onion, chopped
- 1 plum tomato, cored, seeded, and chopped
- ⅓ cup chopped fresh basil
- 1 garlic clove, minced to paste (1 teaspoon), divided
- ½–¾ teaspoon red pepper flakes
- ½ cup whole-milk ricotta cheese
- ¼ cup grated Parmesan cheese, plus extra for serving
- ¼ teaspoon pepper
- 1 teaspoon white wine vinegar

1 Toss two-thirds of bell peppers with 1 tablespoon oil and ¼ teaspoon salt in 12-inch nonstick skillet. Cover and place over medium-low heat. Cook, stirring occasionally, until bell peppers are softened and just starting to brown, about 15 minutes.

2 Add onion, tomato, basil, ½ teaspoon garlic, and pepper flakes and continue to cook, uncovered, stirring occasionally, until onion is softened and bell peppers are browned in spots, 6 to 7 minutes longer. Remove skillet from heat and let cool for 5 minutes.

3 Place ricotta, Parmesan, remaining one-third of bell peppers, remaining ½ teaspoon garlic, remaining ¾ teaspoon salt, and pepper in bowl of food processor. Add cooked bell pepper mixture and process for 20 seconds. Scrape down sides of bowl. With processor running, add vinegar and remaining 2 tablespoons oil; process for about 20 seconds. Scrape down sides of bowl, then continue to process until smooth, about 20 seconds longer.

To serve Reserve 1 cup pasta cooking water when draining pasta. Return pasta to pot and toss with pesto, adding cooking water as needed to reach desired consistency. Serve topped with additional Parmesan.

Olivada

penne | trofie | cavatelli | fileja | filled pasta

WHY THIS RECIPE WORKS: Versions of this ultrarich and intensely flavored olive sauce appear around the Mediterranean, with the most famous being French tapenade. Both sometimes include nuts, but unlike that French condiment, Italian olivada incorporates cheese as well. Olivada is made in a similar fashion to a pesto, and though it's often used as a topping for bruschetta, it makes a dramatic presentation when tossed with fresh pasta. Black olives are more typical than green, and here we choose rich, meaty kalamatas. You can also use gaeta olives; whichever variety you choose, make sure that they are high quality. The anchovy adds flavor but not fishiness, so we recommend you don't leave it out. If you like, serve bowls of pasta with lemon wedges for squeezing over the top.

Makes *enough for 1 pound pasta*
Total Time: 20 minutes

---

3 garlic cloves, unpeeled

1½ cups pitted kalamata olives

1 ounce Parmesan cheese, grated (½ cup)

6 tablespoons extra-virgin olive oil

¼ cup packed fresh parsley leaves

1 shallot, chopped coarse

8 large basil leaves

1 tablespoon lemon juice

1 anchovy fillet

1 Toast garlic in 8-inch skillet over medium heat, shaking skillet occasionally, until garlic is softened and spotty brown, about 8 minutes. When garlic is cool enough to handle, remove and discard skins and chop coarsely.

2 Process garlic, olives, Parmesan, oil, parsley, shallot, basil, lemon juice, and anchovy, if using in food processor, scraping down sides of bowl as needed. Transfer mixture to bowl and season with salt and pepper to taste. (Olivada can be refrigerated for up to 3 days or frozen for up to 3 months. Press plastic wrap flush to surface or top with thin layer of olive oil. Bring to room temperature before using.)

To serve Reserve 1 cup pasta cooking water when draining pasta. Return pasta to pot and toss with olivada, adding cooking water as needed to reach desired consistency.

No-Cook Fresh Tomato Sauce

orecchiette | penne | paccheri | farfalle

WHY THIS RECIPE WORKS: Luscious, garden-ripe tomatoes need little else besides high-quality extra-virgin olive oil and a smattering of fresh herbs to become a bright, summery dressing for fresh pasta. This rendition is our ideal for a no-fuss sauce to enjoy on a summer evening, preferably al fresco. To balance the tomatoes' sweetness and acidity, we mix in shallot, garlic, a generous amount of olive oil, and a hefty amount of herbs—instead of the basil, you can also use parsley, cilantro, mint, oregano, or tarragon. We let all the flavors blend while we assemble the rest of our meal (or just relax outside). The success of this dish depends on using ripe, flavorful, in-season tomatoes.

Makes enough for
1 pound pasta
Total Time:
45 minutes

- ¼ cup extra-virgin olive oil
- 1 shallot, minced
- 2 teaspoons lemon juice, plus extra as needed
- 1 garlic clove, minced
- 1 teaspoon table salt
- ¼ teaspoon pepper
- Pinch sugar, plus extra as needed
- 2 pounds very ripe tomatoes, cored and cut into ½-inch pieces
- 3 tablespoons chopped fresh basil

Stir oil, shallot, lemon juice, garlic, salt, pepper, and sugar together in large bowl. Stir in tomatoes and let marinate at room temperature until very soft and flavorful, about 30 minutes. Before serving, stir in basil and season with salt, pepper, sugar, and extra lemon juice to taste.

To serve Reserve 1 cup pasta cooking water when draining pasta. Return pasta to pot and toss with sauce, adding cooking water as needed to reach desired consistency.

Fresh Tomato Sauce

linguine | garganelli | filled pasta | gnocchi

WHY THIS RECIPE WORKS: Here is the essence of a quickly cooked tomato sauce made with fresh tomatoes—just a short simmer produces such bright and lively results. Plum tomatoes are the best choice, as they have meaty flesh and less juice than other varieties, which translates into a thicker sauce that clings to fresh pasta. Plus, their skins simmer up tender and soft, so there's no need to peel them before adding them to the pot. This simple sauce adapts so well that we offer three variations. The first has you render pancetta at the outset to create a riff on amatriciana sauce. The second features red pepper flakes and minced anchovies for a sauce akin to a Roman arrabbiata. And last up is a pungent Neapolitan puttanesca with briny olives and capers. The success of this recipe depends on using ripe, in-season tomatoes. If you're using very sweet tomatoes, omit the sugar.

Makes enough for 1 pound pasta
Total Time: 20 minutes

- 3 tablespoons extra-virgin olive oil
- 2 garlic cloves, minced
- 2 pounds ripe plum tomatoes, cored and cut into ½-inch pieces
- ¾ teaspoon table salt
- ½ teaspoon pepper
- ½ teaspoon sugar (optional)
- 2 tablespoons chopped fresh basil

Cook oil and garlic in large saucepan over medium heat until garlic is fragrant but not browned, 1 to 2 minutes. Stir in tomatoes, salt, pepper, and sugar, if using. Increase heat to medium-high and cook until tomatoes are broken down and sauce is slightly thickened, about 10 minutes. Stir in basil and season with salt and pepper to taste.

To serve Reserve 1 cup pasta cooking water when draining pasta. Return pasta to pot and toss with sauce, adding cooking water as needed to reach desired consistency.

VARIATIONS

Fresh Tomato Amatriciana Sauce
Reduce oil to 1 tablespoon. Cook oil and 4 ounces finely chopped pancetta in saucepan over medium heat until pancetta is rendered and crispy, 5 to 7 minutes, before adding garlic.

Fresh Tomato Arrabbiata Sauce
Add 3 minced anchovy fillets and ¾ teaspoon red pepper flakes with garlic.

Fresh Tomato Puttanesca Sauce
Add ¼ cup coarsely chopped pitted kalamata olives and ¼ cup rinsed capers to saucepan with tomatoes.

Marinara Sauce

linguine | spaghetti | penne | filled pasta

WHY THIS RECIPE WORKS: While a marinara sauce generally contains tomatoes, onions, garlic, and herbs, variations abound beyond those standards. For our lively marinara, we drain canned whole tomatoes, crushing them by hand and reserving the liquid, and then cook down some of the drained tomatoes along with onion and garlic before adding the juices and red wine, which intensifies the tomato flavor. Using a skillet instead of the more typical saucepan encourages faster evaporation and flavor concentration. We then add some reserved uncooked tomatoes for a bright finishing note before pureeing the sauce in a food processor. We like a marinara that's on the smoother end of the spectrum, but if you prefer a chunkier sauce, give it just three or four pulses in the food processor in step 4. We recommend a Chianti or Merlot for the red wine.

Makes enough for
2 pounds pasta
Total Time:
45 minutes

---

2   (28-ounce) cans whole peeled tomatoes

3   tablespoons extra-virgin olive oil, divided

1   medium onion, minced

2   garlic cloves, minced

½   teaspoon dried oregano

⅓   cup dry red wine

3   tablespoons chopped fresh basil

1–2   teaspoons sugar, as needed

1   Pour tomatoes into strainer set over large bowl. Open tomatoes with your hands and remove and discard fibrous cores; let tomatoes drain excess liquid, about 5 minutes. Remove ¾ cup tomatoes from strainer and set aside. Reserve 2½ cups tomato juice and discard remainder.

2   Heat 2 tablespoons olive oil in 12-inch skillet over medium heat until shimmering. Add onion and cook, stirring occasionally, until softened and golden around edges, 6 to 8 minutes. Add garlic and oregano and cook, stirring constantly, until garlic is fragrant, about 30 seconds.

3   Add tomatoes from strainer and increase heat to medium-high. Cook, stirring every minute, until liquid has evaporated and tomatoes begin to stick to bottom of pan and browned bits form around pan edges, 10 to 12 minutes. Add wine and cook until thick and syrupy, about 1 minute. Add reserved tomato juice and bring to simmer; reduce heat to medium and cook, stirring occasionally and loosening any browned bits, until sauce is thickened, 8 to 10 minutes.

4   Transfer sauce to food processor and add reserved tomatoes; process until slightly chunky, about 8 pulses. Return sauce to skillet; add basil and remaining 1 tablespoon olive oil; and season with salt, pepper, and sugar to taste. (Sauce can be refrigerated for up to 3 days or frozen for up to 1 month.)

To serve   Reserve 1 cup pasta cooking water when draining pasta. Return pasta to pot and toss with sauce, adding cooking water as needed to reach desired consistency.

Creamy Tomato Sauce

penne | garganelli | rigatoni | filled pasta

WHY THIS RECIPE WORKS: Adding cream to a tomato sauce places it in the category of what's sometimes referred to as "pink sauce." In these luxurious pasta sauces, the acidity of the fruity tomatoes is balanced by the richness of dairy. Vodka Sauce (page 216) is probably the most famous example; while this recipe doesn't use vodka, it does up the richness ante even more by including minced prosciutto and sun-dried tomatoes. Before adding our canned crushed tomatoes to the saucepan, we cook a few tablespoons of tomato paste with onion, garlic, and sun-dried tomatoes (in butter, for a touch more richness!). A pinch of red pepper flakes, a splash of white wine, and the prosciutto add depth; a bit of uncooked crushed tomatoes and another splash of wine stirred in before serving make a bright finish. We add the cream to the just-finished sauce to enrich it without masking any of the tomato flavor. Pinot Grigio is a good choice for the wine.

Makes enough for
1 pound pasta
Total Time: 1 hour

---

3   tablespoons unsalted butter

1   small onion, minced

1   ounce prosciutto, minced (2 tablespoons)

1   bay leaf

¼   teaspoon table salt

     Pinch red pepper flakes

3   garlic cloves, minced

2   ounces oil-packed sun-dried tomatoes, rinsed, patted dry, and chopped coarse (3 tablespoons)

2   tablespoons tomato paste

¼   cup plus 2 tablespoons dry white wine, divided

2   cups plus 2 tablespoons crushed tomatoes (from one 28-ounce can), divided

½   cup heavy cream

¼   cup chopped fresh basil

1   Melt butter in medium saucepan over medium heat. Add onion, prosciutto, bay leaf, salt, and pepper flakes; cook, stirring occasionally, until onion is very soft and beginning to turn light gold, 8 to 12 minutes. Increase heat to medium-high, add garlic, and cook until fragrant, about 30 seconds. Stir in sun-dried tomatoes and tomato paste and cook, stirring constantly, until slightly darkened, 1 to 2 minutes. Add ¼ cup wine and cook, stirring frequently, until liquid has evaporated, 1 to 2 minutes.

2   Add 2 cups crushed tomatoes and bring to simmer. Reduce heat to low, partially cover, and cook, stirring occasionally, until sauce is thickened, 25 to 30 minutes.

3   Remove bay leaf from sauce and discard. Stir cream, remaining 2 tablespoons crushed tomatoes, and remaining 2 tablespoons wine into sauce; season with salt and pepper to taste. Stir in basil.

To serve   Reserve 1 cup pasta cooking water when draining pasta. Return pasta to pot and toss with sauce, adding cooking water as needed to reach desired consistency.

Vodka Sauce

shells | penne | garganelli | farfalle | orecchiette

WHY THIS RECIPE WORKS: Chefs in both Italy and America lay claim to the invention of this iconic tomato sauce elevated with splashes of vodka and heavy cream. Whichever country it was born in, it exploded onto Italian American restaurant menus in the 1970s. Despite its reputation as fancy restaurant fare, this classic is easy to prepare. The ratio of ingredients is important to strike the right balance of sweet, tangy, spicy, and creamy. Too much cream will overshadow the tomatoes, and too much vodka results in a harsh taste. To achieve a just-right consistency, we puree half the tomatoes (which helps the sauce cling nicely to the pasta) and cut the rest into chunks. For sweetness, we add sautéed onions; for umami, we use a bit of tomato paste. You do need a liberal pour of vodka to cut through the richness and add "zinginess," but it's important to add it to the tomatoes early on to allow the alcohol to mostly (but not completely) cook off and prevent a boozy flavor.

Makes enough for
1 pound pasta
Total Time:
30 minutes

---

1   (28-ounce) can whole peeled tomatoes, drained, juice reserved

2   tablespoons extra-virgin olive oil

½   small onion, minced

1   tablespoon tomato paste

2   garlic cloves, minced

¼   teaspoon red pepper flakes

½   teaspoon table salt

⅓   cup vodka

½   cup heavy cream

2   tablespoons chopped fresh basil

1   Puree half of tomatoes in food processor until smooth. Dice remaining tomatoes into ½-inch pieces, discarding cores. Combine pureed and diced tomatoes in liquid measuring cup (you should have about 1⅔ cups). Add reserved juice to equal 2 cups; discard remaining juice.

2   Heat oil in large saucepan over medium heat until shimmering. Add onion and tomato paste and cook, stirring occasionally, until onion is light golden around edges, about 3 minutes. Add garlic and pepper flakes; cook, stirring constantly, until fragrant, about 30 seconds.

3   Stir in tomatoes and salt. Remove pan from heat and add vodka. Return pan to medium-high heat and simmer briskly until alcohol flavor is mostly cooked off, 8 to 10 minutes; stir frequently and lower heat to medium if simmering becomes too vigorous. Stir in cream and cook until hot, about 1 minute. Stir in basil.

To serve   Reserve 1 cup pasta cooking water when draining pasta. Return pasta to pot and toss with sauce, adding cooking water as needed to reach desired consistency.

Gorgonzola-Walnut Cream Sauce

gnocchi | tagliatelle | fettuccine | cavatelli

WHY THIS RECIPE WORKS: Tangy, buttery Gorgonzola cheese melts into a decadent sauce to cloak fresh pasta. This cow's milk cheese from northern Italy has origins dating back a thousand years, making it one of the oldest blue cheeses in the world. Today it is produced in the regions of Lombardy and Piedmont (it's named after the town of Gorgonzola, near Milan). Though many varieties are available in Italy, here in the U.S. you will generally find two types: dolce and piccante. The dolce will bring its sweet, creamy, faintly spicy qualities to this dish. The piccante, which is aged longer, also works, but because it's a more crumbly cheese, the finished sauce will be less creamy. The bittersweetness of toasted walnuts, as well as the generous amount of fresh chives stirred in before serving, keep the decadence from going over the top. Pinot Grigio is a good choice for the white wine. This is nice with whole-wheat pasta.

*Makes enough for
1 pound pasta*
Total Time:
30 minutes

1   cup walnuts

1   tablespoon unsalted butter

1   shallot, minced

¾   cup dry white wine

1   cup whole milk

1   cup heavy cream

1   cup crumbled Gorgonzola cheese (4 ounces)

¼   teaspoon table salt

¼   teaspoon pepper

2   tablespoons minced fresh chives

1   Toast walnuts in 12-inch skillet over medium heat, stirring often, until golden and fragrant, 4 to 5 minutes. When cool enough to handle, chop fine.

2   Melt butter in medium saucepan over medium heat. Add shallot and cook until fragrant, about 30 seconds. Add wine, bring to simmer, and cook until reduced to ¼ cup, about 5 minutes.

3   Whisk in milk, cream, Gorgonzola, salt, and pepper. Bring to simmer and cook until cheese has melted and sauce is thickened, about 5 minutes. Stir in walnuts and chives and season with salt and pepper to taste. Serve immediately.

To serve   Reserve 1 cup pasta cooking water when draining pasta. Return pasta to pot and toss with sauce, adding cooking water as needed to reach desired consistency.

VARIATION

Porcini Cream Sauce

Add 1 ounce dried porcini mushrooms, rinsed and minced, to saucepan with shallot. Substitute ½ cup (1 ounce) grated Pecorino Romano for Gorgonzola.

Alfredo Sauce

farfalle | pappardelle | fettuccine | gnocchi

WHY THIS RECIPE WORKS: The fact that this rendition of Alfredo sauce is an Americanized version of the Italian classic makes it no less delicious, albeit in a different way. (The original Alfredo sauce, created in Rome, uses just butter and Parmigiano-Reggiano cheese; for that recipe, see page 77.) When the original Alfredo sauce came to America in the 1920s, restaurant chefs started adding cream to it, since domestic cheeses and butters lacked the richness of their Italian counterparts, and this version continues to be a favorite in Italian American restaurants to this day. A lighter hand is called for when adding two other rich ingredients: ¾ cup Parmesan and 2 tablespoons butter are sufficient to add their distinctive flavors without being overwhelming. Many recipes call for reducing the heavy cream by half, but this makes the sauce unpalatably thick. Here, we reduce only a cup of the called-for cream, and reduce it by only one-third instead of one-half. We then add the remaining ½ cup cream at the very end of cooking, so it doesn't reduce at all. Make sure that the individual serving bowls are warm, which will keep this pasta sauce nice and creamy while you enjoy it. Try this version of Alfredo with herb pasta (see pages 28–29).

Makes enough for 1 pound pasta
Total Time: 20 minutes

1½ cups heavy cream, divided
2 tablespoons unsalted butter
1½ ounces Parmesan cheese, grated (¾ cup)
½ teaspoon table salt
½ teaspoon pepper
⅛ teaspoon ground nutmeg

Bring 1 cup cream and butter to simmer in large saucepan over medium heat. Reduce to gentle simmer and cook until reduced to ⅔ cup, 12 to 15 minutes. Whisk in remaining ½ cup cream, Parmesan, salt, pepper, and nutmeg until combined and cheese is melted. Season with salt and pepper to taste.

To serve Reserve 1 cup pasta cooking water when draining pasta. Return pasta to pot and toss with sauce, adding cooking water as needed to reach desired consistency.

White Clam Sauce

malloreddus | cavatelli | linguine | penne

WHY THIS RECIPE WORKS: It's hard to beat the convenience of canned chopped clams to make a fast and flavorful pantry sauce that's perfect for when you are pulling some of your fresh pasta reserves out of the freezer. (For an in-shell clam sauce, see page 78.) This type of quick clam sauce is an Italian American icon, and here we give you the "white" variety, sans tomatoes. Plenty of shallots and garlic punch up the flavor; clam juice supplemented with chicken broth creates body in this light sauce; and butter, stirred in at the end, provides a velvety texture. We like to sprinkle red pepper flakes over the finished pasta and tuck a lemon wedge into each bowl for squeezing over the top. This would be great with herb pasta or squid ink pasta (see pages 28–29).

Makes enough for 1 pound pasta
Total Time: 30 minutes

2	shallots, minced
2	tablespoons extra-virgin olive oil
4	garlic cloves, minced
2	(6.5-ounce) cans chopped clams
1	(8-ounce) bottle clam juice
1	cup chicken broth
2	tablespoons unsalted butter
2	tablespoons minced fresh parsley

Cook shallots, oil, and garlic in 12-inch skillet over medium heat until shallot is just golden and garlic is fragrant, about 2 minutes. Add clams and their juice, bottled clam juice, and broth; increase heat to medium-high and bring to boil. Cook until sauce is reduced to 2 cups, about 15 minutes. Off heat, whisk in butter and season with salt and pepper to taste. Stir in parsley right before serving.

To serve Reserve 1 cup pasta cooking water when draining pasta. Return pasta to pot and toss with sauce, adding cooking water as needed to reach desired consistency.

Fra Diavolo Sauce

spaghetti | linguine | bucatini | busiate | maltagliati

WHY THIS RECIPE WORKS: This spicy, shellfish-studded extravaganza is often thought to have originated in southern Italy, but it's actually another ingenious Italian American invention. Regardless of origins, it's a celebratory showstopper worthy of both intimate dinners and holiday celebrations. For ease of preparation, we skip the often-included lobster in favor of succulent shrimp, sweet scallops, and briny mussels. Blooming garlic, anchovies, tomato paste, oregano, and red pepper flakes in olive oil lays down an ultraflavorful base. Then we add white wine (such as Pinot Grigio) and steam the mussels until they open. After transferring the mussels to a bowl (leaving all their heavenly juices in the pot), we introduce clam juice and canned whole tomatoes and bring it all to a boil. Last, we add shrimp and scallops to cook through gently before returning the mussels to the pot and finishing with a flourish of chopped cherry peppers and parsley. We prefer shrimp not treated with salt or additives such as sodium tripolyphosphate (STPP). Most frozen E-Z peel shrimp have been treated (the ingredient list should tell you). We recommend buying "dry" scallops, which don't have chemical additives and taste better than "wet." If you can't find fresh "dry" scallops, you can substitute thawed frozen scallops. Try this with squid ink pasta (see pages 28–29).

Makes *enough for 1 pound pasta*
Total Time: 1 hour

12 ounces extra-large shrimp (21 to 25 per pound), peeled, deveined, and tails removed

12 ounces large sea scallops, tendons removed, cut in half horizontally

6 tablespoons extra-virgin olive oil, divided, plus extra for drizzling

7 garlic cloves, minced, divided

¾ teaspoon table salt, divided

3 anchovy fillets

3 tablespoons tomato paste

2 teaspoons dried oregano

1–1½ teaspoons red pepper flakes, plus extra for sprinkling

1 pound mussels, scrubbed and debearded

1 cup dry white wine

1 (28-ounce) can whole peeled tomatoes

1 (8-ounce) bottle clam juice

½ cup chopped fresh parsley

1–2 tablespoons chopped jarred hot cherry peppers, plus 1 tablespoon brine

1 Toss shrimp and scallops with 2 tablespoons oil, 1 tablespoon garlic, and ½ teaspoon salt in bowl. Refrigerate until ready to use.

2 Cook anchovies, remaining ¼ cup oil, and remaining garlic in Dutch oven over medium heat until garlic is just beginning to brown, 3 to 5 minutes, breaking up anchovies with wooden spoon. Add tomato paste, oregano, and pepper flakes; cook, stirring constantly, until tomato paste begins to darken, about 2 minutes.

3 Increase heat to medium-high, add mussels and wine, and bring to boil. Cover and cook, shaking pot occasionally, until mussels have opened, 3 to 4 minutes (discard any unopened mussels). Using tongs, transfer mussels to bowl and cover to keep warm.

4 Add tomatoes and their juice, clam juice, and remaining ¼ teaspoon salt to pot. Using potato masher, mash tomatoes in pot until coarsely pureed. Bring to simmer and cook until flavors meld, about 10 minutes.

5 Stir in shrimp and scallops and cook, stirring frequently, until opaque throughout, about 3 minutes. Off heat, add parsley, cherry peppers and brine, and mussels (along with any accumulated juices) and toss to combine. Season with salt to taste.

To serve Reserve 1 cup pasta cooking water when draining pasta. Add cooked pasta to Dutch oven and toss with sauce to combine, adding cooking water as needed to reach desired consistency. Serve drizzled with extra olive oil and sprinkled with pepper flakes.

Sunday Gravy

spaghetti | linguine | rigatoni | penne

WHY THIS RECIPE WORKS: Sunday gravy is more than just meat sauce—it's a labor of love, traditionally an all-day kitchen affair involving several types of meat, lots of tomatoes, and at least one Italian mother or grandmother. This recipe honors that heritage while shortening the cooking time. Our first step is limiting the meats to one kind of sausage and one pork cut—plus meatballs, naturally. Hot Italian links give the sauce a mild kick; baby back ribs are our preferred pork because they're not too fatty and turn tender in just a few hours. Meatloaf mix, a combination of ground beef, pork, and veal, produces juicy meatballs, especially when mixed with a panade of bread and buttermilk, plus an egg yolk for richness. Browning the meatballs before adding them to the sauce helps them keep their shape. Canned crushed tomatoes are the winner for a nicely thick, bright-tasting sauce. Instead of merely browning the tomato paste, we cook it until it nearly blackens, which concentrates its sweetness. Six tablespoons of plain yogurt thinned with 2 tablespoons of milk can be substituted for the buttermilk. This recipe can be prepared through step 4 and then cooled and refrigerated in the Dutch oven for up to 2 days. To reheat, drizzle ½ cup water over the sauce (do not stir in) and warm on the lower-middle rack of a preheated 325-degree oven for 1 hour before proceeding.

Makes enough for 2 pounds pasta
Total Time: 3½ hours

Sauce

2 tablespoons extra-virgin olive oil

1 (2¼-pound) rack baby back ribs, cut into 2-rib sections

½ teaspoon table salt

½ teaspoon pepper

1 pound hot Italian sausage links

2 medium onions, minced

1¼ teaspoons dried oregano

3 tablespoons tomato paste

4 garlic cloves, minced

2 (28-ounce) cans crushed tomatoes

⅔ cup beef broth

¼ cup chopped fresh basil

Meatballs

2 slices high-quality white sandwich bread, crusts removed and bread cut into ½-inch cubes

½ cup buttermilk

¼ cup chopped fresh parsley

2 garlic cloves, minced

1 large egg yolk

½ teaspoon table salt

¼ teaspoon red pepper flakes

1 pound meatloaf mix

2 ounces thinly sliced prosciutto, minced

1 ounce Pecorino Romano cheese, grated (½ cup)

½ cup extra-virgin olive oil

1 For the sauce Adjust oven rack to lower-middle position and heat oven to 325 degrees. Heat oil in large Dutch oven over medium-high heat until just smoking. Pat ribs dry with paper towels and sprinkle with salt and pepper. Add half of ribs to pot and brown on both sides, 5 to 7 minutes total. Transfer ribs to large plate and repeat with remaining ribs. After transferring second batch of ribs to plate, brown sausages on all four sides, 5 to 7 minutes total. Transfer sausages to plate with ribs.

2 Reduce heat to medium, add onions and oregano; cook, stirring occasionally, until beginning to brown, about 5 minutes. Add tomato paste and cook, stirring constantly, until very dark, about 3 minutes. Stir in garlic and cook until fragrant, about 30 seconds. Add crushed tomatoes and broth, scraping up any browned bits. Return ribs and sausages to pot; bring to simmer, cover, and transfer to oven. Cook until ribs are tender, about 2½ hours.

3 For the meatballs Meanwhile, combine bread cubes, buttermilk, parsley, garlic, egg yolk, salt, and pepper flakes in medium bowl and mash with fork until no bread chunks remain. Add meatloaf mix, prosciutto, and Pecorino to bread mixture; mix with your hands until thoroughly combined. Divide mixture into 12 pieces; roll into balls, transfer to plate, cover with plastic wrap, and refrigerate until ready to use.

4 When sauce is 30 minutes from being done, heat oil in large nonstick skillet over medium-high heat until shimmering. Add meatballs and cook until well browned all over, 5 to 7 minutes. Transfer meatballs to paper towel–lined plate to drain briefly. Remove sauce from oven and skim fat from top with large spoon. Transfer browned meatballs to sauce and gently submerge. Return pot to oven and continue cooking until meatballs are just cooked through, about 15 minutes. Stir basil into sauce just before serving.

To serve Transfer meatballs, ribs, and sausages to serving platter and cut sausages in half. Reserve 1 cup pasta cooking water when draining pasta. Add pasta to Dutch oven and toss with gravy to combine, adding cooking water as needed to reach desired consistency. Serve pasta and meat either separately or together.

Sausage Ragù with Red Peppers

maltagliati | tagliatelle | pappardelle | rigatoni

WHY THIS RECIPE WORKS: Sausage and sweet bell peppers are a beloved pairing that make for a slightly sweet, slightly spicy pasta sauce that all comes together in a Dutch oven. It makes a big batch, so it's great for feeding a crowd or tucking some away in the freezer for another meal. Hot or sweet Italian sausage—your choice—imparts robust flavor, and a few minutes spent browning and breaking it up in the Dutch oven pays dividends. Then we add peppers and onions and cook them in the rendered fat until they're browned and becoming meltingly sweet. We add aromatics and then stir in some red wine to deglaze the pot before adding lots of tomatoes. Tomato paste, crushed tomatoes, diced tomatoes, and tomato puree combine to produce a just-right consistency in this ragù—neither too watery nor too thick. Chianti or Merlot is a good choice for the red wine.

Makes *enough for*
2 pounds pasta
Total Time:
1¾ hours

2   tablespoons extra-virgin olive oil

2   pounds hot or sweet Italian sausage, casings removed

2   red bell peppers, stemmed, seeded, and cut into ½-inch pieces

2   onions, chopped fine

6   garlic cloves, minced

2   tablespoons tomato paste

2   tablespoons minced fresh oregano or 2 teaspoons dried

1   teaspoon red pepper flakes

1   cup dry red wine

1   (28-ounce) can crushed tomatoes

1   (28-ounce) can diced tomatoes, drained

1   (28-ounce) can tomato puree

1–2   teaspoons sugar, as needed

1 Heat oil in Dutch oven over medium-high heat until just smoking. Brown sausage, breaking up large pieces with wooden spoon, about 5 minutes. Add bell peppers and onions and cook over medium heat until softened and lightly browned, 8 to 10 minutes. Stir in garlic, tomato paste, oregano, and pepper flakes and cook until fragrant, about 1 minute.

2 Stir in wine, scraping up any browned bits, and simmer until thickened, about 5 minutes. Stir in crushed tomatoes, diced tomatoes, and tomato puree. Bring to simmer and cook, stirring occasionally, until sauce is deeply flavored and slightly thickened, about 1 hour. Season with salt, pepper, and sugar to taste. (Sauce can be refrigerated for up to 3 days or frozen for up to 1 month.)

To serve Reserve 1 cup pasta cooking water when draining pasta. Add pasta to Dutch oven and toss with sauce, adding cooking water as needed to reach desired consistency.

Ragù alla Bolognese

tagliatelle | pappardelle | filled pasta

WHY THIS RECIPE WORKS: The undisputed pedigree of this delizioso ragù is that it was born in the northern Italian city for which it was named. But there are countless "authentic" interpretations. While ground beef is a common base, many versions add ground pork and often veal as well. Others supplement the ground meat with finely chopped pancetta or prosciutto. Some recipes call for crushed tomatoes; others lean toward the concentrated depth of tomato paste. One version may call for white wine, another for red, another for no wine at all. The inclusion of milk and/or cream is hotly debated. Cooking times range from 90 minutes to 3 hours. The only thing that all Italian cooks agree on is this: The end product should be rich but never cloying, with a velvety, clingy texture. Tomatoes should be a bit player; the true star is the meat. Our for-your-consideration entry uses—count 'em—six types: ground beef, pork, and veal; pancetta; mortadella; and chicken livers. These meats, along with red wine and tomato paste, produce a complex, balanced sauce to cloak fresh egg pasta. Many Bolognese recipes use homemade broth; to get that ultrasilky texture using store-bought broth, we add powdered gelatin. Eight teaspoons of gelatin is equivalent to one (1-ounce) box of gelatin. Chianti or Merlot is a good choice for the wine.

Makes *enough for 2 pounds pasta*
Total Time: 2½ hours

1 cup chicken broth

1 cup beef broth

8 teaspoons unflavored gelatin

1 onion, chopped coarse

1 large carrot, peeled and chopped coarse

1 celery rib, chopped coarse

4 ounces pancetta, chopped

4 ounces mortadella, chopped

6 ounces chicken livers, trimmed

3 tablespoons extra-virgin olive oil

12 ounces 85 percent lean ground beef

12 ounces ground veal

12 ounces ground pork

3 tablespoons minced fresh sage

1 (6-ounce) can tomato paste

2 cups dry red wine

1 Combine chicken broth and beef broth in bowl; sprinkle gelatin over top and let sit until softened, about 5 minutes.

2 Pulse onion, carrot, and celery in food processor until finely chopped, about 10 pulses, scraping down sides of bowl as needed; transfer to separate bowl. Pulse pancetta and mortadella in now-empty processor until finely chopped, about 25 pulses; transfer to third bowl. Process chicken livers in again-empty processor until pureed, about 5 seconds; refrigerate until ready to use.

3 Heat oil in Dutch oven over medium-high heat until shimmering. Add ground beef, veal, and pork and cook, breaking up meat with wooden spoon, until all liquid has evaporated and meat begins to sizzle, 10 to 15 minutes. Stir in pancetta mixture and sage and cook until pancetta is translucent, 5 to 7 minutes, adjusting heat as needed to keep fond from burning. Stir in chopped vegetables and cook until softened, 5 to 7 minutes. Stir in tomato paste and cook until rust-colored and fragrant, about 3 minutes.

4 Stir in wine, scraping up any browned bits, and simmer until thickened, about 5 minutes. Stir in broth mixture, return to bare simmer, and cook until sauce has thickened (wooden spoon should leave trail when dragged through sauce), about 1½ hours.

5 Stir in chicken livers and bring to brief simmer. Season with salt and pepper to taste. (Sauce can be refrigerated for up to 3 days or frozen for up to 1 month.)

To serve Reserve 1 cup pasta cooking water when draining pasta. Add pasta to Dutch oven and toss with sauce, adding cooking water as needed to reach desired consistency.

Beef Short Rib Ragù

tagliatelle | pappardelle | busiate | orecchiette

WHY THIS RECIPE WORKS: For an intensely beefy ragù that spends most of its time cooking hands-off in the oven, we use boneless short ribs, pairing them with porcini mushrooms, tomato paste, and anchovies—all umami powerhouses. After softening aromatics and deglazing with red wine, we add a can of chopped tomatoes, some beef broth, and the rehydrated mushrooms. Then in goes the beef (no need to cut it up or brown it first) and the pot goes into the oven to cook low and slow. Removing the lid partway through cooking facilitates browning, enhancing the meat's flavor. Finally, many Italian beef ragùs call for a touch of warm spices, so we add ½ teaspoon five-spice powder (a mix of cinnamon, cloves, fennel, white pepper, and star anise). Before serving, shred the ultratender meat so that it can be fully coated with the sauce.

Makes *enough for*
1 pound pasta
Total Time: 3 hours

1½ cups beef broth, divided

½ ounce dried porcini mushrooms, rinsed

1 tablespoon extra-virgin olive oil

1 onion, chopped fine

2 garlic cloves, minced

1 tablespoon tomato paste

3 anchovy fillets, minced

½ teaspoon five-spice powder

½ cup dry red wine

1 (14.5-ounce) can whole peeled tomatoes, drained with juice reserved, chopped fine

2 pounds boneless beef short ribs, trimmed

¾ teaspoon table salt

1 Adjust oven rack to middle position and heat oven to 350 degrees. Microwave ½ cup broth and mushrooms in covered bowl until steaming, about 1 minute. Let sit until softened, about 5 minutes. Drain mushrooms in fine-mesh strainer lined with coffee filter, pressing to extract all liquid; reserve liquid and chop mushrooms fine.

2 Heat oil in Dutch oven over medium heat until shimmering. Add onion and cook, stirring occasionally, until softened, about 5 minutes. Add garlic and cook until fragrant, about 1 minute. Add tomato paste, anchovies, and five-spice powder and cook, stirring frequently, until mixture has darkened and fond forms on pot bottom, 3 to 4 minutes. Add wine, increase heat to medium-high, and bring to simmer, scraping up any browned bits. Continue to cook, stirring frequently, until wine is reduced and pot is almost dry, 2 to 4 minutes. Add tomatoes and reserved juice, remaining 1 cup broth, reserved mushroom soaking liquid, and mushrooms and bring to simmer.

3 Toss beef with salt and season with pepper. Add beef to pot and cover; transfer pot to oven. Cook for 1 hour. Uncover and continue to cook until beef is tender, 1 to 1¼ hours longer.

4 Remove pot from oven; using slotted spoon, transfer beef to cutting board and let cool for 5 minutes. Using 2 forks, shred beef into bite-size pieces, discarding any large pieces of fat or connective tissue. Using large spoon, skim off any excess fat that has risen to surface of sauce. Return beef to sauce and season with salt and pepper to taste. (Sauce can be refrigerated for up to 3 days or frozen for up to 1 month.)

To serve Reserve 1 cup pasta cooking water when draining pasta. Add pasta to Dutch oven and toss with sauce, adding cooking water as needed to reach desired consistency.

Beef and Onion Ragù

paccheri | tagliatelle | pappardelle | rigatoni

WHY THIS RECIPE WORKS: This sauce predates the introduction of tomatoes to Italian kitchens. Faced with food shortages, 16th-century Neapolitans created a thrifty yet supremely satisfying gravy of beef and vegetables known as la Genovese. (The provenance of the name is vague: Some theorize that Genoese cooks brought it to Naples; others believe that the name references the reputed frugality of the Genoese.) It began as a dish that was meant for two meals: a meal of cooked beef and a savory sauce for pasta. In the 19th century, onions took center stage, and the dish became one of the region's most beloved. In modern times, more ingredients are added (we use pancetta and salami), and the beef is likely to be shredded and incorporated into the sauce for a substantial single dish—exactly the kind of pasta sauce we love to make in cold-weather months. To eliminate the need for stirring and monitoring the onions during cooking, we move the process from the stovetop to the oven. A surprising ingredient—water—extracts maximum flavor from the onions, turning them to a deliciously sweet, pulpy sauce. We also add tomato paste for a boost of flavor and color and stir Pecorino right into the sauce to add body.

Makes *enough for 1 pound pasta*
Total Time: 2¾ hours

1   (1- to 1¼-pound) boneless beef chuck-eye roast, cut into 4 pieces and trimmed of large pieces of fat

1   teaspoon kosher salt

½   teaspoon pepper

2   ounces pancetta, cut into ½-inch pieces

2   ounces salami, cut into ½-inch pieces

1   small carrot, peeled and cut into ½-inch pieces

1   small celery rib, cut into ½-inch pieces

2½   pounds onions, halved and cut into 1-inch pieces

2   tablespoons tomato paste

1   cup dry white wine, divided

2   tablespoons minced fresh marjoram or oregano, divided

1   ounce Pecorino Romano cheese, grated (½ cup)

1   Sprinkle beef with salt and pepper and set aside. Adjust oven rack to lower-middle position and heat oven to 300 degrees.

2   Process pancetta and salami in food processor until ground to paste, about 30 seconds, scraping down sides of bowl as needed. Add carrot and celery and process 30 seconds longer, scraping down sides of bowl as needed. Transfer paste to Dutch oven and set aside. Pulse onions in now-empty processor in 2 batches, until ⅛- to ¼-inch pieces form, 8 to 10 pulses per batch. Cook pancetta mixture over medium heat, stirring frequently, until fat is rendered and fond begins to form on bottom of pot, about 5 minutes. Add tomato paste and cook, stirring constantly, until browned, about 90 seconds. Stir in 2 cups water, scraping up any browned bits. Stir in onions and bring to boil. Stir in ½ cup wine and 1 tablespoon marjoram. Add beef and push into onions to ensure that it is submerged. Transfer to oven and cook, uncovered, until beef is fully tender, 2 to 2½ hours.

3   Transfer beef to carving board. Place pot over medium heat and cook, stirring frequently, until mixture is almost completely dry. Stir in remaining ½ cup wine and cook for 2 minutes, stirring occasionally. Using 2 forks, shred beef into bite-size pieces. Stir beef and remaining 1 tablespoon marjoram into sauce and season with salt and pepper to taste. Add Pecorino right before serving and stir vigorously to combine.

To serve   Reserve 1 cup pasta cooking water when draining pasta. Add pasta to Dutch oven and toss with sauce, adding cooking water as needed to reach desired consistency.

Rabbit Ragù

orecchiette | tagliatelle | pappardelle | maltagliati

WHY THIS RECIPE WORKS: Rabbit is popular throughout Italy, dating back to the days when the hunter's catch was relied upon to fill the dinner table. Rabbit ragùs are made in Tuscany and the Marches, among other regions. We start our version by browning rabbit pieces and then set them aside while we build the sauce. Porcini mushrooms and tomato paste provide a flavorful backbone. Red wine (such as Chianti) and canned tomatoes contribute acidity, while pancetta adds further complexity. After stirring in chicken broth to give the sauce extra body, we add back the meat and then transfer the pot to the oven to cook through in its gentle, even heat. Once the meat is tender, we shred it and stir it back into the sauce. Tossed with fresh pasta , this is a company-worthy dish that pays homage to classic Italian cooking. While rabbit is usually not readily available in American supermarkets, it is available from butchers, who will also cut it up for you.

*Makes enough for
2 pounds pasta*
Total Time:
2½ hours

---

1   (3-pound) whole rabbit, cut into 7 pieces

½   teaspoon table salt

½   teaspoon pepper

3   tablespoons extra-virgin olive oil, divided

4   ounces pancetta, cut into ¼-inch pieces

2   onions, chopped fine

2   carrots, peeled and cut into ¼-inch pieces

¾   ounce dried porcini mushrooms, rinsed and minced

1   (6-ounce) can tomato paste

6   garlic cloves, minced

1   cup red wine

4   cups chicken broth

2   (28-ounce) cans diced tomatoes

3   bay leaves

½   teaspoon sugar

1   Adjust oven rack to middle position and heat oven to 325 degrees. Pat rabbit dry with paper towels and sprinkle with salt and pepper. Heat 1 tablespoon oil in large Dutch oven over medium-high heat until just smoking. Brown half of rabbit lightly on both sides, about 6 minutes; transfer to plate. Repeat with 1 tablespoon oil and remaining rabbit; transfer to plate.

2   Add remaining 1 tablespoon oil and pancetta to now-empty pot and cook over medium heat until pancetta is lightly browned, about 6 minutes. Stir in onions, carrots, and mushrooms; increase heat to medium-high; and cook until vegetables are just softened, 6 to 10 minutes. Stir in tomato paste and cook until darkened and fragrant, about 3 minutes. Stir in garlic and cook until fragrant, about 30 seconds.

3   Stir in wine, scraping up any browned bits, and simmer until sauce has thickened, about 2 minutes. Stir in broth, tomatoes and their juice, and bay leaves. Nestle browned rabbit and any accumulated juices into pot and bring to simmer. Partially cover pot (leaving about 1 inch of pot open), transfer to oven, and cook until rabbit is very tender and falling off bones, 1½ to 2 hours.

4   Remove pot from oven and discard bay leaves. Transfer rabbit to cutting board, let cool slightly, then shred meat, discarding bones. Meanwhile, bring sauce to simmer over medium-high heat and cook until thickened, 10 to 15 minutes. Stir in shredded meat and sugar. Season with salt and pepper to taste. (Sauce can be refrigerated for up to 3 days or frozen for up to 1 month.)

To serve   Reserve 1 cup pasta cooking water when draining pasta. Add pasta to Dutch oven and toss with sauce, adding cooking water as needed to reach desired consistency.

Ragù Bianco

tagliatelle | pappardelle | farfalle

WHY THIS RECIPE WORKS: White ragùs existed for centuries before tomatoes made their appearance in Italian cuisine in the 1800s. Made with expensive cuts of meat, they were fancy fare for the Renaissance nobility, but they eventually trickled down to commoners, who used whatever meat they could get. Our modern ragù bianco uses two types of pork and eschews anything tomatoey in favor of bright lemon and rich cream, accented by fresh fennel, onion, and garlic. We ensure plenty of savoriness by creating fond twice, first browning finely chopped pancetta along with the onion and fennel in a Dutch oven and then adding water and a touch of cream to create a braising liquid. A pork shoulder, halved crosswise to make cooking faster and shredding easier, simmers in this liquid in the oven, where a second fond forms on the sides of the pot. After scraping this second fond into the sauce, we add plenty of lemon juice before incorporating the pasta. Serve with extra Pecorino and chopped fennel fronds, if your fennel bulb came with fronds. This would be especially nice with lemon-pepper pasta (see pages 28–29).

Makes *enough for 1 pound pasta*
Total Time: 2½ hours

4	ounces pancetta, chopped
1	large onion, chopped fine
1	large fennel bulb, stalks discarded and fronds reserved, bulb halved, cored, and chopped fine
4	garlic cloves, minced
2	teaspoons minced fresh thyme
1½	teaspoons table salt
1	teaspoon pepper
⅓	cup heavy cream
1	(1½-pound) boneless pork butt roast, well trimmed and cut in half across grain
1½	teaspoons grated lemon zest plus ¼ cup juice (2 lemons)
2	ounces Pecorino Romano cheese, grated (1 cup)

1 Adjust oven rack to middle position and heat oven to 350 degrees. Cook pancetta and ⅔ cup water in Dutch oven over medium-high heat, stirring occasionally, until water has evaporated and dark fond forms on bottom of pot, 8 to 10 minutes. Add onion and fennel and cook, stirring occasionally, until vegetables soften and start to brown, 5 to 7 minutes. Stir in garlic, thyme, salt, and pepper and cook until fragrant, about 30 seconds.

2 Stir in cream and 2 cups water, scraping up any browned bits. Add pork and bring to boil over high heat. Cover, transfer to oven, and cook until pork is tender, about 1½ hours. Transfer pork to plate and let cool for 15 minutes. Cover pot so fond will steam and soften. Using spatula, scrape browned bits from sides of pot and stir into sauce. Stir in lemon zest and juice.

3 When pork is cool enough to handle, using 2 forks, shred pork into bite-size pieces, discarding any large pieces of fat or connective tissue. Return pork and any juices to Dutch oven and stir to combine. Stir in Pecorino.

To serve Reserve 1 cup pasta cooking water when draining pasta. Add pasta and to Dutch oven and toss with sauce, adding cooking water as needed to reach desired consistency.

Mushroom Bolognese

fettuccine | garganelli | orecchiette | filled pasta

WHY THIS RECIPE WORKS: Since mushrooms are so successful as a meat alternative, here's our lush Bolognese-inspired sauce using them to full advantage. Because the cell walls of mushrooms are made of a heat-stable substance called chitin, they retain a satisfying, meat-like chew when cooked, instead of breaking down as many other vegetables would. Using two types of mushrooms creates double the complexity. A whopping 2 pounds of fresh cremini mushrooms pulsed in a food processor gives the sauce a satisfyingly chunky, substantial texture, and dried porcini mushrooms deliver concentrated umami flavor. To further boost the savory umami profile, we add tomato paste, red wine, and admittedly unconventional soy sauce. Bolognese often includes a pour of cream, though this is a somewhat controversial topic (and we don't include it in our Ragù alla Bolognese on page 230). With this meat-free ragù, though, we find that a few tablespoons of heavy cream stirred in at the end really rounds out the sauce and makes for a silky finish.

Makes enough for
1 pound pasta
Total Time: 1 hour

---

2 pounds cremini mushrooms, trimmed and quartered

1 carrot, peeled and chopped

1 small onion, chopped

1 (28-ounce) can whole peeled tomatoes

3 tablespoons extra-virgin olive oil

½ ounce dried porcini mushrooms, rinsed and minced

3 garlic cloves, minced

1 teaspoon sugar

2 tablespoons tomato paste

1 cup dry red wine

½ cup vegetable broth

1 tablespoon soy sauce

½ teaspoon table salt

¼ teaspoon pepper

3 tablespoons heavy cream

1 Working in batches, pulse cremini mushrooms in food processor until pieces are no larger than ½ inch, 5 to 7 pulses, scraping down sides of bowl as needed; transfer to large bowl. Pulse carrot and onion in now-empty processor until finely chopped, 5 to 7 pulses; transfer to bowl with processed mushrooms. Pulse tomatoes and their juice in now-empty processor until finely chopped, 6 to 8 pulses; set aside separately.

2 Heat oil in Dutch oven over medium heat until shimmering. Add processed mushroom mixture and porcini mushrooms, cover, and cook, stirring occasionally, until vegetables release their liquid, about 5 minutes. Uncover, increase heat to medium-high, and cook until vegetables begin to brown, 12 to 15 minutes.

3 Stir in garlic and sugar and cook until fragrant, about 30 seconds. Stir in tomato paste and cook for 1 minute. Stir in wine and simmer until nearly evaporated, about 5 minutes.

4 Stir in reserved processed tomatoes, broth, soy sauce, salt, and pepper and bring to simmer. Reduce heat to medium-low and simmer until sauce has thickened but is still moist, 8 to 10 minutes. Off heat, stir in cream.

To serve Reserve 1 cup pasta cooking water when draining pasta. Add pasta to Dutch oven and toss with sauce, adding cooking water as needed to reach desired consistency.

Meatless "Meat" Sauce with Chickpeas and Mushrooms

spaghetti | linguine | penne | trofie | fileja

WHY THIS RECIPE WORKS: Here's another ultrasatisfying, meaty-tasting tomato sauce that contains no meat. We start with cremini mushrooms and tomato paste—both rich sources of umami. As with the Mushroom Bolognese on page 240, using the food processor to chop the mushrooms makes quick work of the prep while creating a ground meat–like texture. Then we incorporate chickpeas, pulsing those into smaller pieces to add body, flavor, and satiating protein. Some vegetable broth stirred in with the crushed tomatoes loosens the sauce without diluting its flavor. Since there's no meat, it needs only a short simmer to bring all the flavors together. Chopped fresh basil add a bright finish. Make sure to rinse the chickpeas after pulsing them in the food processor to rid them of excess starch, or the sauce will be too thick. This sauce would be great with whole-wheat pasta.

Makes enough for
2 pounds pasta
Total Time:
55 minutes

10	ounces cremini mushrooms, trimmed
6	tablespoons extra-virgin olive oil, divided
1	teaspoon table salt
1	onion, chopped
5	garlic cloves, minced
1¼	teaspoons dried oregano
¼	teaspoon red pepper flakes
¼	cup tomato paste
1	(28-ounce) can crushed tomatoes
2	cups vegetable broth
1	(15-ounce) can chickpeas, rinsed
2	tablespoons chopped fresh basil

1 Pulse mushrooms in two batches in food processor until chopped into ⅛- to ¼-inch pieces, 7 to 10 pulses, scraping down sides of bowl as needed. (Do not clean workbowl.)

2 Heat 5 tablespoons oil in Dutch oven over medium-high heat until shimmering. Add mushrooms and salt and cook, stirring occasionally, until mushrooms are browned and fond has formed on bottom of pot, about 8 minutes.

3 While mushrooms cook, pulse onion in food processor until finely chopped, 7 to 10 pulses, scraping down sides of bowl as needed. (Do not clean workbowl.) Transfer onion to pot with mushrooms and cook, stirring occasionally, until onion is soft and translucent, about 5 minutes. Combine remaining 1 tablespoon oil, garlic, oregano, and pepper flakes in bowl.

4 Add tomato paste to pot and cook, stirring constantly, until mixture is rust-colored, 1 to 2 minutes. Reduce heat to medium and push vegetables to sides of pot. Add garlic mixture to center and cook, stirring constantly, until fragrant, about 30 seconds. Stir in tomatoes and broth; bring to simmer over high heat. Reduce heat to low and simmer sauce for 5 minutes, stirring occasionally.

5 While sauce simmers, pulse chickpeas in food processor until chopped into ¼-inch pieces, 7 to 10 pulses. Transfer chickpeas to fine-mesh strainer and rinse under cold running water until water runs clear; drain well. Add chickpeas to pot and simmer until sauce is slightly thickened, about 15 minutes. Stir in basil and season with salt and pepper to taste. (Sauce can be refrigerated for up to 3 days or frozen for up to 1 month.)

To serve Reserve 1 cup pasta cooking water when draining pasta. Add pasta to Dutch oven and toss with sauce, adding cooking water as needed to reach desired consistency.

Braised Kale and Chickpea Sauce

linguine | spaghetti | orecchiette | maltagliati | farfalle

WHY THIS RECIPE WORKS: "Beans and greens" is a classic Italian ingredient pairing that is endlessly adaptable to different preparations. Here, we take the approach of turning it into a hearty pasta sauce, starting by crisping up a couple slices of bacon in a Dutch oven and then cooking the aromatics in the rendered fat to infuse them with smoky undertones. Then in goes chopped kale and broth to simmer and soften. As for the chickpeas, pureeing half of them in a blender along with some of the broth gives this sauce plenty of body, and we stir in this mixture after the kale has gotten a head start on softening. At the end of the simmering time, this flavorful, brothy pasta sauce needs only lemon zest and juice for brightening and Parmesan for added richness. To prepare the kale, it is necessary to remove the tough center stalks from the leaves. Start by cutting away the leafy portion from either side of the stalk using a chef's knife. Stack several leaves on top of one another and then chop them into pieces.

Makes *enough for*
1 pound pasta
Total Time: 1 hour

2   (15-ounce) cans chickpeas, rinsed, divided

2   cups chicken broth, divided

2   slices bacon, chopped fine

1   onion, chopped fine

6   garlic cloves, minced

2   teaspoons minced fresh rosemary or ½ teaspoon dried

¼   teaspoon red pepper flakes

1   pound kale, stemmed and cut into 1-inch pieces

2   ounces Parmesan cheese, grated (1 cup)

1   tablespoon grated lemon zest plus 1 teaspoon juice

1   Process half of chickpeas and 1 cup broth in blender until smooth, about 30 seconds.

2   Cook bacon in Dutch oven over medium heat until rendered and crispy, 5 to 7 minutes. Stir in onion and cook until softened, about 5 minutes. Stir in garlic, rosemary, and pepper flakes and cook until fragrant, about 30 seconds.

3   Add kale and remaining 1 cup broth and bring to simmer. Cover, reduce heat to medium-low, and cook until kale has reduced in volume by about half, about 10 minutes. Stir in chickpea puree and remaining whole chickpeas, cover, and simmer, stirring occasionally, until kale is tender and flavors meld, 25 to 35 minutes. Stir in Parmesan and lemon zest and juice. Season with salt and pepper to taste.

To serve   Reserve 1 cup pasta cooking water when draining pasta. Add pasta to Dutch oven and toss with sauce, adding cooking water as needed to reach desired consistency.

Nutritional Information for Our Recipes

To calculate the nutritional values of our recipes per serving, we used The Food Processor SQL by ESHA research. When using this program, we entered all the ingredients, using weights wherever possible. We also used our preferred brands in these analyses. Any ingredient listed as "optional" was excluded from the analyses. If there is a range in the serving size, we used the highest number of servings to calculate nutritional values. We did not include additional salt or pepper for food that's seasoned to taste.

	CALORIES	TOTAL FAT (G)	SAT FAT (G)	CHOL (MG)	SODIUM (MG)	TOTAL CARB (G)	DIETARY FIBER (G)	TOTAL SUGAR (G)	PROTEIN (G)
CHAPTER 1. HOMEMADE PASTA DOUGH									
Egg Pasta Dough	430	16	4	370	50	52	0	0	15
Semolina Pasta Dough	280	1	0	0	0	59	4	2	9
Whole-Wheat Pasta Dough	310	5	1.5	140	55	55	6	0	14
Buckwheat Pasta Dough	250	4	1.5	140	55	42	2	1	11
Gluten-Free Pasta Dough	360	10	2	185	140	59	3	0	10
Egg Pasta Dough for an Extruder	400	7	2.5	275	45	65	0	0	15
Semolina Pasta Dough for an Extruder	350	1	0	0	0	72	5	2	12
Whole-Wheat Pasta Dough for an Extruder	320	5	1.5	140	55	57	6	0	14
Buckwheat Pasta Dough for an Extruder	300	4	1.5	140	55	51	2	1	12
Gluten-Free Pasta Dough for an Extruder	360	5	1	140	125	70	3	0	9
CHAPTER 2. HOMEMADE PASTA SHAPES									
Potato Gnocchi	290	1.5	0	45	610	62	3	1	9
Ricotta Filling	140	10	6	75	290	0	0	0	11
Three-Cheese Filling	150	11	6	80	360	0	0	0	11
Spinach and Ricotta Filling	100	7	3.5	65	310	2	1	0	9
Pesto and Ricotta Filling	220	18	6	70	370	1	0	0	11
Artichoke and Lemon Ricotta Filling	140	7	3.5	65	480	6	2	1	12
Meat and Ricotta Filling	210	15	6	90	370	1	0	0	16
Braised Short Rib Filling	190	14	6	65	240	2	1	1	12
Ground Pork Filling	180	13	5	80	490	3	0	0	12
Squash, Prosciutto, and Parmesan Filling	110	5	2	60	510	10	1	2	8
Wild Mushroom Filling	140	10	4	65	180	3	1	1	9
Bitter Greens Filling	60	2.5	1	5	290	8	3	1	5
Leek Filling	230	9	5	65	320	32	4	9	7

	CALORIES	TOTAL FAT (G)	SAT FAT (G)	CHOL (MG)	SODIUM (MG)	TOTAL CARB (G)	DIETARY FIBER (G)	TOTAL SUGAR (G)	PROTEIN (G)
CHAPTER 3. FAVORITE PAIRINGS									
Maltagliati with Weeknight Meat Sauce	820	41	12	435	1520	70	4	10	38
Fettuccine Alfredo	640	29	15	335	990	65	0	0	27
Linguine with Clams	460	21	4	275	680	39	1	1	22
Fettuccine with Anchovies and Parsley	570	26	5	280	340	66	0	0	16
Fileja with 'Nduja Tomato Sauce	460	13	3	25	1010	65	5	6	18
Farfalle with Sautéed Mushrooms	820	50	21	445	950	66	3	6	25
Tagliatelle with Artichokes, Bread Crumbs, and Parmesan	800	44	10	385	580	66	0	2	26
Cacio e Pepe	610	22	12	330	700	66	0	0	29
Whole-Wheat Tagliatelle with Oyster Mushrooms and Browned Butter	620	33	15	195	610	62	9	2	24
Farfalle al Limone	640	38	11	390	620	56	0	2	18
Maccheroni di Fuoco	750	48	9	370	570	62	0	1	16
Linguine with Shrimp	590	26	8	395	550	47	0	1	31
Pasta alla Gricia	680	30	11	330	1310	65	0	0	32
Spaghetti alla Carbonara	710	32	11	545	1150	66	0	0	33
Cacio e Uova	520	27	8	325	650	44	0	0	21
Pasta alla Norcina	890	55	22	470	740	58	0	3	30
Creamy Corn Bucatini with Ricotta and Basil	590	16	7	300	430	86	2	8	27
Dill Trofie with Smoked Salmon and Crispy Capers	720	45	16	435	600	55	1	2	22
Pasta alla Norma	670	24	6	285	800	91	9	14	23
Spaghetti al Tonno	690	27	5	300	1380	71	1	3	36
Garganelli with Tomatoes, Crispy Prosciutto, and Peas	740	32	9	415	2080	72	5	9	38
Shells with Burst Cherry Tomato Sauce and Fried Caper Crumbs	730	34	9	295	1480	83	3	7	20
Malloreddus with Fava Beans and Mint	580	15	3	5m	390	88	14	15	26
Linguine allo Scoglio	650	29	6	460	1330	48	2	3	40
Maccheroni alla Chitarra with Lamb Ragù	550	24	7	315	910	45	2	5	32
Pappardelle with Duck and Chestnut Ragù	580	8	2.5	275	1180	93	1	4	18
Pizzoccheri with Swiss Chard, Potatoes, and Taleggio	440	18	10	140	660	50	7	2	22
Busiate with Spring Vegetables	580	24	4	5	720	73	9	8	19
Summer Squash Fettuccine with Ricotta and Lemon-Parmesan Bread Crumbs	870	53	14	405	1340	64	2	4	32
Trofie with Pesto, Potatoes, and Green Beans									
Whole-Wheat Busiate with Lentils, Pancetta, and Escarole	720	28	6	160	1070	87	17	5	32
Orecchiette with Broccoli Rabe and Sausage	470	12	3.5	20	1000	65	7	2	26
Pasta e Ceci	600	25	5	150	1740	71	11	5	23

	CALORIES	TOTAL FAT (G)	SAT FAT (G)	CHOL (MG)	SODIUM (MG)	TOTAL CARB (G)	DIETARY FIBER (G)	TOTAL SUGAR (G)	PROTEIN (G)
CHAPTER 4. FILLED PASTA, GNOCCHI & GNUDI									
Mushroom Ravioli with Browned Butter, Sage, and Truffle Sauce	590	38	17	335	410	40	1	1	20
Three-Cheese Ravioli with Pumpkin Cream Sauce	760	52	27	395	960	41	2	3	29
Short Rib Agnolotti with Hazelnuts and Browned Butter	820	56	25	415	710	40	2	2	34
Cappellacci di Zucca	590	36	19	315	550	48	2	3	16
Pansotti al Preboggion con Salsa di Noci	550	32	7	260	690	44	3	2	22
Tortellini in Brodo	320	18	5	170	730	20	0	1	19
Potato Gnocchi with Fontina Sauce	250	12	7	55	510	26	1	1	9
Ricotta Gnocchi with Garlicky Cherry Tomato Sauce and Arugula	500	25	12	100	1480	38	2	5	28
Spinach and Ricotta Gnudi with Tomato-Butter Sauce	380	23	14	70	1150	19	3	3	21
CHAPTER 5. BAKED PASTA									
Three-Cheese Manicotti with Tomato Sauce	610	35	16	295	1350	36	2	6	34
Cheese and Tomato Lasagna	400	26	12	135	1130	20	2	6	19
Mushroom Lasagna	360	20	8	110	780	27	2	10	15
Spinach Lasagna	340	21	11	145	810	19	2	3	19
Lasagna Verde alla Bolognese	440	30	13	170	810	16	0	3	25
Lasagna with Hearty Tomato-Meat Sauce	500	32	16	190	1220	24	3	8	35
Baked Ziti	570	31	16	255	1300	46	2	9	29
Baked Ziti with Creamy Leeks, Kale, and Sun-Dried Tomatoes	390	12	3	140	450	56	3	5	12
Baked Four-Cheese Penne with Prosciutto and Peas	590	33	19	235	1020	49	1	4	24
Baked Four-Cheese Penne with Tomatoes and Basil	600	33	19	235	1140	51	2	5	25
Baked Penne with Chicken, Broccoli, and Mushrooms	630	26	11	245	530	56	3	5	37
Baked Penne with Chicken, Broccoli, and Sun-Dried Tomatoes	650	29	12	245	570	55	3	4	37
Creamy Baked Tortellini with Radicchio, Peas, and Bacon	670	40	17	265	650	49	2	5	22
Gnocchi, Cauliflower, and Gorgonzola Gratin	200	9	5	30	550	25	3	3	6
Semolina Gnocchi with Browned Butter	280	15	9	70	480	26	1	6	11

	CALORIES	TOTAL FAT (G)	SAT FAT (G)	CHOL (MG)	SODIUM (MG)	TOTAL CARB (G)	DIETARY FIBER (G)	TOTAL SUGAR (G)	PROTEIN (G)
CHAPTER 6. SAUCES TO MIX AND MATCH									
Garlic Oil Sauce with Parsley and Pecorino	180	19	2.5	0	290	2	0	0	0
Garlic Oil Sauce with Lemon and Pine Nuts	290	30	3.5	0	290	4	1	1	3
Garlic Oil Sauce with Capers and Currants	210	19	2.5	0	520	8	1	6	1
Garlic Oil Sauce with Green Olives and Almonds	290	29	3	0	770	7	2	1	3
Browned Butter–Sage Sauce	100	11	7	30	75	1	0	0	0
Browned Butter–Truffle Sauce	120	13	7	30	75	1	0	0	0
Browned Butter–Hazelnut Sauce	140	14	7	30	75	2	1	1	1
Browned Butter–Tomato Sauce	90	7	4.5	20	280	5	1	3	1
Classic Basil Pesto	670	70	10	5	130	5	2	1	7
Toasted Nut and Parsley Pesto	470	48	7	10	250	5	3	1	9
Sun-Dried Tomato Pesto	390	39	6	5	200	8	2	0	6
Pesto Trapanese	250	24	4	5	680	5	2	3	5
Kale and Sunflower Seed Pesto	200	20	3	5	100	3	1	1	4
Pesto Calabrese	220	16	5	15	760	8	2	5	8
Olivada	260	26	4	5	300	3	0	1	4
No-Cook Fresh Tomato Sauce	170	14	2	0	590	11	3	7	2
Fresh Tomato Sauce	140	11	1.5	0	450	10	3	6	2
Fresh Tomato Amatriciana Sauce	180	12	3.5	20	1000	10	3	6	8
Fresh Tomato Arrabbiata Sauce	150	11	1.5	5	560	10	3	6	3

	CALORIES	TOTAL FAT (G)	SAT FAT (G)	CHOL (MG)	SODIUM (MG)	TOTAL CARB (G)	DIETARY FIBER (G)	TOTAL SUGAR (G)	PROTEIN (G)
CHAPTER 6. SAUCES TO MIX AND MATCH (CONT.)									
Fresh Tomato Puttanesca Sauce	150	12	1.5	0	680	10	3	6	2
Marinara Sauce	100	5	0.5	0	360	10	0	6	2
Creamy Tomato Sauce	300	22	13	60	690	19	4	9	7
Vodka Sauce	260	18	8	35	690	11	0	7	3
Gorgonzola-Walnut Cream Sauce	600	54	25	105	580	12	2	6	14
Porcini Cream Sauce	550	47	20	90	280	15	3	6	13
Alfredo Sauce	450	44	27	130	690	3	0	2	12
White Clam Sauce	200	13	4.5	40	320	7	1	1	12
Fra Diavolo Sauce	530	25	4	165	2390	23	2	7	39
Sunday Gravy	540	32	8	105	1390	27	4	12	38
Sausage Ragù with Red Peppers	310	14	4.5	35	1130	29	6	15	23
Ragù alla Bolognese	540	35	12	170	870	9	1	4	36
Beef Short Rib Ragù	850	69	28	150	1030	11	1	5	38
Beef and Onion Ragù	470	16	7	105	1060	32	5	14	37
Rabbit Ragù	370	14	3.5	150	970	12	1	6	43
Ragù Bianco	620	42	19	160	2030	18	4	8	41
Mushroom Bolognese	320	15	4	15	1070	28	2	16	8
Meatless "Meat" Sauce with Chickpeas and Mushrooms	200	11	1.5	0	320	18	4	6	6
Braised Kale and Chickpea Sauce	420	18	6	30	1420	39	13	5	29

Conversions and Equivalents

Some say cooking is a science and an art. We would say that geography has a hand in it, too. Flours and sugars manufactured in the United Kingdom and elsewhere will feel and taste different from those manufactured in the United States. So we cannot promise that the loaf of bread you bake in Canada or England will taste the same as a loaf baked in the States, but we can offer guidelines for converting weights and measures. We also recommend that you rely on your instincts when making our recipes. Refer to the visual cues provided. If the dough hasn't "come together in a ball" as described, you may need to add more flour—even if the recipe doesn't tell you to. You be the judge.

The recipes in this book were developed using standard U.S. measures following U.S. government guidelines. The charts below offer equivalents for U.S. and metric measures. All conversions are approximate and have been rounded up or down to the nearest whole number.

EXAMPLE

1 teaspoon	=	4.9292 milliliters, rounded up to 5 milliliters
1 ounce	=	28.3495 grams, rounded down to 28 grams

VOLUME CONVERSIONS

U.S.	METRIC
1 teaspoon	5 milliliters
2 teaspoons	10 milliliters
1 tablespoon	15 milliliters
2 tablespoons	30 milliliters
¼ cup	59 milliliters
⅓ cup	79 milliliters
½ cup	118 milliliters
¾ cup	177 milliliters
1 cup	237 milliliters
1¼ cups	296 milliliters
1½ cups	355 milliliters
2 cups (1 pint)	473 milliliters
2½ cups	591 milliliters
3 cups	710 milliliters
4 cups (1 quart)	0.946 liter
1.06 quarts	1 liter
4 quarts (1 gallon)	3.8 liters

WEIGHT CONVERSIONS

OUNCES	GRAMS
½	14
¾	21
1	28
1½	43
2	57
2½	71
3	85
3½	99
4	113
4½	128
5	142
6	170
7	198
8	227
9	255
10	283
12	340
16 (1 pound)	454

CONVERSIONS FOR COMMON BAKING INGREDIENTS

Baking is an exacting science. Because measuring by weight is far more accurate than measuring by volume, and thus more likely to produce reliable results, in our recipes we provide ounce measures in addition to cup measures for many ingredients. Refer to the chart below to convert these measures into grams.

INGREDIENT	OUNCES	GRAMS
Flour		
1 cup all-purpose flour*	5	142
1 cup cake flour	4	113
1 cup whole-wheat flour	5½	156
Sugar		
1 cup granulated (white) sugar	7	198
1 cup packed brown sugar (light or dark)	7	198
1 cup confectioners' sugar	4	113
Cocoa Powder		
1 cup cocoa powder	3	85
Butter†		
4 tablespoons (½ stick or ¼ cup)	2	57
8 tablespoons (1 stick or ½ cup)	4	113
16 tablespoons (2 sticks or 1 cup)	8	227

* U.S. all-purpose flour, the most frequently used flour in this book, does not contain leaveners, as some European flours do. These leavened flours are called self-rising or self-raising. If you are using self-rising flour, take this into consideration before adding leaveners to a recipe.

† In the United States, butter is sold both salted and unsalted. We generally recommend unsalted butter. If you are using salted butter, take this into consideration before adding salt to a recipe.

OVEN TEMPERATURES

FAHRENHEIT	CELSIUS	GAS MARK
225	105	¼
250	120	½
275	135	1
300	150	2
325	165	3
350	180	4
375	190	5
400	200	6
425	220	7
450	230	8
475	245	9

CONVERTING TEMPERATURES FROM AN INSTANT-READ THERMOMETER

We include doneness temperatures in many of the recipes in this book. We recommend an instant-read thermometer for the job. Refer to the table above to convert Fahrenheit degrees to Celsius. Or, for temperatures not represented in the chart, use this simple formula:

Subtract 32 degrees from the Fahrenheit reading, then divide the result by 1.8 to find the Celsius reading.

EXAMPLE

"Cook burger patties until meat registers 130 to 135 degrees."

To convert:

$130°F - 32 = 98°$

$98° \div 1.8 = 54.44°C$, rounded down to 54°C

Index

Note: Page references in *italics* indicate photographs.

V

Veal
    Lasagna Verde alla Bolognese,
        170, 170–71
    Lasagna with Hearty Tomato-Meat
        Sauce, *172*, 172–73
    Maltagliati with Weeknight Meat
        Sauce, *74*, 74–75
    Meat and Ricotta Filling, 68
    Ragù alla Bolognese, *230*, 230–31
    Sunday Gravy, *226*, 226–27
Vegetables
    Spring, Busiate with, *128*, 128–29
    see also specific vegetables
Vodka Sauce, *216*, 216–17

W

Walnut(s)
    Creamy Baked Tortellini with
        Radicchio, Peas, and Bacon,
        182, 182–83
    -Gorgonzola Cream Sauce,
        218, 218–19
    Pansotti al Preboggion con Salsa di
        Noci, *150*, 150–51
    Porcini Cream Sauce, 219
    Sun-Dried Tomato Pesto,
        198, 198–99
White flour, 2
Whole-grain flours, 3
**Whole-grain pasta, pairing with sauces,
14**
Whole-Wheat
    Busiate with Lentils, Pancetta, and
        Escarole, *134*, 134–35
    flour, about, 3
    pasta, pairing with sauces, 14
    Pasta Dough, *24*, 24–25
    Pasta Dough for an Extruder, 34–35
    Tagliatelle with Oyster Mushrooms
        and Browned Butter, *90*, 90–91

X

Xanthan gum
    about, 4
    Gluten-Free Pasta Dough,
        26–27, *27*

Z

Ziti
    Baked, *174*, 174–75
    Baked, with Creamy Leeks, Kale,
        and Sun-Dried Tomatoes,
        176, 176–77
    Pasta alla Norma, *110*, 110–11
Zucchini
    Busiate with Spring Vegetables,
        128, 128–29